McDouG⬤AL

McDouG⚽AL

macdonald media publishing

First published in October 2010 by **macdonald** media publishing, 22 Roxburgh Road, Paisley, PA2 0UG. info@macdonald-media.co.uk

ISBN: 0-9553126-8-X

ISBN 13: 978-0-9553126-8-7

A CIP catalogue record for this book is available from the British Library.

Design and typesetting: Cameron Heggie.

Printed and bound by Thomson Litho, East Kilbride.

DEDICATION

To mum and dad, gran and grandad, my daughters, Kelly and Deanna, grandchildren, Casey and Courtney and everyone who helped me on my incredible journey. I've enjoyed (almost) every moment.

But most of all to my lovely wife Isabel...my rock.

C⚽NTENTS

BEING FRANK ABOUT FRANK

Sir Alex Ferguson

Abie Monaghan

Blair Miller

Cowboy McCormack

Jim Duffy

Billy Abercromby

Billy Stark

Gardner Speirs

Ricky McFarlane

Craig Paterson

Frank McAvennie

Alex McLeish

Eric Black

Neale Cooper

Paul Hegarty

Dave Bowman

Joe Harper

F⚽REWORD

By Craig Levein, Scotland manager

I'll sum up Frank the best way I know how.

Hearts versus Aberdeen at Tynecastle on a sweltering hot afternoon. One fantastic team contest; lots of intriguing personal battles going on all over the park and Levein versus McDougall, more often than not, in our penalty box.

Aberdeen had just been crowned league champions and were on the crest of a wave.

It certainly wasn't the first time I'd played against Frank, although it was one of my better performances against him. Only trouble is, we lost 3-0 and he scored a hat-trick. How do you fathom that one out?

As I say, I came off at the end believing I'd played him well, but he still had three goals and a win bonus bulging his back pocket. Strange game. But that was the mark of Frank McDougall - the player.

He had this unbelievable knack of scoring goals. I mean, he didn't really do much else that day, but did he have to? He was an out-and-out goalscorer; the closer he got to the penalty box, the more dangerous he became. My philosophy was, keep him thirty or forty yards from the box where he can't do any damage. Easier said than done.

It was as though he was just going along with your philosophy then, bang, he's away from you and the goalkeeper is picking the ball out of the net. Was he lulling me into a false sense of security? When it came to the area in and around the penalty box he was as good as there was. His goals record was second to none and he scored on a consistent basis.

Sure, he may have been surrounded by quality players at Aberdeen, but he still had to put the ball in the net. And we're not just talking tap-ins either. He scored some pretty spectacular goals in his career.

Fast-forward 20 or so years and I'd have to liken him to the Kris Boyds of the world - the type of guy who comes alive in the penalty box. As manager of the national team, how lucky would I be to have a player of Frank's calibre at my disposal?

That match against the Dons may have been 25 years ago, but I remember it as though it were yesterday.

PR⚽LOGUE

I HAD the football world at my feet and in a few devastating seconds it was cruelly snatched away. One act of madness left my fledgling football career and life in tatters.

Two months prior to that fateful night of August 25, 1973, I had signed an S-form with Hearts on the strength of four second-half goals in a juvenile match through in Edinburgh. Me, Frank McDougall, the boy from Cadder (a housing scheme in the north of Glasgow), joining one of the biggest clubs in Scotland.

It took a while to sink in, but suddenly I was rubbing shoulders with the likes of Donald Ford and Drew Busby; guys you normally only saw on television, read of in the national papers, or had in your bubblegum card collection. But what should have been the happiest time of my life was soon to spiral into a period of eternal darkness and everything I'd worked towards was slowly spirited away.

My gran hadn't been keeping too well and was in the Western Infirmary. I had just been to visit her. I was 15-years-old and required two buses to get home to Cadder. I was on the second of these buses, the No 24, which made the relatively short journey from Maryhill to Cadder, a stretch of maybe a mile or so, with a childhood friend, John Docherty. As the bus travelled up hilly Sandbank Street through Gilshochill, a small scheme of maybe 5000 people, the bulk of whom lived in three sprawling tower blocks, danger lurked in the shadows.

As usual, John and I would be talking football, and dissecting the previous weekend's results and performances. It was what we did. We could spend hours pouring over the ins and outs of the game. It was a passion and while we would invariably disagree on many points, we always stopped short of falling out.

We were halfway through our journey and, as the double-decker bus slowed down to take a sharp right into Thornton Street, I broke off from chewing the fat to look out the window. It was the worst decision of my life.

Unknown to me, a large crowd had congregated just inside a nearby close mouth. The 'Gilshy Boys' and, of course, we were from a rival scheme. Intruders on their territory, or at least, that's probably how they saw it. Regardless, we weren't welcome.

Me, I was just coming back from hospital after visiting my sick grandmother. That's the way I saw it. What I didn't see, though, was a hulking great brick hurtling its way towards the bus. By the time I noticed it heading in my direction, it was too late.

The rock smashed through the window and the glass shattered into a thousand pieces. Unfortunately, the shards sprayed my face like shrapnel and many ended up nestling deep between both eyes. I screamed at John, 'My eyes!' and he immediately started searching for them, believing the brick had taken them clean out. Looking back, that may have been the easier option, because the next six months would be the toughest of my life.

The next thing I remember is the shrill of sirens and an ambulance arriving to take me to hospital. I don't recall much chat between the paramedics, but I didn't need experts to tell me I was in big trouble. Despite being in my early to mid teens, I was well aware of the severity of the incident.

The pain was excruciating and a million thoughts began racing around in my head: family, friends, football. My career had barely started. What was going to happen to me? I was also a promising boxer; a sport I enjoyed immensely. It had been running quite nicely alongside my football career. Of course, I knew that one day I'd have to choose between the two, and football would always win, but for now I was happy to indulge in both.

The paramedics patched me up best they could and 'loaded' me into the ambulance. My mind worked overtime as the vehicle sped along Maryhill Road in the direction of the nearest hospital. In an extreme case of irony, I was headed for the Western Infirmary, the place I had just come from. Fate would cruelly decree that I should end up in the bed next to my gran, although I couldn't see her.

I can only imagine what that must have been like for her. I know it was tough for me, but for my gran to see me lying there in a crumpled heap must have been a nightmare; helpless in the knowledge that she couldn't do a damned thing for me. It must have been awful.

I didn't deserve to be there. I was no angel, but like most teenagers growing up in a tough housing scheme, I was no villain either. The attack had been as cowardly as it gets. I couldn't even tell you if police ever arrested the people responsible, as I was never told, but over the ensuing days and weeks many friends and acquaintances would approach me with offers to seek out and administer retribution. I always refused.

Eventually the name of the perpetrator was handed to me on a little piece of paper. He knew exactly what he'd done. It was a cheap shot and the type of attack I would have expected from one so cowardly. But I had a bigger battle on my hands than seeking revenge.

I was a teenager in trouble - blind in both eyes and struggling to accept my fate. I've faced many challenges in my life, but this was undoubtedly the toughest and one where destiny really wasn't in my hands. I would come to rely on a dedicated and truly gifted team of surgeons, and would eventually owe them everything.

For the first time in my life, football wasn't top of my agenda.

ONE SMALL STEP FOR MAC-KIND

OAKBANK Hospital was a typical Victorian building. Grey and drab and built for a purpose, which certainly wasn't vanity. It was no more than 100 yards from the Round Toll, which lies on the periphery of Glasgow's Maryhill district.

On the morning of February 21, 1958, patients at the dowdy hospital, which has long since been demolished, awoke to the sounds of baby Douglas Francis McDougall exercising his lungs for the first time. It was just a week after Valentine's Day and the first of four McDougalls who would have love bestowed upon him at 4 Farnell Street, just a goal-kick away from the hospital, and a couple of closes along from Granny and Grandad Reilly. My mum, Margaret, spent a lot of time at her parents' house and, being a real granny's boy, I was also in and around her humble abode more often than not - although there was another reason for that.

Like many of the flats in the Maryhill area, mum and dad's house was overrun with rats and they reckoned it would be safer for me to reside in a rodent-free zone. Imagine missing out on all those furry pets. What I remember of the very early days was happy. Sure, life was tough for everyone in the inner cities of the 60s, but we just got on with it, and dad, Frank, who was employed as a crane driver, brought home the bacon.

Everything changed though when he was made redundant. It was a pivotal moment in my life, even though I was too young to understand it at the time. The key decisions were made on my behalf. I was just four years old when dad decided he had no alternative but to chase work. In doing this, the family, which had been swelled by two, would leave Scotland.

With nothing doing in their native city, the McDougalls would head south, eventually settling in Bury, Lancashire, where my dad found a job. Everyone, that is, apart from me. My sister Margaret and David, the second eldest, were born this side of Hadrian's Wall, while James, the youngest, was born in Lancashire. Margaret went on to run a pub in Bury before getting a job in the local college. David was a long-distance lorry driver and, as we'll find out, James made his way as a steel worker.

Me? I stayed with grandparents Dick and Jeanie Reilly and they were like parents to me, bringing me up as one of their own. There was never a moment when I felt abandoned or disowned. Growing up with my granny and grandad seemed the most natural thing in the world, and there would be the cushion of regular trips down south to visit my parents.

My grandparents already had two boys, Robert and James (Chico), the eventual kit-man at Partick Thistle, and a girl, Hannah, who would settle in Rochdale, but there was always room for their little Frankie. We were soon on the move from Farnell Street though and our destination, and the place I would come to regard as home, was a small housing scheme called Cadder. It was 'landlocked' by larger areas such as Maryhill, Milton and Lambhill, and had been purpose-built at the end of the 1950s to ease congestion in overcrowded, nearby areas. Cadder was home to around 10,000 people and we lived at 148 Tresta Road, which spanned the length of the graveyard.

My primary school would be St Agnes's, which was located at the other end of Tresta Road. It sat directly in front of an old, disused coal bing, which could be a great source of entertainment, what with its rugged terrain and myriad hiding places. Like so many other primary schools it has since closed its doors.

St Agnes's, or the 'Aggie's' as it was affectionately known, holds mixed memories for me. On one hand I was quite comfortable there, although I don't have great memories of playtimes, and not because of school bullies. There was no room for bullies as the janitor ruled the school playgrounds with a dictatorial authority normally reserved for the Army drill hall. In fact, I have these awful visions of him constantly taking marbles from me. Cynics may suggest that's when I truly lost them. Subject-wise, I didn't really have any favourites and only attended school because it was mandatory.

But our soccer battles with great rivals Cadder Primary were worth turning up for. I suppose that's when I learned the art of competitiveness and self-preservation. To football-playing pupils of Cadder Primary and St Agnes's, it was the Rangers v. Celtic of its time. Looking back we were mere children, but the intensity reserved for these occasions was the stuff of legend.

Unfortunately, we were more often than not on the losing side, which was in no small way down to a player called Alex McLaren, the captain of the Cadder team and a giant among, well, primary seven pupils. Alex and I would meet up again on the football field a few years later, but this time we would be on the same side, thank goodness.

Academically, I was something of a no-hoper. I wasn't in the slightest bit interested in learning to count to 100, or who had been the king of England in 1066. Every waking moment was spent kicking a ball down at Cadder pitches or playing keepy-uppy and learning to shield the ball like Kenny Dalglish.

Football was soon vying for my attention with another sporting passion though; that of boxing. I was a regular visitor to Cadder Youth Centre and a few of us would mess around with an assortment of odd, dishevelled gloves, pretending to be Mohammed Ali or Joe Frazier. We took it seriously. So much so, that we decided to approach youth centre leaders and ask for a proper boxing ring to help fulfill our growing passion for the sport.

The youth centre was the heartbeat of the community and was split into two buildings. The smaller acted as a sort of clubhouse and was the area where games such as pool, table tennis and darts took place. It would also host regular Friday night discos.

The bigger hall was home to the five-a-side pitch, badminton courts and, once given the all clear, our brand new ring. Our ring really was a knockout, but had just one small flaw. It had no canvas floor – that was just outwith the budget. It meant though that when you bit the dust, which I tried my level best NOT to do, you landed on a rock hard surface.

Cadder was a pretty tough place and, with quite a few of us into boxing at that time, it meant you would inevitably meet your match and end up on the floor. Maybe my memory has faded with age, but I don't recall ending up on my bum too often.

Jamie Webster was one of the main leaders at the youth centre. Later, he was to become a high-profile shop steward at the shipyards and at one time, was never off the television. Jamie was a great guy, but took no prisoners. If anyone dared start trouble at the centre, they had him to answer to. In all the years I've known him I can't recall him ever starting a fight, although I reckon he finished loads.

Many teens perceived him as a bit of a take-on. He had a mild-mannered demeanor and wore glasses quite a bit. Maybe he genuinely was mild-mannered, but disturb that raging inferno inside and he'd come down on you like a ton of bricks. Thanks to Jamie, the youth centre was a safer place to be.

But, while football and boxing were huge attractions for me, the first of life's many hurdles was lurking just around the corner. While the little angel on my right hand shoulder represented everything that was good in life, the devil perched menacingly opposite had a bottle of cheap wine in his hand to compliment his nasty scowl. I may have been just 11 years old, but that didn't stop me wanting to sample the demon drink.

En route to school one morning I bumped into a few boys I knew from the scheme. They were bigger lads of around 12 or 13 and had finished with primary school. One of them produced a carrier bag with several bottles of spirits.

Foolishly, I decided to polish off the best part of a bottle of neat gin on my own and within just a few moments of the last drop slipping down my throat I was on my way to hospital in a speeding ambulance. It was time for little McDougall to get his stomach pumped. It felt as though my insides were on fire and the relief on being 'cured' by medics at Stobhill Hospital was immense. I didn't touch another drop for weeks.

My next brush with the 'Don Revie' (bevvy) saw me pinch a bottle of whisky from my gran's house. I retired to the nearby graveyard with a friend, Brian Smith, to sample its delights. I had even remembered to take a couple of nice glasses in which to sup the contents from. I had thought of everything. Well, not quite everything.

My big mistake, apart from actually drinking the stuff in the first place, was to head for school at around 11am, immediately after the last drop had been drained. Smiddy had a bit more sense and went for a snooze.

One look at my contorted face, rubber legs and all-round disorientated state and I was hauled up before the head teacher. After being read the riot act by Mrs Dolan, I was sent straight home. She was furious, and no wonder.

While I lived on the same street as my school, the Aggie's was at the other end, a good 15-minute walk – sober. On this occasion though, it took me almost three hours to get home. Apart from taking two steps forward and three back, I apparently stopped for a couple of naps along the way. That would explain the reason for my inebriation going largely unnoticed on arriving home, because I was sober by the time I got there.

I loved my granny and grandad to bits and would never have done anything to hurt them. They were strict, but always fair. The last thing I wanted was to let them down, but it seemed as though I was fighting a never-ending battle with those two little opposites on my shoulders. But if the truth be told, I don't regret drinking at such an early age. It's what a lot of kids did back then and I just went with the flow. By doing so I didn't miss out on anything and it's not as if I was hammering it every night. I was just at that experimental stage.

I was by no means the youngest drinker in the scheme and I refuse to wheel out that age-old excuse that there was nothing for kids to do in Cadder. That simply wasn't true. We had lots to pass the time. Maybe it was down to peer pressure and the need to impress those around about me. Thankfully, drinking illegally wasn't a regular occurrence and I could more often than not be found with a ball at my feet.

I was determined to be a footballer and, at the risk of sounding big headed, I knew that it wasn't just Britain that had talent. God knows I practised often enough, although that's not the only ingredient you need to make it big. I reckon certain people are born talented, but that its then up to you to make something of that gift.

At the youth teams I played for I was often picked out by opposing coaches and managers as the player to watch - the danger man. And when local managers were looking for players to supplement their squad, they quite often looked in my direction. I felt privileged, but at the same time I wasn't comfortable with the attention. I was happiest on the pitch, scoring goals and linking up with team-mates. Even at the end of my senior career, attention was something I never courted.

I practised from the age of four, when grandad would take me out into the garden and kick the ball around with me. Despite never really playing at a high level himself, he knew a thing or two about the game and imparted his knowledge in a way I understood.

He was a great teacher. Any spare time he had was spent with me and a football. I would also practice ball skills and keepy-uppy till bedtime and spend hours studying idols such as Gerd Muller, Kenny Dalglish, Gunter Netzer and Pele. Of course, there wasn't wall-to-wall football coverage in the 1970s, but I grabbed the opportunity to watch football on TV whenever it arose.

Many of the skills I was to take into my professional career were honed as a youngster. The control, balance and ghosting were practised to death - while running away from the police no doubt contributed to my general fitness.

We would often head up to a piece of spare ground in the graveyard for a kickabout and I always wanted to be Dalglish or Muller. Well, I couldn't exactly be Frank McDougall - who had heard of him? Part of the fun was pretending, no, believing you were a top footballer and when you scored a goal it wasn't actually you that had scored it, it was Dalglish or Muller. It was etched in your mind and helped make the whole game more realistic. But that was the good thing about growing up. Most things were make-believe and it was acceptable to reside in fantasyland.

The drinking aside, my childhood was fantastic and I have nothing but good memories. Mum and dad may have been 200 miles away, but I didn't miss out on a thing. But one incident, which took place just after I left primary school, could so easily have mapped out an entirely different future, and ensured I was sent straight to jail.

I was standing in a close in Skirsa Street with three mates one night, and we were knocking back a few bottles of cheap wine. Unlike the others, I was taking it easy because I was Bury-bound early the next morning to visit mum and dad. It was approaching 10pm and I said my goodbyes before making the short five-minute walk to Tresta Road.

Next morning I awoke to the news that there had been a murder at a secluded house near the top of Skirsa Street. It was just off Balmore Road and adjacent to the back end of the graveyard.

For some reason, the guys I had been with had entered the house and the occupant was killed. The scheme was awash with gossip, but a lengthy trial ensued, which I didn't attend, and one of the guys, who lived directly opposite me in Tresta Road, was sentenced to Her Majesty's Pleasure, which more or less meant he would be detained without limit of time.

The terrible tragedy was to cast a giant shadow over Cadder for many years to come.

DISCOVERING THE ROUND BALL

FOOTBALL more or less ruled my life but the first rung of the ladder to 'fame and fortune' was played out under the leadership of a man named 'Pimmy the Penguin.' I never did find out why Jim McCue came to acquire such a nickname, but one thing I do know is that he was a damned good manager and a great guy.

He gave lots of kids from Cadder and surrounding areas their big chance and I was just one of a number of burgeoning footballers he took under his wing. Pimmy ran Scotland Boys Club, and they were based, like most other Cadder organisations, at the youth centre. We played our football at Cadder pitches, which were different, but adjacent to, the Cadder School pitches.

Don't mention dressing rooms though. We used to get changed at Pimmy's house, well, his garage to be exact. We'd walk from his home in Cadder Road, down Langa Street, and under the railway bridge, which eventually brought you out at the pitches: probably a walk of a good three-quarters-of-a-mile. It must have been the longest distance between any set of changing rooms and a pitch. But football was everything and I would've hiked from Timbuktu to Cadder just for a game.

Cadder pitches were massive and there was always a decent sprinkling of locals to watch us tackle teams from other parts of north-west Glasgow. One game in particular stands out. We played host to Knightswood and I was having a right ding-dong battle with one of their players. The tackles were flying in and we crunched one another repeatedly.

On one such occasion, the last for us both, we squared up and even though it was handbags at dawn, the referee promptly sent us both packing. The other player was John Wark, who would go on to carve out a highly successful career south of the border with Ipswich Town, when they were a real force to be reckoned with, and Liverpool. He also won many caps for Scotland.

On another occasion, we found ourselves just minutes from kick-off and minus a pretty important player – the goalkeeper. At the time I felt I could do the business in any position and offered to fill in between the sticks. Big mistake. With just a few minutes on the clock, I ran up to take a goal kick, stubbed by foot on the turf before hitting the ball and pulled up immediately. It was pretty sore, but not excruciatingly, so I was shocked to discover I'd broken my leg.

My time at Scotland Boys Club came to an end with a cup final at Maryhill Juniors' Lochburn Park. It was great to play on such an important ground and I thoroughly enjoyed the occasion. I'd played for the Under-12s, 13s and 14s, but that was it and it was time to move on. I would never forget my time with the club and, especially, that walk from changing rooms to pitch, which became even longer after a defeat.

Once I'd outgrown 'Scotland' I spent most of my spare time playing football with pals, one of them a guy called Tam Bennett. He played for Rangers Athletic, a well-organised Under-16 outfit run by a gentleman called Dan Isdale, or Mr Isdale, if you were fortunate enough to get a game for them.

I was at a loose end one Saturday and was hanging around outside the Cadder shops. I didn't have a club at the time, but what I did have was a king-sized hangover following a night on the booze. I bumped into Tam, footie boots slung over his shoulder, and he was on his way to Edinburgh for a Scottish Youth Cup match against Tynecastle Boys Club, a feeder side for Hearts. He was waiting for his lift and asked if I fancied a day out. As I wasn't doing much else I decided to go along for the ride.

It was quite an experience for a lad of my age to visit our capital. It was just 45 miles away, but may well have been in another country. Quite a few folk turned up to watch and the match started at a terrific pace. Tynecastle were a decent side and were quick to force the play. So good, in fact, that they were 3-0 up at the break and Athletic were facing a bit of a tanking.

Off trundled the boys at half-time to the inevitable tongue-lashing.

Mr Isdale didn't look best pleased and let rip at his beleaguered players. I kept my distance and the manager got on with telling his players how they could arrest the slide in the second-half. Even though I was a good bit away, I could still hear him launching into 11 very sorry looking individuals. Strangely, a few of the players started looking over at me. I hadn't been overly critical of them in the first half. In fact, I hadn't said a word. Then Tam Bennett came bounding over and asked if I fancied playing the second half. Absolutely. He told me after the game that he'd said to Mr Isdale, 'my mate can play a bit'. No pressure then, huh.

I had no kit, but quickly pulled on a strip at the side of the park. Players were staring at my feet. I had a pair of white sandshoes on. No boots, just sandshoes. It was a massive grass park and as it had been raining, I had visions of sliding all over the place - more ice-skater than footballer.

The advice from Mr Isdale was simple. He was calm and collected by this time and asked me to play up front. I was to try and get the team back into this cup-tie. It was incredible, but this 14-year-old boy from Cadder had just been charged with getting Rangers Athletic into the final of the Scottish Cup.

And I did just that, with interest. Four second-half goals from yours truly helped the team ease past this tough opponent, the cream of Edinburgh, and into a final. I was elated – and TWO teams signed me up just moments after my incredible four-goal romp. First of all, Mr Isdale shook my hand warmly, offered his congratulations and asked if I wanted to sign for the team. I accepted.

I had grown up a big Celtic fan and was well aware that Rangers Athletic were affiliated to Rangers, and that they wore the full Rangers kit. I may also have been the first Catholic to play for the team, but you know what, none of that stuff bothered me in the slightest. I just wanted to play football and here I was being offered a team place. Sorted.

Sure, I would get stick from my Celtic-supporting mates back in Cadder when they saw me parading around in my smart blue blazer and grey flannels, but it was all light-hearted and didn't really bother me. At that time I wasn't really aware of the pitfalls thrown up by the religious divide in the West of Scotland. Most of it went straight over my head.

I was then approached by a gentleman, asking for a word. Having scored four goals moments beforehand, I was in the mood to talk to anyone. He introduced himself as Bobby Seith, manager of Heart of Midlothian FC. Did I just hear him correctly? Manager of Hearts?

He told me I'd both played and taken my goals well. He asked if I would like to come and train with Hearts, with a view to possibly signing an S-form (schoolboy form). I was absolutely gobsmacked. I was definitely interested, but said I'd need to talk it over with my grandad. Thankfully he was perfectly happy to wait.

I went home walking on air, talked it over with grandad and eventually put pen to paper for the Jambos. I was a professional footballer, well, not quite. It was great to have another club so soon after finishing with Scotland Boys Club, and I mean Rangers Athletic, not Hearts. I had thoroughly enjoyed my finest hour, well, 45 minutes, and was thirsty for more.

Boxing was also playing a bigger part in my life around this time. I loved to fight when I was younger, but felt I'd be better off doing it legally, than on street corners after a few gulps of cheap wine. A guy called Bobby Keddie attended Cadder Youth Centre and offered his services as a coach.

We had the ring in the big hall and it was now time to knuckle down and see what we could achieve. Regardless of the sport, I've always tried 100 per cent in everything and wanted to be the best I could. Boxing was no different. I would go into the ring with everyone and anyone and taking a punch was never a problem. Boxing also taught me discipline. The amateur game was hell for leather, but that's where you learned your trade.

The fitness required to box was far more intense than football. It was all bodywork; heart, stomach, legs etc. – it was hard work, but I coped okay and I'm sure it helped a lot with my football. I reckon I was around two years ahead of most of my contemporaries in terms of fitness and physical development, even though we were all the same age.

In 1975 I fought in the Palace of Art, at Bellahouston Park, for the Scottish ABA title. In the final, I was up against a guy called Willie Black from Milton. He was a tough opponent and put up a good fight, but I defeated him in the end. Tragically, Willy died a fortnight later after being hit by a train. He was a big loss.

I always knew there would come a time when I'd have to choose between football and boxing. Little did I know, however, that choice would be taken out of my hands, but more about that later.

I never lost sleep over the negative effects of boxing. I was a teenager, interested only in reaching peak fitness before a fight. Nothing else entered the equation.

I fought a guy called Willie Anderson in the semi-final of the ABA. I won the contest, on a unanimous decision and was naturally delighted. At the time, he was going out with a girl called Lily Kavanagh, whom I would eventually marry. Spooky, or what?

My granny and grandad didn't mind me boxing, which was pleasing. In fact, one of my grandad's brothers, Owen Reilly, was a world champion fighter. Another of his brothers played for St Johnstone. I was free to pursue my passion.

A few weeks after scoring four against Tynecastle Boys Club, Dan Isdale asked if I'd like to be included in the squad for a prestigious youth tournament in Germany. I didn't have to be asked twice, even though I'd just turned 15. Apart from the day trip to Edinburgh, I'd barely been outside Cadder, but the 'long-haul' to Europe sounded like fun.

I counted down the days and it seemed an eternity between being asked and actually heading out from Central Station on the first leg of our marathon adventure. But the experience was everything I could have hoped for and more.

We played eight games in a week, and it was something of a personal success for me. I scored 36 goals and drew comparisons to German football legend Gunter Netzer. Mind you, I still believe that was down to the blond flowing locks and not the football ability. The compliments were phenomenal though and when we arrived home the Evening Times ran a feature on Gunter and I. Happy days.

We played against the likes of Hamburg and Stuttgart Boys Clubs and it was just a magical experience. After every match, an opposition player would invite a member of our team to stay overnight at their place in an effort to foster relations between the different clubs. It worked a treat and was a real eye-opener to see how other kids lived. I came from a tough backdrop of fighting inside and outside the ring, so going over there and meeting nice young lads the same age was a pleasurable experience. It was all about the football for them and I learned a thing or two in the process.

While I won't deny for a minute that I was in the local gang, I was more or less a peripheral member. I could always get myself away from the gang culture because I had pals that weren't into it all, although there was a definite attraction for me. I was fairly polite and I'm sure that my 'alternative' outlook on life was just part and parcel of growing up in a Glasgow housing scheme. Part of the reason I took up boxing was to channel the aggression positively.

You here so many stories about footballers misbehaving on foreign trips, but our behaviour was impeccable. Mr Isdale wouldn't have had it any other way. In fact, I believe he still has a street named after him in Germany to this very day. We all loved playing for Rangers Athletic, but knew that if you stepped out of line you were out. The manager didn't mess around.

Mr Isdale lived in Oran Street, in Maryhill, and I would go down to his house occasionally. He was a fantastic man and treated me like a son. I only played for the club for one season, but it was among the most enjoyable of my career. And the fact I'd been to Germany with the Athletic was definitely responsible for my new found love of German football. I idolised guys like Netzer and Gerd Muller. I loved the way they played the game and cheered them on at every opportunity. My grandad probably couldn't understand the attraction, but he let me get on with it nevertheless.

The Germans were a great side and I decided to adopt them as 'my team', until I laid eyes on Pele. Then it was over to Brazil.

OFF TO THE BIG SCHOOL

IT'S fair to say that primary school hadn't exactly filled me with inspiration but it was soon time to move on to pastures new and leave St Agnes's behind. My new school would be St Augustine's Secondary, which was situated within the heart of Milton and deep behind enemy lines.

Milton was just another tough housing scheme, although I was about to find out just how tough. If that school taught me anything, it was how to run extremely fast – to escape the clutches of rival gang, the Milton Tongs. A group of us from Cadder, which included Brian Smith, Paul Healey and 'Ludo,' were leaving St Agnes's at the same time and decided to meet up every morning outside the shops to walk to school together. Strength in numbers was the idea and it worked more often than not.

It was a fair trek to Augustine's – which would soon be home to one Frank McAvennie – and we would head up Skirsa Street and into Balmore Road, where we would pass Mallon's Bar, before cutting through Balmore Industrial Estate.

The school wasn't far from there and all the while we'd be keeping an eye out for potential dangers as we gingerly crossed a street daubed with the infamous words, 'Keep Out – Tongs Land.'

There was often the odd skirmish with our rivals although, no matter who won or lost, there was always a fair chance that it would all kick off again the following day. It's fair to say I hated school. There really is no other way to describe it.

Those who insist that schooldays are the happiest of your life should keep their opinions to themselves. They were anything but for me, or most people I knew.

Being at secondary school in the 1970s is a little bit different from these days, when a high percentage of pupils stay on for a further one, or even two years. I couldn't wait to leave. In fact, I only managed to clock up two of the statutory four years at secondary and more or less cut my ties as a 14 year old.

What was the point in staying on? I was academically bankrupt and knew that any talent I possessed lay in my feet. What was to be gained by remaining at St Augustine's and wasting both their time and mine? I didn't see the point.

I spent the bulk of third and fourth year playing football, so I suppose I did do something educational with my time. Of course, it meant leaving without any qualifications.

Granny Reilly missed out on being able to proudly slip O-Grade certificates into transparent plastic polly pockets, before depositing them into her 'Frank's Schooldays' album. She would, of course, be able to see her grandson reach the top of the class in other pursuits, which, she told me, had more than compensated for any lack of educational paperwork. My grandparents didn't know that I had decided to leave 'early', but on the few occasions I did get caught, I was 'rewarded' with a slap on the wrist and a flea in my ear.

Sadly, grandad died when I was 14. He was just 58-years-old and cancer got the better of him. His death hit me hard because, even though mum and dad were special, my grandparents were two of the greatest people I had ever known.

By and large, Cadder was a great place to grow up. Apart from the youth centre and football pitches, there were wide, open spaces galore in which to muck around in. One such open space was the old concrete works, which lay at the back of the houses in Vaila Street.

It was certainly expansive and incorporated the 'Rabbit's Foot Bar,' the remains of an old outbuilding and, no doubt, part of the original concrete works. We spent a lot of time at the 'Rabbit's Foot Bar' and visits normally included partaking in a small libation. I suppose it was a sort of unofficial gang hut, as one of my favourite pastimes included that of 'running' with the local tribe. It sounds terrible now, but at the time it didn't seem such a big deal.

Cadder was surrounded by many schemes, which meant we were

pretty much hemmed in. Going anywhere involved travelling through rival territory and was dangerous, hence most young guys from Cadder tended to remain on their own patch.

Main rivals in the 1970s were the 'Barnes Road,' a gang that took their name from a street in their native Ruchhill. Mostly, fights with the 'Barnes Road' consisted of standing on the opposite side of the canal bank (the 'nolly'), calling each other names or chucking stones at one another. Nothing too serious.

Below the canal bank was a tunnel called the 'Halloween Pend,' which linked both Cadder and Ruchhill. It was a fearsome passageway with a couple of bends, which meant it was in perpetual darkness, and with conditions constantly wet underfoot, it wasn't a nice place to be.

Occasionally, when we were feeling bold, and had sufficient numbers, we would venture through to their side and chase them up over Ruchhill Golf Course. Only on one occasion did I ever get as far as deepest, darkest Ruchhill. Then you really were in bandit country.

Normally we would congregate in the tunnel and prepare our charge. I once decided to lead such a charge and regretted my stupidity instantly. The enemy was positioned on top of the 'Pend' - ready to drop a fridge on top of whoever was daft enough to pop their head out first.

Unfortunately, that was me, and as I ran through they let go the metal contraption and it hit my shoulder. It was agony, so I turned on a sixpence and sought immediate refuge back inside the 'Pend'. It had taken the skin clean off the shoulder and, while it was bleeding profusely, I was well aware that it could've been a whole lot worse.

The bottom end of Cadder had three grass squares. One night a few of us were standing chatting in the middle square (Skirsa Place) when one of them screamed at me to 'watch my back.' I turned round to see this maniac coming straight at me with a meat cleaver. He lashed out, but somehow I managed to dodge the ragged metal blade and it missed me by inches. That was my cue to leg it.

Members of the Barnes Road gang had sneaked into Cadder and we weren't about to start mixing it with them. We were vastly outnumbered. But, we knew exactly which close doors would be unlocked and made our getaway. Thankfully we were faster runners and there were no real casualties. It really was too close for comfort though.

Thankfully, incidents like that weren't the norm and most of our activities could be filed in the 'mischievous' category. Such as stealing our rivals' bonfire wood and lugging it up to our patch - only to find that boys from other street had taken ours. It would inevitably end in a free-for-all. I played football during the day and the twilight shift was strictly for getting up to no good.

I suppose there was a fine line between getting caught up in the gang culture full-time and being able to walk away. Thankfully, I was able to plump for the latter more often than not.

It has been many years now since I lived in Cadder and people may find it strange that someone who has been all over the world playing football can still be attracted to an incidental little scheme in the north of Glasgow, but I still look upon Cadder as the greatest place in the world. For so long it was the centre of my universe and I'll keep heading home every time I have the opportunity. My Uncle Robert and Aunt Marion still live there and that suits me just fine. It gives me the excuse I need to visit any time I'm in Glasgow. I try to get down a couple of times a year and, while the old place may have changed slightly, due to much-needed regeneration, I still look upon it as home.

Recently, I was heading along to the shops for the morning rolls when I stopped all of a sudden and just stared at the youth centre. Anyone clocking me would've been forgiven for thinking I'd lost the plot. The youth centre's future is up in the air and councillors want to bulldoze the place. They obviously don't live local because if they did, they would realise it's a major part of the scheme's social fabric. It's a necessary part of Cadder and will be for as long as folk want to use it.

I've great memories of Cadder and they will be with me forever. And the thing is, it doesn't seem that long ago. It has to be almost 30 years since I last lived in the place, but it seems like yesterday.

Sometimes you read about people who have grown up in housing schemes and made good. They often use the word 'escape' when describing how they managed to move to a nicer area. I certainly don't look upon myself as an escapee.

Of course, I've been lucky in many respects, but I prefer to say I simply used my talents to move on. I was in no hurry to leave the scheme, but football dictated that I would. While I loved living in Cadder, I often wondered what my life would've been like had I moved south with the rest of my family to Bury.

Would I still have pursued a career in professional football? Would boxing have been my number one passion, or would I have stuck in at school and ended up working in a job unconnected to sport? Monday to Friday, nine-to-five in an anonymous office block. Doesn't bear thinking about, does it? One thing I'm sure of though, is that I would've hated the thought of being brought up elsewhere. Cadder was my home. I loved it and it still conjures up a host of magical memories.

TYNECASTLE CALLING

WITH computers but a twinkle in the eye of Mr Bill Gates, it was the ambition of most young lads growing up in the 1970s to become professional footballers. Kids of all shapes and sizes could therefore be found with a ball at their feet, or taking part in a mass kickabout on the nearest bit of spare ground.

When I headed through to Edinburgh that Saturday to watch Tam Bennett and Rangers Athletic tackle Tynecastle Boys Club, the last thing I thought I'd be leaving with was an offer from a professional football club. It was the stuff of dreams. But that's exactly the way it transpired and it was the talk of the 'Steamie' as we headed back to Glasgow. The fact that the team had a cup final appearance to look forward to had paled into insignificance.

On arriving back in Cadder, I rushed up the road to tell my grandparents. They were thrilled, although once the euphoria had cooled, I sat down with grandad to talk through the pros and cons before he would allow me to phone Mr Seith and accept his offer.

'Right,' he said, 'what exactly did Mr Seith say to you? What was his offer? How often does he want you through at training?'

I didn't have the answers. I'd stopped listening after he'd said: 'How would you like to come and train with Heart of Midlothian…?'

Of course, there were no agents in those days and I leaned pretty heavily on grandad, trusting him implicitly to make all the right decisions. After administering lots of helpful advice, he said: 'It's up to you son. It's your career and your life. I'm here to help you make the right decisions, but ultimately it's up to you. Do you want to play for Hearts?'

Of course I did, and we jumped on the train the following week to head through to Tynecastle at the invitation of Mr Seith. He sat there before us in his office along with right hand man, John Cummings, and we plonked ourselves down on a couple of large, imposing leather chairs.

Grandad did most of the talking while I sat like one of those little nodding dogs people normally display on the back sill of their car. It was indeed a proud moment, but I wish I could've comprehended it a bit more. They say that 'youth is wasted on the young'. How true is that?

I was just 14 years old when I signed for Hearts, but my attitude was first class. I knuckled down and got on with the job of discovering exactly what it took to become a professional footballer. I was incredibly lucky and I knew it. I was living the dream and wasn't about to do anything to jeopardise it.

It helped that a mate of mine, Ian 'Bertie' Todd, a Maryhill boy and the nephew of former Lisbon Lion, Bertie Auld, had also signed for Hearts after impressing with Rangers Athletic.

There was a lot to learn and I started off, like all young players do, by sweeping the terracing after home matches. The dressing rooms also needed mucking out and then there were the players' boots to clean. It was so far removed from the glamorous lifestyle of fast cars and WAGs, but it was certainly enjoyable and just being around a stadium as striking as Tynecastle was a tremendous buzz.

Guys like Willie Johnston and Donald Ford were at Hearts in those days and for two days a week during school holidays I travelled through on the train with Drew Busby, who was a top player and a fantastic goalscorer during that period. Normally, I would travel through to Edinburgh two nights a week for training. Like most other lads of my age, I was collecting football cards at the time, and I remember having several of Drew, moustache and all. And here I was, travelling with this guy. It didn't get much better than this.

My train fares were covered and I received the princely sum of 75 shillings (£3.75) a week for my efforts. It was my first ever wage and I was incredibly excited when I received my first pay packet. I thought I'd struck gold. The way I saw it, as long as I was playing football I was happy. I was still at school and was still playing with Rangers Athletic. It was the perfect scenario.

During the week I'd be learning my craft at Hearts, playing football at the weekend and earning a few quid to boot. I was too young to play for Hearts Reserves and they didn't have a youth team, so I was happy to continue playing for Rangers Athletic.

I didn't train with the first team, but was in with the rest of the apprentices who were put through their paces by John Cummings, a first-class coach and a gentleman. He was an ex-professional player and seemed to genuinely enjoy passing on his pearls of wisdom to us youngsters. When John spoke, we listened. He was how I had always imagined a real coach to be, if that makes sense.

I only ever saw Bobby Seith now and again, but when I did he was nothing but pleasant and we had a good relationship. Years later there was a rumour doing the rounds suggesting I'd left Hearts because I didn't get on with Bobby. I don't know how these tales start, but nothing could've been further from the truth.

I was only at Hearts around four months, but I had a ball and learned so much in a short space of time. If anyone asks, I always say that Hearts was my first club; that's a measure of how much I enjoyed it. When it came down to leaving it was purely my decision, and there were a few deciding factors. The incident on the bus, but more of that later, had a huge bearing on my decision.

But there were also a number of occasions when I had to travel through to Edinburgh straight after school. I found that quite tiring and while I wasn't exactly worried about my studies suffering, I did find the whole thing exhausting. But I'll never forget departing the train at Haymarket Station and walking along Gorgie Road towards the stadium. Tynecastle was such a grand arena and I used to pinch myself every morning and tell myself that was where I worked.

When I did eventually decide to leave, John Cummings and Bobby Seith did everything they could to get me to stay and that spoke volumes about how highly they rated me. I felt proud that I had obviously made quite an impact in such a short space of time. But I decided to go and that was that, although there would always be a place in my affections for Hearts.

They had given me my first big break in football and I would never forget that, but now it was time to get on with the rest of my life.

A DREAM SHATTERED

MY dreams of playing professional football for Heart of Midlothian were shattered in a moment of madness. That's all it took to turn my world upside down. A mate, John Docherty, and I had just been to the Western Infirmary, in Glasgow's West End, to visit my gran. She hadn't been keeping too well.

It was two buses there and the same back. I was just 14 at the time, but she meant the world and I wanted to make sure she had someone visiting that night. The visit went well and she was glad that John and I had made the effort. So were we, even though we probably talked shop (football) for the entire hour.

I was still at school and didn't have much money, but when we left the hospital we nicked into the University Café, in Byres Road, pooled our funds and purchased a big a bar of chocolate before catching the bus up to Maryhill. It was a largely uneventful journey, apart from the ceremonial munching of the chocolate, but little did I know what lay in store on the final leg of the trip.

We jumped off the bus at Gairbraid Avenue, in Maryhill, and waited on the 'wee 24' as it was still called, despite a more recognisable double decker bus replacing the original quaint single decker. The fact that the double decker was now the bus of choice would contribute immensely to my downfall.

Even hanging around Gairbraid Avenue was potentially dangerous, as the 'Valley' boys didn't take too kindly to outsiders frequenting 'their' patch – even though the bus stop was directly outside the front door of the main police station. They were a hardy bunch.

It was all very territorial in the 1970s. We felt a bit like cult film characters 'The Warriors' trying to make their way home through gang-riddled New York following a bad boy convention. Gairbraid Avenue was no place for Cadder boys. Technically, the gangs were at 'war' but we were lucky that night. It was relatively quiet and we didn't have too long to wait for our bus. The moment the No.24 arrived we jumped straight on and were mighty relieved when it crawled away from the terminus.

As the bus climbed hilly Sandbank Street, home to another rival gang, 'The Gilshy Boys', from Gilshochhill, we were chatting happily and blissfully unaware that a large group had gathered at the close mouth of No 239. At this point the bus had to slow down to make a sharp right turn into Thornton Street, where it stopped just outside the Gilshy flats. Then it would move off into 'neutral' territory before turning into Cadder – and safety. Unfortunately, we didn't get that far.

Each time I travelled through Gilshy I was always on the look out for signs of potential danger. That night I hadn't seen anything suspicious, so believed the coast to be clear. They must have been hiding in that close though. As the bus slowed down I turned to look out the window - and that's the moment that almost changed my life forever.

A huge brick came crashing through the window and hit me full force in the face. It was a painful thump, and that would've been bad enough, but the majority of shattered glass ended up embedded in my eyes.

I can't recollect seeing who threw the brick – although I was subsequently given a name – or noticing if the perpetrator, or gang members, ran away or remained there to gloat and boast of their cowardly act. I was in too much pain for any of that.

I remember screaming at John Doc, 'My eyes, my eyes.'

He countered with 'I'm looking for them.'

John thought my eyes had been taken clean out by the force of the brick, and that may as well have been the outcome, as the pain I was experiencing at that moment was excruciating. Within seconds of the brick coming through the window, there was darkness, awful pain and fear, in that order. I didn't know what was going to happen to me.

The brick had hit me somewhere between the face and forehead and I could feel the gash just above my eyes, but that was the least of my worries. I remember the bus was stationary. Nothing was happening. It was as though my world had paused. I was also in shock, although I wasn't totally aware of that at the time.

Then the sound of sirens punctured the night air. All the time I was in darkness. I couldn't see a thing, not even shadows in the night. Nothing. I remember hearing the wail of an ambulance in the distance and as the piercing sound appeared closer, I knew it was for me.

The noise intensified and became more distinctive and it duly arrived. The paramedics soon got to work. Naturally, I was oblivious to what they were doing. Part of me wanted to ask, but I didn't dare. I was afraid of the truth. How would I cope with being blind? Did this mean my promising boxing career was over? Would I never be able to fulfil my childhood dream of becoming a professional footballer?

So many questions needing answered. So many answers I didn't want to hear, but I would soon learn the truth because medics were working on me furiously. Eventually, one said, 'We need to get this lad to hospital, and fast'. The 'H' word.

Even though I knew it was inevitable, I still didn't want to hear it. I didn't want to go to hospital. The thought of going there made me feel sick. It made it all seem so real and so serious.

And the dreadful irony is that I was to end up in the same hospital as my gran. But not just the same hospital, or the same ward, but in the bed right next to her. How awful was that? How awful was it knowing that your gran was right next to you, but that you couldn't see her, nor anyone for that matter? I was worried about her being worried.

I was carefully moved from the upstairs deck of the bus to the ambulance. The paramedics were incredibly sensitive to my plight and I simply did as I was told. I was aware of people all round, watching every moment of the drama unfold. Was the perpetrator there? Was he gloating?

The ambulance driver switched on the siren, always a worrying sound, and quickly ferried me back to where I had just come from. At least John was with me and would help me cope with the trauma. It was a nightmare and I was hoping, no, praying, that I would wake up soon.

But, unfortunately, it didn't turn out that way and my worst fears were later confirmed when a doctor – I couldn't tell you what he looked like – informed me of an impending transfer to Gartnavel Hospital, which was something of a relief as it meant gran wouldn't have to lie there looking at me 24/7.

Gartnavel is more of a specialist hospital and I quickly realised that this problem wasn't going to be solved overnight. Surgeons, meanwhile, battled to clean away the glass shards that had infiltrated my eyes, outside and inside.

Glass had worked its way round behind the retina and this alone presented these talented medics with their greatest challenge. To remove the glass without causing even more damage was a slow and painstaking process.

Initially, I had 50 stitches inserted in one eye and 10 in the other. I was told that my eyes were a complete mess and it had all been caused by one moment of madness. I didn't have time to hate the person responsible at that point, but that would come. For the moment, I was concentrating solely on winning this battle. There was little doubt in my mind though that I had been targeted purely because of where I lived.

During the early days in hospital, I had a visit from a 'Gilshy boy' called 'Tich.' Realistically, it could have been anyone as I still couldn't see a thing. He assured me that it wasn't him that threw the brick. We were old street sparring partners and I believed him. But who did what wasn't really my main concern.

I had been in the Western Infirmary for around a fortnight before being transferred a couple of miles along the road to Gartnavel, which is situated on Great Western Road, one of the main routes from Glasgow to Loch Lomond, although I wouldn't be going anywhere pretty for quite some time.

I spent almost six months in Gartnavel and it seemed like an endless stream of operations. At the time I probably didn't appreciate the complicated nature of the injuries, but looking back, I realise that surgeons had faced an uphill battle to save my sight.

The main consultant came round to see me one day and explained the main problems they were facing. The internal stitches were continually bursting and it really was touch and go at that point as to whether or not they could restore my sight, fully or even partially. There were huge complications and each time they thought they were making progress, stitches would again burst and they would be back to square one. But they didn't stop trying - they never once gave in.

Initially the news had devastated me and I was resigned to spending the rest of my life with a white stick and guide dog. It was easily the lowest point of my 14 years to date. I was still young and reasoned that had I been born blind it may not have been so bad, but to have your sight cruelly snatched away would be ten times worse.

Everything had to be reconstructed at the back of my eyes. Absolutely everything. At this point I had been in hospital a couple of months, but still hadn't been able to fully accept my fate. I had frequent visitors. Family and friends would come and go, their presence helping to break the monotony and, more importantly, playing a vital role in maintaining my spirits.

Then one afternoon I had a couple of surprise visitors. Bobby Seith and John Cummings made the trip through from the capital. What a massive boost. They assured me that I still had a future at Tynecastle. You've no idea how much these few words lifted my spirits.

Then senior Jambos such as Drew Busby, Willie Johnston and Donald Ford visited the hospital and soon had me laughing. It was an incredible feeling. Their support was fantastic and their very attendance proved to me that I was appreciated at Tynecastle. I was a junior player with Hearts, but these club legends had taken the trouble to come and see me. The whole series of visits had me feeling upbeat for the first time in months.

Evenings were the longest though. It was during these that I began to revisit that dark night. Why did I look out the window? At least if I'd kept my face turned away the worst that could've happened would've been a sore head and I would've got over that pretty quickly. Some might even suggest it wouldn't have done that much damage.

The hours, days and weeks passed and all the time, surgeons fought to save my sight. I spent hours in the theatre but there was never any indication of whether things were going well or not. I'm convinced they didn't want to say anything in case they couldn't deliver on their promises.

One day, I was taken to theatre and they operated, as they had done many times previous. Naturally I was out cold, but when I came round, and had my tea and toast, a nurse told me that the consultant wanted to speak to me. I didn't think anything of it. My eyes were covered in bandages and, once again, everything was just audio, nothing visual, although I was starting to get used to it.

Later that day the consultant came to see me and we had a brief chat about nothing important. He leaned forward and said he just wanted to take a look. He started to take off the bandages. It was as though someone had switched the lights back on. I was ecstatic, although he urged caution, insisting it was early days and that I wasn't yet out the woods.

I soon was though. This incredibly gifted man had won a long and bloody battle and to this day I am eternally grateful to him and his dedicated team. They worked a miracle. The bandages remained off from that moment. I wasn't allowed home for a few days – for observational reasons – but I could handle that.

Nurses brought me football magazines and comics. The daily papers, in fact anything at all. I even started reading notices on the walls. I would go to the toilet and stop to read posters about eating healthy. I could see. Of course, there were moments when I was too frightened to be truly happy, just in case it was all a false dawn and I was again plunged back into the abyss.

On the day of my release, I was like a new man – or teenager – and I left Gartnavel walking on air. A family member was at the hospital to pick me up and even though it was just a short drive home, some 15 minutes or so, I took in every sight as though seeing for the first time. Sure, I knew I still had a mountain to climb in terms of my recuperation, but the major battle had been won and the rest was up to me.

The first thing I did was call time on a promising boxing career. It had been a short, although successful one, but it was too much of a risk and one I wasn't willing to take. I had experienced months of complete darkness and it was a place I didn't wish to re-visit. One punch would've put me back on the canvas. There was no way I was taking that chance.

Football? Now that was a completely different matter. It was my life and as soon as I was able, I was out and about and down at Cadder pitches playing till it was dark. But there was one more legacy from the horror time I'd just endured, and that was the moron who had thrown the brick in the first place.

Believe me when I say that retribution was a viable option. No, make that the only option. I thought of it many times, but decided against seeking revenge, although there was a string of people only too willing to take up the baton for me. I refused their kind offers. God knows, it would have been so easy to say yes and see him pay for everything he'd put me through. I felt it was more important though to put the entire, sorry episode behind me and move on.

No sooner had I come out of hospital than the newspapers were at the door. They all wanted a piece of the promising young footballer whose career had been tragically cut short by a brick-throwing thug.

My grandad was brilliant. He was a hardy lad and chased those who didn't appear to have my best interests at heart. He allowed the Evening Times access. They had been good to me in the past. Their people came in and took some photographs and I offered a few quotes. It seemed the right thing to do.

For the pictures, I had a ball that had been given to me by some friends. They had scribbled certain words on it (a reference to the original incident). The Evening Times' photographer took quite a few pictures of me holding the ball, then asked me to throw it up in the air and head it.

I still had the bandages on and the sun was causing a few problems, but I couldn't believe it when the article was printed and the accompanying photograph had the ball positioned perfectly with the words... '***** is Dead'... slap bang in the middle and naming the alleged brick thrower.

I know who was solely responsible for throwing the brick through the window, but haven't seen him since the night it happened. I felt utter hatred for that individual. He was obviously a coward because if he'd had anything against me and wanted to do something about it, I would have obliged by fighting him one-to-one. But people like that don't do one-to-one - it's not in their make-up. It would probably have been easier to accept if he'd done it in a boxing ring, toe-to-toe, and not in the cowardly manner he chose.

The thing is that could've been my granny on that bus or someone else's kid. That's the worrying thing. Had that been the case, there would've been hell to pay. He would NOT have got off Scot free, no way. There would've been a backlash, big time, and I would not have been responsible for my actions.

To this day I still suffer from double vision and that'll be with me until the day I die. One pupil is bigger than the other, but to think of where I was, at my darkest hour, and where I am now, there is no comparison. What happened, happened and I have to live with it. Thankfully it wouldn't affect my career. I was too passionate about football to let anything get in the way, although for a while it really was touch and go

A B⚽Y AMONG MEN

MENTALLY I was still feeling the effects of the brick-throwing incident in my latter days at Hearts. The trauma was ongoing and was one of the reasons I swapped Tynecastle for Cadder. That's where I spent the bulk of my time immediately after leaving Hearts, and where I felt most at ease.

Nightmares continued long after I'd left Edinburgh behind as the frightening incident was proving difficult get over. The Evening Times ran a story called 'Frank McDougall: Why I'll never sit on a bus again.'

It was all true. Something happened to me that night. I had always been quite a confident guy, with a swagger. That swagger remained to a degree, but there was something niggling away at the back of my mind, something that made me apprehensive about a lot of things, even to this day.

Immediately after leaving Hearts I decided to finish with football completely. I can't put my finger on the reason, but I'd made my mind up and that was that. Maybe I felt cursed, or that getting my sight back after four months in the dark was so good that I didn't want to push my luck.

I was still playing football with my mates down the pitches, but refused point blank to take part in any organised games. I got a job as a labourer in the local brickworks. It was out past Cadder on the Balmore Road and I worked there for a few months. It was hard graft and certainly much tougher than I'd envisaged the life of a professional footballer would have been. That was all in the past now anyway, or at least that was the plan.

A friend of a friend soon found out I wasn't playing any more and convinced me that quitting the game was such a waste of talent. Slogging my guts out at the brickworks certainly wasn't my idea of fun, but I was earning an honest living and I was content.

But he wasn't for giving up and continually asked if I wanted a game with junior side Duntocher Hibs. They played out past Milngavie, at a little place called Hardgate, and I decided to go along one Saturday. It was at the Duntocher Hibees that I first teamed up with John 'Cowboy' McCormack and we would go on to become life-long friends – and both marry Lilys. Cowboy was such an amazing character.

I only played a couple of games for Duntocher, but they were instrumental in helping me regain my appetite for a game I had first fallen in love with as a four year old. It wasn't long before another junior team was waiting in the wings and it was based a bit closer to home. I was friends with a guy called Abie Monaghan, a native of Possil and an incredibly talented player - one of the best I ever played alongside. I suppose that's saying something considering some of the players I lined up with at both St Mirren and Aberdeen.

Abie asked me along to Glasgow Perthshire and I was happy to accept. Keppoch Park, in Possil, would be home for two seasons and I loved my time there. I ended up with more than I bargained for though, when I bagged myself a wife. But to the football, and the reason I enjoyed the experience so much was the standard of player – and person – that frequented 'Shire's black ash park on a Saturday.

No sooner had I arrived at Keppoch though than my 'Shire career looked as though it had ground to a premature end. I'd only played a couple of games when I was approached by legendary Celtic star, Bertie Auld after a match one afternoon. Now this guy really was one of my heroes (yes, another one). He was a major part of the first British team to win the European Cup – the Lisbon Lions – and stood head and shoulders above most midfielders of his time.

Bertie was manager of Partick Thistle and he asked me down to Firhill for a trial. I jumped at the chance and said goodbye to my old team-mates (of just a few weeks) at Keppoch Park. 'Shire manager Ian Wallace was great about the whole deal and assured me that if it didn't work out, he'd have me back in a flash. That was music to my ears, and very comforting, although I hoped I wouldn't have to take him up on his offer.

I trained at Thistle, but was farmed out to Sighthill Boys Club for my competitive fix. I also trained with Sighthill. Their manager, Eddie McCulloch, put us through our paces at a facility way out Maryhill Road near Bearsden.

Back at Firhill one morning, I was brushing Alan Hansen's boots. It was the week before he left to sign for Liverpool and I couldn't have been happier. After 'passing up' an opportunity to make the grade at Hearts, here I was having a second shot at pro glory with the nearest senior team to my Cadder home.

Hansen was the type of guy who wanted to see his face in his boots though. I didn't really care for him, if the truth be told, because he never once gave me the time of day, even after I'd finished sparkling his boots. But I'd just finished polishing them this day when someone came into the dressing room and told me to go and see the gaffer.

Off I trotted along the corridor to Bertie's office. I knocked the door and stood waiting for the ok to enter. It didn't come. I knocked again, but nothing. I went back along to see if I could see the guy that had passed on the message. I was walking past the other dressing room and the door was ajar. I noticed a cloud of smoke inside and popped my head round the door. There was Bertie, lying in the bath puffing on a huge King Edward, looking and acting every inch the 'King of Firhill.'

'You wanted to see me, boss,' I asked. He nodded and told me to brush out the dressing room, which I did. I was then asked to bag a pile of dirty towels that were lying about the room. When I finished, Bertie motioned me across. I wish I'd never heard the words he was about to speak.

'You'll never make a football player, son,' he said, hardly looking at me as he dragged on his shortening cigar. 'You're not good enough, I'm letting you go.'

As I'd said, Bertie Auld was my idol, but he'd gone down in my estimations. I was absolutely gutted. Couldn't he have let me down a little gentler, or even before I'd been ordered to carry out those menial tasks? I suppose it was harder to take from a guy I'd hoped to impress, but there was life after Partick Thistle and there was definitely life after Bertie Auld – I'd make sure of it.

He had been a tough guy on the field and, for sure, I learned that he was every bit as hard off it. Partick Thistle was my local club and I had wanted to make something of myself there, but unfortunately happy endings aren't mandatory. Many might say 'back to the drawing board', but for me it was 'back to the 'Shire'.

I called Ian Wallace and asked the question. 'Absolutely', he said. At least they wanted me. I slotted back in as though I'd never been away. It was a relief to get back playing with guys like Abie, John Pelosi – who would later go senior and make his mark with St Johnstone – Pat Smyth, Patsy Fagan and many other great players.

And it showed in my play because the goals started to arrive with incredible regularity. Maybe it's because I was happy. Or could it have been something else? After home matches we would 'retire' to the Brothers Bar, at Saracen Cross for a couple of pints and a bite to eat. The camaraderie between the players was first class and that old adage about 'those who drink together, win together', was certainly true of 'Shire's Class of '78'.

I didn't always make it back to the pub though, because directly facing the exit gate at Keppoch was a single tenement block in Closeburn Street, and I was drawn to one house in particular. It was the home of Lily Kavanagh and she was normally at her window as I was leaving the ground. It started off with a simple wave and a smile and then she would come down to the closemouth and we would chat for a while.

We eventually progressed to dating and before too long, probably around a year, we were married. Whirlwind romance or what? We bought a tenement flat in Kilfinan Street in Lambhill, just at Mallon's Bar, and goal kick away from Cadder. I had my eldest daughter, Kelly, with Lily and we would later move out to East Kilbride and build our dream home.

The fact that I had been at Hearts, and 'enjoyed' a short stint at Partick Thistle, gave me the drive and ambition necessary to succeed at the top level.

I knew I could play in the Scottish Premier League and I knew I would hold my own. I would tell myself – 'I will be good enough, I will make it'. I always had faith in my ability and knew that I would score goals at any level. It had been my decision to leave Hearts and I never once regretted it. I wasn't big headed, but knew I was a decent player. Cockiness was a trait I never possessed, but all strikers need confidence and that is a completely different thing altogether.

Joe McHugh was the owner of the 'Shire during my time there, and he also owned the Brothers Bar. He was an absolute gentleman and one of the nicest guys I've ever met. Joe had installed Ian Wallace as manager and he really knew his stuff. Ian had a great knowledge of the junior game and it showed. The players had great respect for him, which was so important. I loved working with Ian and the team spirit he built up was second to none.

Abie and I played up front together and he was just such a star. He had played at Hibs and a few other clubs and when I was at the 'Shire, he had been around the block. As one of the youngest players at Keppoch Park at the time, I would get the benefit of that experience.

I was a good listener and learned a lot. You couldn't fail to learn from these guys because experience oozed through the very core of the team. I scored lots of goals for 'Shire, but much of that was down to hard-working and selfless team-mates.

At the 'Shire, our local derby was against Petershill, and not Ashfield, who were just over the wall. The Peasie came from Springburn, just a mile or so up the road from Possilpark. Games against them were always full-blooded encounters and not for the faint-hearted. I relished them. They had guys like Norrie Fulton and Tam Gourlay, who was the first player ever to save a penalty kick against Celtic and Scotland defender Tommy Gemmell. Gourlay had been with Airdrie at the time, but had dropped down to the juniors to sign for Petershill.

We had them at our place one day and it was a match we had to win to clinch the league title. No pressure then. It was 2-2 with just under a minute to go and suddenly I recalled something our team captain, Davie McKnight, had said to me in the dressing room before the game.It went something like, 'That big Tam Gourlay's a soft touch. He's a bottle merchant. If you find yourself one-on-one with him, just go right through him, he'll pull out the challenge at the last minute. Believe me.'

Well, I was young at the time, and just a touch naive. Of course I believed senior guys like Davie. After all, he was our club captain and wouldn't lie to me. How wrong could I be?

As I said, the clock was ticking down and I suddenly found myself one-on-one with Gourlay. Recalling Davie's words, there was nothing to fear so I ran straight at him, expecting him to jump out the way when he saw this ferocious centre forward bearing down on him.

As I was being stretchered off, my team-mates were all around me, congratulating me on scoring the winning goal and securing another trophy for the 'Shire.

I was informed later, after being given the all-clear by medics, that the ball had been played through to me by one of our midfielders and that I confidently beat Gourlay to the ball. Then someone switched the lights off.

Now, if we were going by the script, he was supposed to dive for cover as I bore down on him, growling in an effort to scare him off. It came down to a straightforward 50-50 and did he pull out of the challenge? Not a chance. And I felt the full force of his studs on my chest. But I had got to the ball first and knocked it past him for the winning goal. So I ended up with a few holes on my torso. Big deal. The fact that I had then been carried off – and him sent off – really was incidental.

Later that night we were celebrating in the Brothers Bar when a proud looking Davie joined me. 'You were fantastic today Frank,' he said, with a grin as wide as the River Clyde. I looked at him challengingly, before saying, 'I thought that Gourlay was a bottle merchant.'

He replied, 'I was only winding you up, Frank, but if you didn't see the ball hit the back of the net, I can assure you, it was a cracker'.

He shook my hand and walked off to join some of the others in the celebrations. I had to admire his cheek. It had worked a treat and we had won the game, but my head was still thumping, and it wasn't the drink.

On another occasion, we were down at Port Glasgow for a Scottish Cup replay after drawing the first game 2-2 at our place, in which I'd scored twice. Did we think we'd missed our big chance? No way, we were a confident lot and knew we could win down at the Port, although it would be tough. They were a hard team to play against on their own patch and some of their supporters really did take the biscuit.

Midway through the second period, we were well on top and again I'd managed to score twice. A few of their fans weren't happy and I discovered exactly how unhappy one of them was when I completed my hat-trick. It was a decent goal and as I ran to our small band of fans to celebrate, this guy swigging from a bottle of Eldorado (the 1970s equivalent of Buckfast) obviously wasn't feeling the love. He came right up to me and threatened to smash the bottle over my head, and stick the remainder in my neck. I cut the celebrations short and returned to the centre circle. As they prepared to re-start the game, I said to Abie, 'I think that guy's gonna do me after the match.'

He told me not to worry. Abie insisted the guy was full of hot air and that it was just a hollow threat.

The ref eventually blew the final whistle and as we headed for the sanctuary of the pavilion I noticed that the Port Glasgow nutter was still hanging around. I was all for jumping straight on the team bus and heading up the road to Possil, but the lads persuaded me to come into the Port club for a quick pint. Once inside, and within the bosom of the 'Shire lads, I felt a little safer, until the door opened – cowboy style – and in walked the Lone Ranger. Thankfully he didn't feel the need to share his tonic wine with me and we left after a single drink.

Yes, the Port was a hard place. Although the junior game in general is a tough place to learn your trade, it stands you in good stead for the seniors and, I suppose, it was all part of growing up.

The 'Shire's pitch, Keppoch Park, was one of the last junior grounds to have a black ash playing surface and it often gave us a great home advantage – or, at the very least, proved to be a great leveller. Lots of teams would turn up, take one look and you could tell from their reaction that they just didn't fancy it one bit. That gave us the edge because from the first minute wee Davie McNight would have us flying in for some meaty challenges, just to show that we weren't afraid of a nasty black ash rash. Later, in the post-match shower, we would be scrubbing out bits of ash and the water would be jet black.

The black ash surface didn't ever frighten me, but I could never quite work out the bounce of the ball. It could make even the best of players look extremely stupid, as they would go one way, and the ball the other.

We won the old Central League Second Division title in my first season at 'Shire, and then claimed the league play-offs, which were played for between the winners of the first, second and third division champions.

That meant we were in among the big boys in my second and final season at Keppoch and it was a great way to see how I would handle the step up. Seamlessly, I would have to say and we went so close to becoming one of the very few sides to have won both leagues in successive seasons. We had more or less set the pace all season, but lost a couple of games at vital times.

Regardless, we still topped the league table with just a few matches to play and our main threat came from Lesmahagow. We had just two games left and the 'Gow had four.

Our destiny wasn't in our own hands because if they won all their games, they would be champions – regardless of what we did. But they slipped up and that gave us a chance – until we came a cropper against Shettleston. It meant we had to win our last game by 26 clear goals at Benburb. Suffice to say we didn't and the 'Gow won the league. We finished runners-up, which wasn't too bad an effort considering we'd just come up from the second division.

But we weren't finished there and I had an opportunity to grab some silverware before seeking out pastures new. We travelled the short distance to Maryhill's Lochburn Park for the Maryhill Charity Cup final against the hosts, who had just won the third division. I managed to score a couple as we won a full-blooded encounter 3-2 after extra time. Marking me that day was none other than Jim Duffy, who would sign for Celtic the following season.

I couldn't believe that we were still playing at the end of June. In the juniors, the seasons seemed to merge into one another and more often than not the close season would consist of a week or two, which was great for me. Naturally, there was very little time for pre-season training, which I loathed and that suited me down to the ground.

But, when the time eventually came to move on from the 'Shire it was tough, especially as I'd made so many great friends. Heading for pastures new, which in this case would be Clydebank, was made that little bit easier when Joe McHugh informed me that he had managed to insert a special clause into my contract with the Bankies. 'Shire would get ten per cent of any future sell-on fee.

So, when St Mirren eventually paid £180,000 for me, the Possilpark side netted a cool £18,000. Now that's what I call good business. Joe may have been an incredibly likeable guy, but he was also a shrewd operator.

Personally, I was bursting to play at a higher level. My Tynecastle experience, if not my time at Partick Thistle, had merely whetted the appetite and I wanted more – and I was determined that given the opportunity again, I would grab it with both hands.

By this time I had left the brickworks behind and moved to a job as a scaffolder. I had always wanted to reach the dizzy heights in my career – but not up a 300-foot scaffolding rig. It was time to say goodbye to 'Shire and hello Bankies, although my time at Kilbowie Park would be a dizzy mixture of highs and lows.

CASH IN THE BANKIES

I HAD apparently been on the Bankies radar for a while. Scouts had been up at a few 'Shire games as manager Bill Munro looked to reshape his side following relegation from the Scottish Premier League the previous season.

Bill had just sold talented winger Davie Cooper to Rangers and the £100,000 transfer fee had helped purchase brand new floodlights for trim Kilbowie Park. The surroundings were fantastic and the envy of many a bigger club. But due to their large outlay, the Bankies were on the lookout for a bargain buy and I wasn't the only new face to join up during the close season.

But my strike partner, Blair Miller, had been with the Bankies the season previous, albeit he had spent the biggest part of the campaign in the reserves. He was a bank clerk and a quiet spoken lad, but he didn't take any nonsense from opposing defenders, and I liked that. Blair and I clicked almost immediately and linked up well. I also managed to pick up more than a few scraps from his legendary knock downs. We forged a great partnership.

Initially the gaffer had called me up and asked if I'd like to join the team for training. That approach seemed par for the course in those days. I had no hesitation in agreeing, realising it was a genuine opportunity to make something of myself. Third time lucky in the seniors?

During my first training session he said to me, 'I hear you've been scoring regularly for the 'Shire. The reports are positive and I reckon you could do a job for me. We're keen to get back to the Premier League and we need goals.'

Bill offered me a signing-on fee of £2,000 and I didn't need to think twice. I was just 20-years-old but, while I wasn't quite ready for the knacker's yard, I was well aware that the clock was ticking on my career. But what would prospective suitors think if I added Clydebank to Hearts and Partick Thistle as senior clubs I'd failed to make the grade at?

There comes a time when you have to lay down a permanent marker and shape up, or ship out. That time was now. Of course, I again had the safety net of the 'Shire to fall back on, but I couldn't use that forever. It was time to stand on my own two feet.

I started off with the obligatory pre-season training and it was tough. It was the first time I'd been involved in anything like it and I struggled. I worked at it though and eventually the fitness came. In any case, fitness would become vital as the season wore on, as the lads liked their post-match drink in nearby watering hole, The Atlantis. Hard work was the order of the day as I battled to keep the legacy of my excesses at bay.

The new season was almost upon us and Kilmarnock were our opening day visitors. I took a moment to reflect on the journey I was about to embark on – and one thing was missing. My grandad. He had helped so much, but passed away before getting the opportunity to watch me in action in the Scottish League. I'm sure he was looking down proudly when Killie came to town though.

I found out the day before the match that I'd be on the bench, one of the two substitutes permitted in the 1970s. Nerves were prevalent and I didn't get a wink of sleep the night before. I tossed and turned from dusk till dawn and it was a bleary eyed, but excited, yours truly that leapt from his bed just as the milkman was delivering his bottles.

Making my way to Kilbowie, I realised that this was it. It was Saturday, August 12, 1978 and my day of reckoning had finally arrived. Bring it on, I thought. We met up for a pre-match meal of steak at the club and then started to prepare for the match. Later in my career, Alex Ferguson would ban steak as our pre-match meal because, he claimed, it took too long to digest. I certainly don't think it ever did me any harm.

I remember sitting in the dressing-room, legs like jelly and thinking how far I'd come from playing down at Cadder pitches with Scotland Boys Club. I had never been this nervous before. After a goalless first-half, Blair notched the opener, although Killie pegged it back to one apiece through Cairney.

The gaffer threw me on with around 15 minutes to go and at first I simply soaked up the atmosphere. There were just over 2,000 people inside Kilbowie, the biggest crowd I had ever performed in front of. I was desperate to do well and chased down everything. I wanted the Killie players to know they were in a game. And I got my reward in the 82nd minute when I used my pace to latch on to a through ball to prod home what proved to be the winner.

When it eventually sank in, I was overjoyed. I remember Davie McCulloch, the ex-Ayr United player, being one of the first over to congratulate me. He was a smashing player and the whole experience felt fantastic.

Future Celtic and Scotland star Davie Provan was playing with Kilmarnock that day and they were a big scalp. I was on top of the world and couldn't believe it when the Press wanted a word after the game. I remember thinking, 'This is what it's all about'.

I went home that night, lapping up every minute of my winning goal. I was elated, but my feet were still firmly planted on the ground. I was well aware that one swallow didn't make a summer.

At work on the Monday morning, people were talking about my goal. At first I didn't really know how to handle it, but as the goals started to flow, I became used to it, although I never quite mastered the art of being centre of attention.

I was part-time at the Bankies and was on £50 a week basic wage plus £30 win bonus – and I had just got the players their first of the season. What a feeling. I've always been big on team spirit and what better way to endear yourself to a new group than by sticking some extra cash in their back pockets?

Cowboy McCormack was in our starting line-up that day and we had laid down our marker, although we lost 4-2 at Raith the following Saturday. I was in from the start, but Rovers hit three in the first eight minutes to leave us reeling. We found it hard to get back into the game despite Blair scoring twice.

We were desperate to get the club straight back up into the Premier League, so we had to knuckle down and roll up the sleeves. I failed to score for a couple of games, but bounced back with goals in a League Cup win over Stenhousemuir and a league victory up at Montrose.

In mid-September we faced a tough home match with Hamilton Accies, but I managed the first goal in an impressive 4-1 win. The two points from that game took us to second top of the league, just one behind Dundee. One of the most pleasing aspects of our impressive form was that we seemed to have gelled in a relatively short space of time. The gaffer was first class, although he wasn't too chuffed when I was sent-off in a 1-1 draw at Airdrie.

As a measure of just how far we'd come in a short space of time, we travelled through to Easter Road to face Hibs in the third round of the League Cup. They were unbeaten in all competitions, but we put them under massive pressure and were gutted to leave with a 1-0 loss.

The following Saturday, it was up to Perth to play St Johnstone and we won an absolutely cracking game 3-2. I got the first goal and it started off a run in which I scored in six out of our next seven matches. This confirmed my earlier theory that I could score goals in almost any company.

I was still working as a scaffolder at the time and as things were going well enough, I didn't see any need to change it. We had a great bunch of boys at Kilbowie and, as well as Cowboy, we had the likes of Jim Gallacher, an excellent keeper, Norrie Hall and Billy Fanning.

Blair was a fantastic centre-forward, although I like to think that I did most of his running. In fact, when he ventured 'outside' the box, he was prone to the occasional nosebleed.

One source of frustration was that I had missed out on the chance to play alongside Davie Cooper. He had exited one door just as I was coming in the other. We would've made a great team. How many goals would Coop have set up for Blair and I?

I was a relatively quiet guy at the time. I just listened and occasionally chipped in with pearls of my wisdom. I never overstayed my welcome in any serious team debates though.

One vice I did enjoy was a cigarette. In that first game against Killie I had been sitting on the bench lapping up the action. When the ref blew for half-time I was preparing to go out for a warm-up when Norrie, our right-back, approached the bench.

He had enjoyed a good, solid first-half, but I couldn't believe that as the rest of the players disappeared up the tunnel for a slice of orange and some boss-chat, he came over to the bench and lit up a ciggy. I was absolutely desperate for one and asked if he wouldn't get into trouble for lighting up during a match. He assured me that Bill Munro allowed him to smoke just before kick-off and at half-time. Once I got to know Norrie a bit better I told him that I shared his 'passion' and we used to enjoy a not-so-fly drag before and during matches.

Dundee were the early pace setters in the division and we felt that if we could keep up with them, we had every chance of joining them in the Premier League. Near the end of November, we hosted the Dark Blues at Kilbowie and 2,500 fans packed in to see the game. Our last home game, against Montrose, had attracted just 700 so you can imagine the atmosphere was electric.

Former Lisbon Lion Tommy Gemmell was the Dundee manager and he'd built a solid side at Dens Park. We also had good players though and fancied our chances of an upset.

We got off to the best possible start when I headed home inside the first 20 minutes. That's the way it stayed until the break, and we could hear big Tommy giving what can only be described as an inspirational team talk through the wall. But Blair doubled our advantage and, despite a late consolation, Tommy couldn't prevent us joining his side at the top of the league. It was a great feeling to be riding so high in my first season of senior football.

A couple of weeks before Christmas, Santa paid us an early visit. We had St Johnstone, at Kilbowie in a must-win match, but trailed 2-0 at half-time and were being played off the park. Then all of a sudden, the lights went out. There had been a power cut for miles around and the game had to be abandoned. Shame.

Kilmarnock and Dundee were well in the mix, so we had definitely got out of jail, because even the most optimistic among us couldn't see a way back.

One of my greatest memories at Clydebank arrived in the middle of January, 1978, when Rangers manager John Greig called Bill Munro to ask for a challenge match.

The Old Firm were due to meet in a Scottish Cup semi-final, but Rangers' game had been called off due to ice. The managers arranged a game for the midweek. We hadn't exactly been cramming the games in ourselves and hadn't played for a month.

A couple of weeks beforehand, Rangers had pulled off a real shock in the European Cup when they travelled to Holland and became the first foreign club to beat PSV Eindhoven on their own patch. I remember watching that match and thinking that Rangers had one heck of a team.

So imagine my surprise when we thumped them 4-1 at Kilbowie in the midweek friendly – and I scored a hat-trick. For my first, I lobbed Peter McCloy, which in itself was no mean feat. As his nickname, the Girvan Lighthouse, suggests, big 'Gas Meter' was around six feet four inches. Blair put us two up after the break and I sealed a decent performance with two goals in as many second-half minutes to complete the rout.

The following day, Rangers drew Cologne in the European Cup and I remember thinking that they'd have to play a wee bit better if they were to brush aside the German cracks. The ground was so hard that night that I played with training shoes on. It was an incredible feat for tiny Clydebank and was made all the more remarkable as Rangers had their first choice eleven out.

To thump a team 4-1 that included the likes of Sandy Jardine, Davie Cooper, Bobby Russell and Alex MacDonald was just amazing. It gave us great confidence. We were a decent side, but Rangers were far better. It was our cup final. When you play against either of the Old Firm you always want to do your best in the hope that they'll sign you up.

It was all over the papers the following day and once again I found myself subject to a barrage of Press attention. The papers wanted to know all about this guy who had scored a hat-trick against the mighty Glasgow Rangers – with a pair of sandshoes on. I thought back to my first game for Rangers Athletic, and my four goals against Tynecastle Boys Club. What was it with me and sandshoes?

Six months beforehand, I had been playing for the 'Shire and the Press wouldn't have cared if I'd been wearing clogs, but now that the Old Firm had been on the receiving end they wanted to know even the tiniest detail.

Being thrust into the media glare was something I'd never contemplated while growing up in Cadder. Nothing can prepare you for a group of people shoving microphones and notepads in your face, but it's certainly not all bad.

Blair and I had struck up an excellent partnership and for two guys who hadn't even known each other a few months previous, and who both came from the juniors, albeit at different times, it was good going.

It wasn't long before the gaffer handed me a licence to roam. I was switching from one flank to the other and playing through the middle. I thrived on the freedom and it definitely contributed to our success. Bill was a shrewd manager.

Another highlight that season was my Hampden debut. We drew Queen's Park in the Scottish Cup at home, but they battled well and held us to a 3-3 draw. I scored, but we had to rely on good old Cowboy, with virtually the last kick of the game, to earn us a replay. There may only have been a few turnstiles open at the National Stadium for the replay that night, but it was still a fantastic feeling to run out onto the hallowed turf.

I briefly thought back to my childhood, when we would play games on any spare piece of ground and pretend it was Hampden. Now I was actually there. Dreams can come true.

A re-arranged match at Dundee was scheduled for midweek and the club were that desperate to win they flew Jim Fallon up from London. It mattered not though, we lost 2-1. We then crashed out of the Scottish in a competitive local derby with Dumbarton.

Things went from bad to worse, on a personal level, the following midweek when we squared up to Queen of the South. Every point was now a prisoner and although we won 3-1, with Blair (twice) and me getting the goals, I was gutted to be shown a red card for absolutely nothing.

It was a tough encounter at Palmerston and the tackles were flying in. I became embroiled in an incident after a few players had gone in heavy to win the ball. I squared up to an opponent in a 'handbags' incident and the referee came charging in to sort it out.

He told a couple of us to stand aside while he consulted his linesman. I was totally shocked when he showed me a straight red card for spitting on an opponent.

He said it within earshot of the guy I was supposed to have gobbed on and he was straight over, assuring the ref, 'Frank didn't spit on me, we just clashed, there was nothing in it'. But he had made his decision based on the ludicrous opinion of the linesman and off I went. I didn't spit on the guy and yet I was convicted of that very offence. Mud sticks, but it didn't seem to bother the referee, even though he'd been reassured by my supposed victim.

And it wasn't even just a case of my opponent trying to get me off the hook. Spitting in someone's face is one of the most disgusting things a player can do to a fellow professional, so the other guy was hardly going to lie about it.

I missed the match at Rugby Park the following Saturday as we drew a blank with Killie. It looked as though Dundee were red-hot favourites to win the league and we would be left fighting it out with Killie for the scraps. At this point the Ayrshire side were top, two points ahead, but we'd played two games less.

In a midweek game at the start of March, Blair and I scored three between us (I got two) as we demolished St Johnstone 3-0. Papers described us as the league's deadliest double act. At this point, leading scorer Blair had 26 goals in domestic competition and I had 18. I felt as though we could score every time we played. We managed two apiece against Airdrie near the end of March in a 4-1 win. That took us top of the league.

There was a great buzz around the club and the players were desperate to do well for one another, the management and supporters. The last day in March was D-day as we hosted Kilmarnock. A large crowd turned up only to leave disappointed: we lost 2-1. That defeat certainly gave Killie the upper hand in the race for promotion, although fate was still in our own hands. Three wins from our final three games and a place in Scottish football's elite was still ours.

The first match was against Dumbarton and, as well as desperately needing the points, we also wanted revenge on the Sons for dumping us out the Scottish. And revenge was sweet. We beat them 3-1 thanks to a double from yours truly and a Cowboy thunderbolt.

I was only at Clydebank for a season, but it was a thoroughly enjoyable and invaluable experience. The Bankies were a great club and treated me well. Unfortunately, though, we were to miss out on promotion in the penultimate game of the season.

We were up at Arbroath and had to win. I opened the scoring after around 15 minutes, but the Red Lichties pegged us back. There were 900 folk there and most were dressed in red and white. With the clock ticking down, we knew just one goal would see us back in the top flight. Promotion was so near, yet so far.

Then, with a couple of minutes remaining, I was hauled down in the box and the ref pointed to the spot. Penalty. Cowboy offered to take it and no one was arguing. I believe they're still looking for the ball in the North Sea, somewhere between Arbroath and Norway.

I had taken quite a few penalties that season, but I left that one to Cowboy and I've no regrets on that score. Cowboy had the bottle for the big occasion, but unfortunately that particular kick went askew. The match finished 1-1, which left us with the proverbial mountain to climb.

Killie's league programme was over and they sat proudly at the top on 54 points. Dundee were second with 52, although they had four games in hand over the Ayrshire side, while we were third, also with 52 points, but with an inferior goals difference. We had just one game left.

Oh, how I wish, like today, there were three points up for grabs for a win. In saying that, we would've been nailed-on certainties to go up had we not shipped 50 league goals that season. A place in the top flight was still up for grabs, but to gain promotion, we had to beat Raith Rovers by at least 11 goals at Stark's Park.

In the end, we won the game 2-1 and I had the consolation of scoring, according to the Evening Times, 'one of the greatest goals ever witnessed at Stark's Park.' It was a decent goal, even if I say so myself, but it wouldn't mean a thing in the final analysis. Or would it?

Kilmarnock may have pipped us to promotion, but there was still the small matter of Dundee having to win at least one of their last four games, three of which were at home. They lost the first one, against St Johnstone and when Arbroath beat them at Dens Park, we started to believe. Could the unthinkable really happen? The answer was 'no' because a 2-0 win over Raith finally put us out our misery.

We'd still had a good season and Blair and I had managed 58 league and cup goals between us. That contributed in no small way to Bankies being top scorers in the first division with 78 goals, which meant a place in the following season's Drybrough Cup.

I was chuffed with my individual haul of 28 goals. It proved to me that I could score at any level. I'd left the juniors and jumped up three senior divisions, and still managed to finish second top scorer in our division...to my team-mate.

I had a two-year contract so it looked as though I'd still be around the following season and, to be honest, I wasn't in any hurry to leave Kilbowie. But soon after our last game, my future made the sports pages when Jack Steedman, the Bankies owner, issued a public 'hands-off' to clubs hoping to sign me. He then congratulated Dundee on winning the league.

Celtic were obviously in the market for a striker because just days later, they had a £100,000 bid for Motherwell's Willie Pettigrew knocked back and speculation began in the papers over who Billy McNeill would turn his attention to next. Moving from Clydebank hadn't even entered my head at that point.

With the season over, Jack Steedman told us all to gather round as he had an announcement to make. Conjecture was rife in the dressing room and some of the lads even thought we were for the bullet after failing to gain promotion to the Premier League. How wrong could we be?

Jovial Jack came walking in and declared, 'We're sending you to Majorca for a week on an all-expenses paid holiday'.

Wow, we certainly didn't see that coming but Jack was as good as his word and we were soon winging our way to sunny Spain. Our place of rest for the coming week would be a fantastic hotel, in fact the best I'd ever stayed in. This was the life of a footballer.

The first of my two years had flown by and I had enjoyed every minute. Well, almost every minute. There was just no accounting for Cowboy's terrible sense of humour or dress code, but here we were, heading to Majorca for a break, despite missing out on a one-way ticket back to the top flight.

We had hardly touched down in Palma and Cowboy and I were planning our week-long itinerary. Lager, curry, lager and so on. We had it all mapped out and would hit every bar in Magaluf and drink the resort dry. Well, we weren't that unprofessional, but we did plan to have a good time.

The most incredible thing happened on our first night out. We were sitting in a bar having a beer when in walked Roy Aitken and Davie Provan of Celtic. 'How you doing Frankie Boy?' they said, much to my amazement. Celtic were also on a week's break in Majorca having just edged Rangers for the title.

'Looks like we'll be seeing a lot more of each other next season,' continued Aitken, who was known as The Bear throughout his long and illustrious career.

'Oh, why's that then?' I asked with burning curiosity.

It turned out that 'McDougall joins Celtic' stories were splashed all over the sports pages of newspapers back home in Scotland. I was in shock, so the first thing I did was to rush out into the street and find a payphone. I had to call home.

Thankfully, my gran answered quickly and I asked, 'Is it true?'

There was no need for her to ask what I was on about. 'Yes,' she answered, 'you're now a Celtic player. Congratulations son.'

Celtic were my boyhood heroes, I had never hidden that, and now I was getting the chance to play for them. How good was that? Of course, those were the days when you could go from one team to another and not necessarily know anything about it.

Clubs did all the bartering and you were told that you now played for so-and-so. On this occasion, it didn't matter a jot that I had been left out of the negotiations altogether. As the season had been drawing to a close I'd heard murmurs that certain clubs were interested in me, but you tend to take these rumours with a pinch of salt.

Celtic had been mentioned in despatches, but I had been professional enough to push it to the back of my mind. I still had a job to do for the Bankies and would never have given them any less than 100 per cent. Anyway, I had dismissed it all as mere paper talk. I had forgotten all about that until Roy and Davie walked into that bar in Magaluf.

The rest of the holiday was just amazing. We had a great time, and enjoyed the odd glass of Sangria, but the thought of playing for Celtic was never far from my mind.

We arrived home on the Sunday and I didn't even have time to take my jacket off, but the phone was ringing off the hook. It was Jack Steedman. He assumed I'd heard the speculation, but I denied it.

'Anyway,' he said, 'I want to see you at the ground tomorrow night.' I agreed and replaced the receiver. I was apprehensive about the meeting, but went along nevertheless and when I entered the office, Jack, his brother Charlie and Bill Munro sat before me. I was nervous, but thought the reason for being summoned was to say my goodbyes. I played it cool though. Jack invited me to sit down and said, 'Well, Frank, you'll be aware that Celtic have made a £100,000 bid for you.'

Again I denied all knowledge, but thanked him for letting me know. What he said next shocked the living daylights out of me.

'But you won't be going.'

It took me a couple of minutes for his comments to sink in. Had I just heard correctly? Did he say I wasn't going to Celtic? If he did, I was certainly having none of it. It was out before I realised, 'Oh, I'm going alright, believe me.'

He countered with, 'Believe me, you're not. You have another year of your contract to run and you'll see it out, I'll make sure of it.'

I decided the best course of action was to leave it at that. There was nothing to be gained from a slanging match. I said my goodbyes, although not in the manner I'd envisaged beforehand. The steam was coming out my ears. This was the chance of a lifetime and no one would stop me grabbing it with both hands.

I went home and spoke to my gran and she could see I was hurting like mad. She was great but I missed not being able to talk things over with grandad because he had never, ever let me down where football was concerned.

I was summoned to the ground two days later and was determined to reach a satisfactory conclusion in an adult manner. Falling out with people who'd been good to me wasn't on the agenda, but that didn't prevent me from feeling a little down.

Ironically, the draw for the Drybrough Cup had been made earlier that day and Bankies had pulled Celtic. Who would I be playing for?

I walked into Jack's office and forced a smile.

'St Mirren offered £100,000, which we knocked back, but they've now upped the ante to £180,000. You're going there,' he said, bluntly.

I countered with, 'Jack, I'm not going to St Mirren. I'm going to Celtic, end of story'.

He was becoming a little perplexed by my reluctance to conform and roared, 'For the last time, you are not going to Celtic'.

I said, 'Fair enough, but I'm not going to St Mirren either'.

He said, simply, 'Okay, let's forget the whole thing. You'll play your football with Clydebank next season'.

And with these words I stormed out the office. We had reached an impasse and neither party was budging. He had flippantly told me to forget the whole thing, but how can you when a club as big as Celtic has just made it clear they want you, and you can't go?

I was a young guy with no agents, or anyone else for that matter, to help with advice. Oh how I needed my grandad at that moment. Jack called me back into the office and said, calmly, 'Look, Frank, why don't you at least talk to St Mirren, you might be pleasantly surprised at what they're offering'.

Curiosity got the better of me and I agreed to speak to St Mirren – and I'm so glad I did.

Jim Clunie was the manager of Saints at the time and when he offered me a signing-on fee of £50,000, I almost fell off my seat. Fifty grand. That was a heck of a lot of money and I'd be lying if I said the pound signs registering before my very eyes didn't influence me.

Jack still wasn't letting me speak to Celtic, but the game had changed. That £50k was a lot of money and I decided to speak to Jim Clunie again. I also liked what I heard regarding the football side of things and put pen to paper at the end of that second meeting. I was now a fully-fledged St Mirren player – and would be playing Premier League football in season 1979/80. What an amazing thought.

At the time, it was a record transfer between two Scottish league clubs and that's a statistic I am very proud of.

I don't think for a minute that Jack had been playing St Mirren and Celtic off against one another because he'd refused me permission to speak to Celtic even before Saints had registered an interest. He didn't know about the Saints bid at that time, or did he?

It soon became common knowledge that St Mirren had entered the race to sign me and that must surely have alerted Celtic. Why didn't they up the ante? Maybe they simply weren't able to raise the bar in financial terms and if that was indeed the case, all the old 'biscuit tin' stories about the club were true.

In fact, on the day I signed for Saints, Billy McNeill was quoted in one of the papers as saying he had been forced to bail out of the race once St Mirren went to £180,000. Sad days indeed for such a massive club.

Regardless, I was now a proud member of an exclusive club of just seven players to be transferred between two Scottish clubs for a six-figure sum.

For the record, the others were: Davie Provan (Kilmarnock to Celtic) £145,000, Doug Somner (Partick Thistle to St Mirren), Murdo MacLeod (Dumbarton to Celtic), Davie Cooper (Clydebank to Rangers), Gordon Strachan (Dundee to Aberdeen) and Colin Stein

(Hibs to Rangers) who had all cost £100,000. Exalted company indeed.

Folk have often asked if I'd have joined Rangers, had they shown an interest. Would I have done a 'Mo Johnston' and signed for the other side? Of course I would. The opportunity to play for either of the Old Firm doesn't come round too often and I believe it's something players should grab with both hands if given the chance. Everyone knew I was a Celtic fan, but looking back, I think moving to St Mirren was the right career choice. Try telling me that at the time though.

Overall, Jack Steedman was okay, although he did go down in my estimations when he refused to allow me even to speak to Celtic. That was bad news. I may have spent just a year at the Bankies, but I loved the club and the fans. They were great to me and I'll never forget that. There aren't many places that I hold in such high esteem, but Clydebank is definitely one.

The Bankies were my introduction to senior football and for that I'll always be grateful. But at least I was able to leave a legacy as I was told that my transfer fee paid for the stadium to become all-seated, the first of its kind, I believe, in the country. It was a good feeling knowing the club had benefited from my departure.

And it was sad to leave behind The Atlantis, our watering hole of choice. A few of us enjoyed a beer or three, but we also trained hard.

It was time for pastures new. A fresh challenge awaited and one that would see me move another rung up the footballing ladder. Would I be able to hack it in the Premier League, playing against the likes of the Old Firm, Hearts and Hibs, on a regular basis?

If I'm being totally honest, I never gave it much thought. My mind was focussed on another forthcoming event. Lily was due to give birth and all thoughts of football were put on hold.

L⚽VE IS IN THE AIR

MY PARKHEAD dream may have been over, for the time being anyway, but I was still incredibly excited and looking forward to the new season with St Mirren.

When I awoke on the morning of my first training session, I did so with the realisation that I was the most expensive footballer in Scotland. And with that, comes a certain responsibility to prove to people that the club were right to shell out such a large sum of money. That fee of £180,000 may not seem much these days, but it was a heck of a lot in the 1970s.

But the pressure I was feeling wasn't just connected to the size of the fee. Saints had just punted Frank McGarvey to Liverpool for £400,000 and I was purchased to fill his boots, and they were big boots to fill.

In reality, I had just a single season of senior football behind me and while I'd made the switch to Clydebank effortlessly, it was another substantial hike from First Division to Premier League.

Those 28 goals for Clydebank proved I could score in decent company, but time, and fate, would tell if I would succeed. If determination was the only ingredient needed I would have no problems adjusting to life in Scottish football's top flight.

At the time, I wasn't aware that I was the most expensive player in Scotland until I read it in the papers. No one had mentioned it and I wasn't a 'stato' when it came to juggling facts and figures. It was a great feeling knowing that Saints had wanted me badly enough to up their initial offer of £100,000. I wanted to repay that faith.

It was just over a year since I'd been playing for the 'Shire and it was an almighty step up from juniors to Premier League, but Clydebank had provided me with that vital stepping-stone.

It certainly helped bed me into the seniors and was an important part of my football education. It may just have been a single season, but playing in the first division week in, week out worked wonders for my confidence.

Following the move to Saints, a couple of papers reported that I'd turned my back on Celtic, but they didn't know the truth. That aside, I was genuinely happy to be a St Mirren player.

After speaking to Jim Clunie for a second time, I'd headed over to Love Street for talks with the chairman, William Todd. We quickly agreed terms. I wanted to be there, no question.

St Mirren were an established top four, or five, Premier League side and expectation levels at Love Street had grown. There were good players at the club and I knew it would be a battle just to get my hands on a jersey each Saturday.

At the time, manager Jim Clunie, who had previously worked as Lawrie McMenemy's assistant boss at Southampton, had just signed another striker, Dougie Somner, from Partick Thistle. Future team-mates would also include Jackie Copland, Billy Stark, Billy Abercromby and Lex Richardson.

My remit at Saints was simple. The gaffer wanted me to go out there and score goals and I believe I did just that. I enjoyed playing alongside Dougie, he was a big lad, but could play a bit, and he also chipped in with plenty of goals, including more than 30 in our first season.

Dougie wasn't a party animal, like Frank McAvennie and me, but he was a great lad and we didn't hold it against him for heading straight home after training and passing up the opportunity to play snooker with the 'gang.' I formed a good partnership with the former Jag and we got on well, both on and off the park. He was a fantastic signing for Saints.

I was soon into my stride in Paisley and the step up in class was achieved easier than I'd first thought. If you can score goals early on the confidence boost is priceless and it takes some of the pressure off.

I always knew I had goals in me, but scoring in the Premier League was extremely fulfilling, especially with defenders such as Alex McLeish and Willie Miller at Aberdeen, and Paul Hegarty and Dave Narey at Dundee United on the beat. And that's not to mention the Old Firm and Edinburgh sides.

As time wore on, the gaffer would trust me with free-kicks. It was something I practiced a lot in training and, I'm afraid to say, is the reason behind some mischievous team-mates christening me Zico.

I took some beauties and managed to curl a few round the wall and into the top corner. I was beginning to believe I had Brazilian blood coursing through my veins, although the whole Zico thing was most definitely tongue in cheek, courtesy of Mr Abercromby, the quickest wit in all of Paisley. That's one quality that certainly wasn't missing from the Love Street dressing room, where the banter was free flowing.

One thing that I was enjoying was the increase in my standard of living. I was full-time at Saints and was being paid accordingly. I was on £220 a week and invested the signing-on fee wisely in bricks and mortar.

Lily and I were married, and Kelly was born during my first season at Love Street. We bought a little flat in Lambhill, not far from where I grew up. Kilfinan Street was as small as they come. Just one close, but still room for a chip shop, pub and bookies.

It's fair to say I spent quite a bit of time in Mallon's bar and that probably acted as a catalyst for us moving to pastures new. That, and the fact that we wanted a garden for Kelly to run around in. Lambhill's a nice area, but we eventually decided we wanted somewhere that could offer a bit of open space. That's why we chose East Kilbride. We bought a bungalow in the new Gardenhall Estate and promptly moved the 25, or so, miles to our new home.

It was great all round, apart from the time I decided to buy a car, my very own Austin Allegro, in a bid to get to training at Love Street on time. I didn't have a licence, but I was a decent enough driver. I only had the car two days and was heading home one afternoon when I forgot to take my foot off the gas as I turned a corner. Bang. I went slap bang into a lamp post and the car was bashed up pretty badly. It really was quite a prang.

It happened in Hairmyres Street, just 100 yards from the house, so I nursed it along to the driveway and had a peek to see who'd witnessed my little faux pas. There wasn't a soul in sight and I swear I didn't see a single curtain twitch.

Imagine my horror a few hours later when there's the type of knock on the door that's normally reserved for coppers…and bad news. And sure enough, when I opened the door there they were, standing there with that knowing smirk, although they still felt the need to ask such an obvious question.

'That car in your driveway sir, is it yours?'

Doh. Of course it's mine and the bash in the side and the lopsided lamppost outside our Wimpey home were also a bit of a giveaway. My spell as a latter day Stirling Moss was well and truly over. At least for another 30 years.

I had to go to court and was represented by the St Mirren lawyer. It was a strange experience being advised to plead guilty to something I hadn't done, and not guilty to the charge I was actually guilty of. Nevertheless, I received a £350 fine and that was the end of it.

The house was great and the neighbourhood fine, but I was finding it tough living a rural life after being brought up in a housing scheme, and at times the whole business just overwhelmed me. I was okay during the football season, when my mind was taken up with training and games, but during our six weeks off, I was like a little boy lost. How do you top up with lager and vindaloo in the middle of nowhere?

It was a lovely house in a lovely area, but it just wasn't me. We stayed for three years, but sadly we split up and I went back to living with my gran in Cadder.

Naturally I had given up my job as a scaffolder and was free to concentrate full-time on improving as a footballer. It's every boy's dream to be a full-time footballer and I was no different from the thousands of others growing up in the west of Scotland.

When you're part-time there's only a certain standard you can reach due to restrictions on the time and resources you can put into it. If you're able to work on your game all day, every day, then you're a dead cert to come on leaps and bounds.

During my time at Saints we all but matched the Old Firm and all the others, but we were always just that bit short of taking the next step to winning honours.

Personally, scoring against Celtic and Rangers wasn't a problem, but when the Saints team bus pulled up outside Ibrox and Parkhead, some players would take one look at the massive stadium, imposing gates and marble entrance and think, 'We can't compete with them'.

I reckon it was the mentality that so-called provincial teams possessed when going to face the Old Firm in their own backyard that held them back. Both of these sides were on a higher pedestal – and we put them there, which was the galling thing.

That all changed when I signed for Aberdeen. Fergie made us believe 'We will win there.'

But to a certain extent I could understand the mindset of the smaller clubs. You would leave a stadium like Love Street and roll up outside these big grounds. Enter the inferiority complex. It had an effect on the players and was probably noticeable in our play. The manager has a huge roll to play in such situations and Alex Ferguson was the master.

At St Mirren I bonded instantly with guys like Dougie, Aber, Lex and Alex Beckett, in fact, there wasn't a single player I didn't get on with. There was a great atmosphere at Love Street. And then along came my shadow, Cowboy McCormack. I just couldn't shake him off. Jim Clunie paid Clydebank £55,000 for his services and I can still see his big grinning face on the back page of the Evening Times. I often joked that if I signed for Timbuktu Wanderers then Cowboy would join them the following week. Thank God Fergie didn't take him to Aberdeen.

The St Mirren club shop sold keyrings of all the players. I remember a shop assistant mentioning that mine normally sold out first and that they usually had to sell Aber's at half price just to clear some room on the shelves. I reckon there may still be a box of Aber keyrings at the club shop even now.

And I remember football cards were all the rage among kids in those days and I can just picture the scene. Dozens of kids in the school playground with football cards at the ready, eager to do a swap in order to be the first to complete the set.

'I'll give you 100 Cowboy McCormack's for one Frank McDougall.'

You don't think about kids idolising you, but I'm sure they did. I know I did when I was growing up. I remember getting this strange, but enjoyable, feeling the first time I set eyes on a Frank McDougall card. Was I really that handsome?

There was a fantastic team spirit at St Mirren in the early days and a crowd of us would go for a game of snooker and a couple of beers after training. I suppose you could say there was something of a drink culture at the club, but it was accepted in those days to a certain extent.

We had a lot of time on our hands and it was easy to slip into that way of life. When you do something every day it soon becomes the norm, but we were training hard so it didn't impact on match days. We trained till around lunchtime and, in that respect, I don't think too much has changed today.

Nevertheless, Aber fancied himself as a bit of a Jimmy White, although regular starts of 30 and 40 didn't help his cause. But in true

Aber spirit he would come back for more and I started to feel sorry for him – eventually. But did I ever let him win? Not a chance, although I did let him get close a couple of times.

In fact, to this day I still play to a decent standard in a snooker league in Aberdeen, although I reckon the skills were honed in the clubs of Glasgow.

I was enjoying my time at Saints and the whole Celtic 'episode' was in the past. Don't get me wrong, I don't think I ever got over missing out on a dream move to Parkhead, but St Mirren proved a great distraction and it was a pleasure going into work there every day.

Of course, at that time, Celtic didn't have a great deal of money, which was obvious as Saints had beaten them to my signature and they weren't exactly the most affluent club in the country.

I can say though, with hand on heart, that I couldn't have signed for two better clubs than Saints and Aberdeen. At the time it may have been a disappointment, but things couldn't have worked out any better for me.

When I joined up at St Mirren I didn't know any of the players personally. It was a whole new set of boys, but I'm comfortable with meeting people for the first time. I may have been taken out of my comfort zone in Cadder and thrust into the limelight, but not many people get that opportunity and I was determined to make the most of it.

I've never been a good trainer, but I know what has to be done and I try my best to get on with it. In nine years as a pro, I looked upon pre-season as a form of cruelty - a necessary evil. But with my first season in the Premier League almost upon us, it was time to knuckle down and put in a shift.

On the eve of the campaign though, Saints fans were dealt a major blow when club legend Tony Fitzpatrick followed Frank McGarvey out the exit door. Fitz was snapped up by Bristol City for £250,000 and suddenly Saints fans were two old favourites short. Dougie Somner and I would have to go some way to appease supporters, naturally distraught at losing the big name duo.

We prepared for the new season at St Mirren's version of Jock Wallace's notorious Gullane Sands. It was a piece of rugged terrain near Erskine. It may not have been as well known as Gullane, but by all accounts it was just as back breaking.

Jim Clunie and his assistant Ricky McFarlane certainly knew how to get the excess pounds off their players. In fact, at one point I thought I was Red Rum training on the sand.

We had a club doctor at Love Street and he would accompany us down to Erskine and monitor our progress. It was all very professional, although running on the sand felt a bit like running on the spot. You didn't really get anywhere. I suggested buckets and spades and caught my first glimpse of the 'Clunie stare.'

Jimmy Bone was due to meet up with the rest of the squad soon after his exertions across the pond, where he'd been knocking in the goals for Toronto Blizzard.

In fact, so successful had his spell been that it was suggested he might miss the start of the Scottish season because Blizzard were on the periphery of the play-offs. 'Papa,' as he would become known, had been playing against guys like Johann Cruyff and Franz Beckenbauer in North America and I was looking forward to hearing all the stories.

I was all set for my Saints debut on Saturday, August 28 against Hibs in the Anglo-Scottish Cup when disaster struck. A midweek ankle injury during training meant a fitness test on the day of the game. Despite managing a light training session the day before, I was still doubtful. It was so frustrating because a debut is among the most important games a player can play in.

As it turned out, I beat the crock, but fell awkwardly on the ankle and it was game up for me at half-time. I was hooked as a precaution. It was just one of those games. Dougie was also in the wars and ended up with three stitches in an eye wound.

The tie finished 3-3, which made Hibs favourites to progress to the quarter-finals. It was so frustrating after being 3-1 up and cruising at one point.

We had a friendly arranged against Watford for the Monday night, but I missed out on our 2-0 win thanks to that pesky ankle. And I missed the return match against Hibs, which we won 1-0 to progress to the last eight.

It was stop-start from there on in as I was sidelined for our last pre-season friendly, a 1-0 defeat at Grimsby, but was given a run-out with the reserves in a match against junior side Beith. I scored in that one, but then drew a blank in our opening league draw with Kilmarnock.

Our next game was a pretty bizarre affair. We played well at Dundee but lost out to four goals from future Rangers star Ian Redford. Not the best of starts for either me or Saints.

I got four of my own the following midweek for the reserves in a 7-1 mauling of Partick Thistle. I wonder if Bertie Auld was watching. And in the week leading up to the first Renfrewshire derby of the season against Morton, Lil gave birth to Kelly, and I was on cloud nine. Unfortunately, I was brought back down to earth with a bump as we lost 3-0.

I missed our next five games and my dream move to the Premier League was turning into a nightmare. We were lying bottom of the league with just one point from four games. I was in and out of the team and struggled to find any sort of rhythm or consistency, but returned to face Dundee United at Love Street and we desperately needed a win. Thankfully, Doug Somner and I scored as we bagged our first league win of the season. It was a good feeling and helped us off the foot of the table.

My first-ever competitive match against English opposition arrived a couple of days later against Bolton Wanderers, in the quarter finals of the Anglo-Scottish Cup and we got off to a dream start.

We were 4-0 up inside 25 minutes and a cricket score looked on the cards. Billy Stark and Jimmy Bone scored and I added a double. I was unfortunate not to complete my hat-trick with a second-half effort, but when Bolton scored twice to half our lead it seemed like a defeat.

In the second leg a fortnight later at their place, big Sam Allardyce, now a successful Premiership manager, scored twice to give them a 2-0 win, and an aggregate of four apiece. Thankfully Papa Bone popped up in extra time to send us through on a 5-4 aggregate.

Just before that second-leg match, we went to Easter Road and yours truly scored in a 2-0 win. It looked as though we had finally turned the corner, although it's always dangerous to presume in football. One moment you're in seventh heaven, next, you're lying on your backside feeling sorry for yourself.

After the Bolton match, I remember chatting to big Sam and he was a gentleman. He was a tough guy on the pitch, as I found out, but once in the sanctuary of the player's lounge, he was extremely relaxed. Willie Morgan, the former Manchester United player, and legendary England forward, Frank Worthington, also played for Bolton in that game.

I managed to get on the score sheet again as we disposed of lower league Hamilton 3-1 at their place in the League Cup. However, we lost at Celtic Park on the Saturday, the first time I'd visited the ground since the close season transfer tug-of-war. Not a lot was said about it and I just got on with my job.

But, unfortunately, it was to kick-start a drop in form for both me and the team. It seemed as though our decent spell was all too brief and it was a case of 'as you were' for another few weeks.

Celtic scored first and I thought I'd equalised with a diving header, but it came crashing back off the post. The difference that day between success and failure was the thickness of the post. Had that gone in, it would no doubt have put a different complexion on the game. As it was, Celtic ran out 3-1 winners.

We then lost to Bolton, although, as I said, we scraped through in extra time before dropping a point at home to Aberdeen; although in truth we had actually stolen one.

With the Dons leading 2-1, I forced an equaliser with virtually the last kick of the ball – Fergie was raging. Some things never change. He went ballistic with the referee, claiming that he'd played too much stoppage time, and that the goal should never have stood.

It was around this time that Alfie Conn started training with us. He had launched his career with Rangers, headed south to play for Tottenham Hotspur before coming back north to play for...Celtic.

He was searching for training facilities after leaving Parkhead and Jim Clunie offered them. He never did sign for Saints though, which was a pity because he would have been a great addition to the team, and his creativity would've made sackloads of opportunities for Dougie and I. He had tremendous ability and still had plenty to offer.

I don't know if Alfie brought us bad luck or not, but as soon as he turned up we lost 2-0 to Hamilton at Love Street in a League Cup tie. That meant 3-3 on aggregate and spot kicks. We lost 4-2 and the media, as well as our manager, slaughtered us.

And we were roasted again on the Saturday when Partick Thistle, complete with cigar-smoking Bertie as manager, beat us 2-1 at our place. I scored what I thought was a perfectly good equaliser, although the guy with the flag thought otherwise.

Oh how I would've loved that goal to have stood and to have gone up to Bertie and said, 'Not good enough, huh?' after he'd given me the boot at Thistle. That would keep though.

After that, I seemed to fall out of favour and the gaffer preferred to play Somner and Bone up front. There was nothing I could do, but bide my time and score for the reserves when picked. I was desperate to get back in the first team though.

We'd endured a terrible start to the season, results wise, but the lads fought back and secured an excellent win midway through November. Rangers travelled to Love Street and we were determined to make sure they knew they'd been in a game. There was a full house and we edged it 2-1. Peter McCloy pulled me down in the box and Dougie smacked home the winner from the spot.

A couple of weeks later, Hibs came to town. Nothing too exciting about that, but this Hibs team contained a genuine footballing legend: George Best. It was a pleasure to play on the same pitch as the former Manchester United star and he managed to score. Thankfully we got two. We had a wee chat after the game and he was great company. Unfortunately he wasn't tempted by a night on the tiles in Paisley.

That slender win pushed us up to third and suddenly we started to believe that a European slot was achievable. The following weekend we completed the Old Firm double by beating Celtic 2-1, and again I managed to score against one of the Glasgow giants.

The Renfrewshire Cup isn't one of the most prized competitions in football, but try telling that to the supporters of Saints and Morton. That season though, fans from 'doon the watter' at Greenock were crying into their beers as we hammered their favourites 10-1 on aggregate. I helped myself to a treble in a 6-0 mauling at Love Street. Our fans were in raptures. Performances like that are guaranteed to endear you to your own supporters.

We were at it again in our first match of 1980. I opened the scoring at Ibrox and we went on to win 2-1. Things were starting to go pretty well and I was soon joined by another McDougall at Love Street. My young brother, David, had come up from England after being freed by Oldham. I had a word with Jim Clunie and he told me to bring him along to training.

Unlike me, David was more of a preventer of goals than a scorer and he impressed enough to get a run-out in a couple of reserve games. I watched him in a challenge match at Keanie Park against Johnstone Burgh and he did well, but didn't get offered a contract, which was a pity. After Saints, he had trials at both Celtic and Leicester City.

Not long after time was called on David's brief stint at Love Street, so was mine...after a tackle by a one-time idol of mine.

It was on my 22nd birthday that Danny McGrain's challenge broke my leg during a Scottish Cup quarter-final replay at Love Street. On the Saturday prior to the game, we'd gone to Parkhead and almost knocked them out at the first time of asking. Oh, how I wish we'd managed that.

There were 35,000 spectators at Celtic Park and I opened the scoring with a diving header. Billy Stark hit a shot from outside the area and it was going wide until I re-directed it into the corner of the net. Unfortunately Murdo MacLeod equalised with virtually the last kick of the ball.

So it was that we lined up on the Wednesday night at our place, confident of booking a semi-final slot. Why not? We'd just run Celtic close a couple of days beforehand.

Ian Foote was the ref and 27,000 fans packed into Love Street, most of them hoping for a shock. In fact, the crowd was so vast that the kick-off was delayed to let everyone in. But while this was fantastic for the bank balance, it didn't do the players any good having to hang around, clicking heels in the dressing room.

When the action finally got underway, things were going pretty well, although I got involved in a 'handbags' incident with big Tom McAdam a few yards outside the Celtic box. He'd left me lying on my backside and as he stood over me menacingly, I kicked my legs up in the air and caught him with my boot. Honours even? It seemed not. McAdam was sent-off for his part in the incident and I was booked.

Immediately following the clash, Celtic's midfield 'enforcer' Roy Aitken came running over to me and said, 'You're getting it'.

'Charming', I thought. Then I countered with, 'If you get me, Aber will see to you.'

To think it had only been a couple of months since I sat in a Majorcan bar with Aitken calling me his 'buddy'. Changed days.

Just moments later, I was clean through and had taken a touch as McGrain came sliding in. It all happened in a split second, but he caught me big time and that was it - game over.

It was crystal clear exactly what our fans thought of McGrain's tackle as ball boys spent a fair bit of time clearing lager cans off the park after I was carried off. Many fans were arrested during the game as tensions boiled over.

Jim Clunie told me a few days later that while he was keeping his fingers crossed I wasn't badly hurt, he believed, at the time, that my leg was broken. The pain I felt after that challenge was excruciating. I was taken to hospital and x-rays revealed a broken bone in my leg. No surprise there then. I was told I would miss the rest of the season, but I had other ideas. I loved playing football and was determined to get back as quickly as possible.

The next day, the papers came up to the house to photograph me with my stookie on. I was asked to hold up my daughter, Kelly, who was just six months old. I remember speaking to a reporter from one particular paper and telling him that I didn't believe it was intentional on Danny's part. The following day I was horrified to read 'my' comments insisting, 'Danny McGrain meant to break my leg'.

That led to a distrust of the media on my part, which may or may not have been fair, because I know there are as many honest and reliable journalists out there as there are bad guys, who will work anyone over just to get a story.

Danny McGrain is a friend of mine, and is probably one of the greatest Celtic players ever, although that said, it was still a shocking tackle. Oh, we lost the game 3-2, although that wasn't foremost in my mind as medics attached a plastercast before dispatching me off home with a pair of crutches.

As if being laid low with a broken leg wasn't enough, I was dumbfounded and annoyed when Saints carpeted me for saying 'exclusively' that McGrain had meant to do me. Whether he did or not is immaterial, because I didn't say that. Yes, I spoke to the Press and I was asked if I thought it had been deliberate, but all I said at the time was, 'You would have to ask Danny McGrain that'.

How would I know if he had deliberately set out to hurt me? I had my own private thoughts on the matter, but there was only one man in the ground that night capable of answering that question and it was Danny McGrain himself.

I also suffered a serious injury during a match with the other half of the Old Firm. Rangers defender Tom Forsyth was known to many as 'Jaws' and there was good reason for that – he was hard as nails. On one occasion I mixed it with big Tam and ended up in hospital. I wouldn't say a bad word against him either, though, because while big Tam could put it about, I genuinely didn't believe that injury was his fault.

Maybe 'winning' was just a vital ingredient of being an Old Firm player. And so it was that I had to watch on from stands up and down the country as the lads continued to battle towards a European place.

By the end of April, we were still in third spot with just four league games to go. Four 'cup finals', as the gaffer described them. There were mixed feelings as we lost the first of them to Aberdeen. Days after the game I was handed the best news imaginable.

Our club doctor gave me the green light to start playing again, just ten weeks after the leg break. I was back training and while I knew I wasn't anywhere near ready for a return to top team action, just being told I could play again was like winning the pools.

I took part in a top-of-the-table reserve league match against Aberdeen and it felt great to be involved again. It wasn't the European Cup final, and it was only the second-half, but it was football and I was back.

I wasn't interested in sitting in the house moping around. I wanted back out on that pitch and I drove myself on in a bid to get back playing ASAP. That's right, 'Frank McDougall in voluntary extra training' sensation. I remember asking our reserve team coach, Eddie McDonald, if I could play the whole game that night, but he thought it better to build up to a full 90.

I had a few more reserve team outings before the end of the season, but my top team involvement was limited to willing on the lads to that UEFA slot which, if successful, would be Saints first-ever foray into European football.

We lost our next game to Hibs and the nerves were beginning to kick in. Our last two games were against the Old Firm and we got a well-deserved point at home to Celtic. The last game against Rangers was incredible - our most impressive win of the season. Rangers were on the wrong end of a 4-1 drubbing and ironically it was Alex Miller, our future manager, who scored their consolation.

It was a tremendous victory, but all it achieved was to give us a more than decent chance of qualifying for the UEFA Cup. Celtic were due to meet Rangers in the Scottish Cup final the following weekend, and a Celtic win would guarantee our place.

For the moment though, we had managed third place in the Premier League, Saints highest-ever finish and a tremendous achievement for a provincial side. And seven days later our season was complete when a George McCluskey goal handed Celtic the Scottish Cup, and rubber-stamped our UEFA Cup qualification.

It was time to look out the passport – we were on our way to Europe.

SAMBA, SUNSHINE... AND ZICO

IT'S incredible to think that I eventually married a Brazilian girl, given that one of the greatest adventures of my life played out in that exotic South American country.

It was the close season of 1980, May to be exact and after finishing third in the Premier League, there was talk of a close-season tour to Rio by way of a reward. Naturally it was the main topic of conversation, but until anything could be confirmed it remained pure conjecture.

Of course, I'd suffered the leg break against Celtic in the Scottish Cup replay, but was back playing reserve team football just ten weeks later.

As the Brazilian trip became more of a reality, the gaffer announced his intentions to take just seventeen players. I reckon a miraculous recovery booked my place on the plane. If the gaffer did indeed take that into account then I am forever in his debt. I had a ball.

Despite initial plans being formulated, we still had buckets to sweat before we were to hear those well-known words, 'we are now cleared for take off.' However, there was much wrangling going on behind the scenes and the tour was anything but certain. One minute it was on, next it was off.

A few weeks before our planned leaving date, it was put back, and Saints insisted it would only go ahead if both they and the Brazilian authorities could thrash out a few niggling problems.

St Mirren director Harold Currie was involved in the organisation, and it was proving anything but an easy ride. At that time, Brazil was anything but the destination of choice for holidaying Brits.

The problem seemed to centre on certain financial terms being honoured, as well as the promise of three attractive matches. Initially it was mooted that we'd be playing against top sides Vasco de Gama, Corinthians and the winners of the Brazilian Gold Cup, which was the equivalent of our Scottish Cup. That turned out to be a false dawn though.

Secret negotiations were taking place that would hopefully see St Mirren become one of the first Scottish clubs to tour Brazil, although it was proving difficult for Mr Currie to get the Brazilians to commit to anything in writing.

Jim Clunie was desperate for the trip to go ahead. He was insistent that our exertions in finishing so high up the league deserved, as he put it, 'an ambitious and attractive tour'. It was certainly both of those all right and you have to take your hat off to the board of directors for coming up with something so innovative.

But no sooner had the plans become public knowledge than the tour was off. It was announced to all and sundry that the club had decided to cancel because the Brazilian authorities were struggling to come up with our 'three attractive fixtures'.

They reckoned it was far too long a journey just to play two games, and they were probably right. It was the end of a dream and the players were gutted. It was a bit like scoring the winning goal in a cup final and having it ruled out, incorrectly, for offside.

But, lo and behold, less than a fortnight later, the tour was back on, although I for one wasn't counting my chickens. We were scheduled to fly to London at the end of May and hook up with another flight, which would take us directly to Rio. It was a 13-hour jaunt, but I reckoned it would be well worth it...if it happened at all.

Then it was confirmed that we would indeed be travelling to South America and let's face it, there weren't many of my mates heading for Brazil that year. Blackpool, maybe, but I was eyeing the trip of a lifetime.

Our first match would be against first division Rio side Bangu. That's when it started to become real. Bangu were described as the 'Partick Thistle' of Brazil - a mid-table, first division side.

On the eve of the tour there was a real blow for one of our defenders, Iain Munro, who was told he wouldn't be part of the travelling squad as he hadn't signed a new deal. Club officials insisted they would only take players who wanted to be at St Mirren.

As we boarded the flight at Glasgow Airport, on the first leg of our marathon 6,000-mile journey, we had something extra to celebrate. Ricky McFarlane, who had previously been a part-time coach, had just been promoted to Jim Clunie's full-time assistant. We were delighted for Ricky; he was a smashing guy.

It was a 'cool' 80 degrees when we touched down in Rio. I couldn't believe my luck as I stepped out onto Brazilian soil for the first time. Brazil has always been the epicentre of total football and I was just so privileged to be there. We were based at a beautiful hotel called the Rio Horsa Nacional and it had everything, from tennis to golf. Our every need was catered for.

It was still the intention to face Bangu in our opening match and the gaffer soon informed us of our other fixtures: next up was a game against Santos Victoria, who were equal in status to Bangu. They played some 200 miles north of Rio.

The final fixture was against Coritba, a top-four side who played their football 300 miles south of our iconic base.

Before squaring up to Bangu, we were treated to the incredible spectacle that is the Maracana Stadium, probably the most famous sporting venue in the world. The occasion was the Gold Cup final between Flamengo and Athletico and 154,000 spectators turned up to witness the occasion.

It was probably the most amazing atmosphere I've ever witnessed and I wasn't even playing. It was an incredible game, full of absolute passion from both spectators and players, and despite Athletico having three men sent off for dissent, Flamengo just shaded it 3-2.

But there I was, standing on the terracing of the Maracana watching players such as Zico, my idol, Nunes and Julio Cesar in the flesh. It is an experience that will live with me until my dying day. Suddenly the jet lag seemed insignificant.

The following morning we went for a stroll along the equally famous Copacabana Beach and it was jam-packed. It was a sight to behold, seeing volleyball courts set up all along the golden sand and kids playing barefoot. We could hardly walk on it never mind play football.

It was soon time to play our first match and we were walking tall as we entered the Bangu stadium. One look at the pitch told you it was going to be a bumpy ride, and I don't just mean because of the quality of opposition. The pitch was like a ploughed field.

I played the first half, but due to a lack of match action, and the humidity, I came off at half-time to be replaced by young Alan Logan. We eventually lost the match 2-0, but witnessed the rare sight of Dougie Somner missing a penalty after Billy Stark had been brought down. It was still an incredible occasion, and it got even better.

After the football, there was a samba festival on the pitch and we were mesmerised by the sight of all these incredible dancers and musicians. There were literally hundreds of them. It looked like some sort of Guinness world record attempt. We were also treated to a nice reception and went back to the hotel a happy bunch of campers, despite the result.

Another afternoon at the beach was on the agenda the following day, and I wish I hadn't bothered. Now, the Copacabana, as I said, is a sight to behold, but it wasn't the only sight after I spent a couple of hours topping up my tan.

I awoke with Cowboy's dulcet tones ringing in my ears. 'You're burning, ya clown'. And how right he was too. I was beetroot and my shoulders were red raw. I thought dumb blonde jokes were the normal preserve of the fairer sex. It was agony and I just wanted to get back to the hotel.

There, Cowboy and I managed to put our big feet in it again by visiting the hotel restaurant and indulging in some decent grub - steak sandwiches and a couple of cold drinks, to try to take away the pain you know. I can tell you, Saints director John Corson wasn't in the slightest bit impressed by the bill we racked up and he let us know it.

All was forgotten the following day, Saturday, when we headed north to play Victoria Santos. I had picked up an injury and had to make do with a seat in the stand. There were around 2000 people there, including a few exiled Scots who became Saints supporters for the day.

We all know that the Brazilians are famed for their stylish and silky soccer, but let's just say that the prototype manual obviously hadn't made it 200 miles north of Rio. Santos were a strong, physical side, with the added sideshow of a few cloggers to boot, literally. And big Dougie Somner, no shrinking violet himself, bore the brunt of a couple of tasty challenges.

One of their players was ordered off for a waist-high challenge on the big man that wouldn't have looked out of place in a Kung-Fu movie. Bruce Lee, eat your heart out. It was an absolute shocker. In fact, many of their tackles were dreadful and the referee could be described as no more than a joke. He let them away with murder and they repeatedly took advantage of his generous nature.

But just to show them that there's no place in the game for thuggish behaviour, we won 1-0, thanks to a goal from my replacement, Alan Logan. And the wee man's counter earned us a beautiful trophy, which had been put up by a local businessman. I'm sure it looked lovely sitting next to the Renfrewshire Cup and Anglo-Scottish Cup in the Love Street trophy room, although it was a touch on the big side.

The weather was far cooler and the pitch much better than our first game – and another significant event took place in this game. The bold Cowboy made his Saints debut.

We also changed our travel plans to take in a Brazil Select v. Mexico Select match. But soon it was onwards to our final game - this time 300 miles south of the magnificent Rio de Janeiro and Coritiba, a top-four side, awaited. I must admit I felt a bit surplus to requirements, being out of commission, especially after waiting so long to get back into the fold after my broken leg.

Coritiba were a decent side, but we were more than a match for them. Once again, Alan Logan was on target and we managed a 1-1 draw. One abiding memory from this match was the incessant drumming and flag-waving of local supporters. They were magnificent and added to a tremendous atmosphere. Cowboy sold the equaliser and I had great pleasure in reminding him afterwards.

Although we'd really enjoyed the trip, I was starting to look forward to getting home, although I wasn't particularly looking forward to the journey. Rio to Lisbon, then on to London, before catching the final plane to Abbotsinch Airport.

That was almost postponed when the Brazilian Football Association invited us to stay on for a few extra days to take on their triumphant national youth side at the magnificent Maracana. As tempting as it was, many of the players and officials had already booked a short break back home, while others had commitments.

We were told that the invitation was a reward for our impressive conduct and discipline on the tour (although they obviously didn't see us in Rio's famous Sunset Club, where absolutely anything goes) but, unfortunately, it had to be turned down.

And so it was that we packed our bags and bid farewell to an amazing country – although I would be back a few years later. It was a weary, but fulfilled, party that made their way to the sprawling Rio Airport for the journey home. But what happened on that first flight simply couldn't be put into words.

Jackie Gough was our kit man and all round good guy. We got on well and often shared a laugh and a joke. He was especially helpful as I was recovering from the leg break and always had words of encouragement.

We were over the worst of the flight and weren't too far from Lisbon when I first realised something was wrong. Ricky McFarlane had been asked to take a look at Jackie. He'd taken some sort of bad turn, but as he was only 42 years old, we didn't expect anything really serious to happen to him. How wrong could we have been?

When the club doctor, Stewart McCormick was summoned, we realised something awful had happened. There was nothing Stewart, or anyone else, could do - Jackie was dead.

We sat in stunned silence as the plane landed at Lisbon. Jackie's body was taken off for a post-mortem and it was a couple of hours before we were ready to resume our three-leg journey.

Silence engulfed the final part of the journey from London to Glasgow and when we walked through arrivals, there was a scattering of friends, family and club supporters there to greet us. They already knew the awful news and many tears were shed.

The club directors jumped into a waiting car and headed straight to Jackie's house in Paisley to visit his family. Jackie had been with the club 15 years and suddenly he was gone. It took us a long time to get over that tragedy.

FROM ERSKINE TO ST ETIENNE

THE close season was a short one. We hadn't long arrived back from Brazil and tragic Jackie Gough was still in everyone's thoughts.

We normally enjoyed a six-week close-season break, but that was cut to a mere ten days, not because we had just returned from South America – but because we were off on our travels again. This time we were heading in the opposite direction, to Northern Europe and the mystical Scandinavian country of Finland. At least it was a mystery to me.

Vice-chairman, Gordon Foulds, was the link this time, due to business interests in the timber industry and we were to take part in a short, three-match tour against Lahti Reipas, Ilves Tampere and HJK Helsinki. Before leaving though, it was back to the sands of Erskine for our annual training ritual. I wasn't keen on pre-season, but was well aware that I had to make an impact because of the amount of game time I'd missed due to the broken leg.

In saying that, I wasn't about to do anything daft like go full throttle. I had a reputation to preserve. Because our break had been curtailed, I had less time to get stuck into my usual pre-season of lager and vindaloo, although not all team-mates preferred the 'McDougall Fitness Regime'. One such guy was Billy Stark. I had known Billy since our youth days, but we became good mates at Saints and also played together at Aberdeen.

On arriving back from South America, I spent time with the family, as well as squeezing in sporting pursuits such as snooker and greyhound racing. After just seven days relaxation though, the phone rang. It was Billy and he asked me out – for a run. He was keen to hit the ground running at pre-season training.

Billy was a stick insect and a fitness fanatic. Me, I still had a few curries and pints to enjoy before reporting back to our military style 'boot camp'. My answer was a firm, but polite, 'no'. I promised to think of him pounding the streets while at the snooker club enjoying my forbidden fruits.

On day one at Erskine Beach, we found out just how close we had come to parting company with Ricky McFarlane. Apparently he'd received a cracking offer to take up a coaching role in the United Arab Emirates, (where, I'd imagine, they had lots more sand) £40,000 tax free for two years' work. That was unbelievable money 30 years ago. Their loss was definitely our gain.

The trip to Finland was timely, as we'd drawn Scandinavian opposition, IFS Elfsorg, of Sweden, in the UEFA Cup, and the gaffer was looking forward to tackling like-minded opposition.

Everyone was looking forward to being involved in Saints first ever Euro campaign. Off we went to Finland and played our three matches, securing two wins and a draw. Now, I'm well aware that Scandinavian countries didn't enjoy the best of reputations at that time, but we weren't exactly Real Madrid ourselves, so it was a decent show.

We arrived back in Scotland just three days before the start of the Drybrough Cup, a competition consisting of eight teams who had qualified by means of being top scorers in Scotland the previous season.

It was a straightforward knockout competition that was popular enough among players and supporters. They did introduce a rather bizarre offside rule for the competition though, which consisted of moving the offside line from halfway to the 18-yard box. It wasn't utilised in any other competition and took a bit of getting used to. I suppose it meant less running for yours truly.

Nevertheless, we beat Falkirk 2-0 in the quarter-finals, before edging past Ayr United (2-1) en-route to meeting Aberdeen in the final. Unfortunately we lost 2-1, but it was a good workout for the lads and the opportunity to take part in a cup final at Hampden was always welcome.

When I'd picked up the injury in Brazil, young Alan Logan had stepped in and taken his chance, scoring in two of our three games.

He had enjoyed a good pre-season and the gaffer decided to go with him for the start of the league campaign. I had no complaints.

We started off with a home match against Fergie's Aberdeen side, the reigning Premier League champions. I came on for Alan in the second half and missed a gilt-edged opportunity late on to salvage a point. As it was, Drew Jarvie's goal won the match.

I was on the bench again when Hearts came calling a couple of weeks later, and a certain gentleman came back to haunt us. Alfie Conn scored after two minutes and we lost again.

We travelled to Firhill for a League Cup tie with Partick Thistle and I was at my lowest ebb since joining Saints, and that includes the broken leg. Benched again.

I spoke to the gaffer and he was as blunt as always. He insisted I hadn't done enough against Albion Rovers in the first round of the League Cup and hinted that, since joining Saints, I'd failed to make the type of impact he'd hoped for. That hurt, but Jim didn't say these things just to irk you. He was as straight as a dye and I knew I had to take it on board.

The Saturday before we were due in Sweden, it was back to Firhill for a league encounter. Again, I wasn't in the pool, with the gaffer plumping for ex-Jags Bone and Somner up front. We lost and while it was only the middle of September, our league position was perilous.

When the tie with Elfsborg came around I was desperate to be involved, and I got in by default. Jimmy Bone had arrived back late from the USA and was therefore ineligible.

Apparently the Swedes had made an unusual request to St Mirren before the tie. Their goalkeeper, Roger Svensson, was desperate to work with the new UEFA ball, so they phoned and asked if we could send them one over. They didn't make them in Sweden and they were too expensive to import. What a cheek.

There was a real buzz about the place and everyone was looking forward to being part of history. From the moment the draw was made, I thought, 'this is what it's all about'. I was on the cusp of playing European football for the first time – if you discount my German experience with Rangers Athletic.

Paisley was a great place to be. The whole town signed up for the ride. When I spoke to Buddies about the draw, not many had heard of Elfsborg, although I'm sure it was a similar story in their neck of the woods. Saints weren't exactly perennial challengers in Europe either so it was a good match up.

When the tie eventually arrived, we headed off to Abbotsinch Airport, dressed smartly in our club blazers and, to a man, brimming with pride. Hundreds of supporters had booked flights to Sweden and we travelled with a fair degree of backing...and expectation.

Nowadays, Sweden isn't too far away. A hop, skip and a jump and you're in Stockholm. In 1980, it may as well have been on the other side of the world. Elfsborg played in a town called Boras, 30-odd miles outside Gothenburg. It was a small, textile town and we were certainly wrapped-up in this cup-tie. Of course, we had players with European experience in the squad, but it was thin on the ground. For most of us, this was our maiden voyage. Saints fans had shelled out £300 a time just to cheer us on, so we were determined to give them something to shout about.

We were at the airport at noon on the Monday and weren't scheduled to get to Boras until around nine o'clock that night. We had a couple of hours to wait for our flight and a few of the lads went to the airport cafe for a cuppa. Not me, I made straight for the games arcade to see what model of Space Invaders machine they had. In no time at all I was surrounded by team-mates and, to a man, they were dishing out advice on how to wipe out the pesky little aliens.

I remember club secretary Laurence Rew coming over to dish out plane tickets and everyone blanking him because we were all so wrapped up in this state-of-the-art games console. Very dated now, I know. I loved Space Invaders and found it a great way to relax – by getting stressed out.

Before long we were on the plane and heading off on the first leg of our journey. Around 30 minutes from Stavanger, in Norway, we were served a beautiful meal of venison and salad. Did they think we were Real Madrid? We had half-an-hour in Norway and it gave us a chance to stretch the legs. No one had heard of deep vein thrombosis in those days.

Then it was back on the plane for the 70-minute jaunt to Copenhagen, where we had to endure another two-hour stopover before taking to the air once again, this time bound for Gothenburg. We were travelling in instalments. Eventually arriving in the picturesque Swedish city around 7pm, we waited on the bus to take us to Boras, another 40-minute trek.

But it was all worth it when we arrived outside the Grand Hotel. This was one gaffe that lived up to its name. We checked into our rooms before heading off to explore our base for the next few days. And guess what I found? Only a casino and disco. I didn't want to ever go home. Naturally, we went to bed early that night.

After breakfast the next morning, we walked out through the hotel foyer to be greeted by the most amazing sight: a fleet of luxury Mercedes cars waiting to take us to training. Talk about travelling in style. Cramming into a messy mini-bus to head to Erskine Beach for training would never again be the same.

We were ferried to Elfsborg's neat training ground where we put in a decent session. At the ground, we were greeted by a group of Saints fans playing a bounce game on an adjacent park. We stood and watched them for a while. Talk about role reversal.

After working up quite a sweat, we returned – by luxury Mercedes, of course – to our hotel and relaxed ahead of the 6pm kick-off. A couple of hours beforehand a monsoon, the likes I'd never before witnessed, fell from the heavens. Surely the game was in doubt.

At 5pm we were chauffeur driven, again in luxury (not that I was complaining, but were there no buses in this town?), to Elfsborg's Ryavallen Stadium, with the rain still teaming down.

We walked the pitch about 15 minutes before kick-off and it was sodden. There and then, some of the guys considered switching from boots to flippers. We all believed there was still a greater than 50 per cent chance of the game being postponed, but we had to prepare as if it was going ahead, and it's just as well we did.

We disappeared back to the dressing room to get changed and the gaffer gave us our final team talk. We emerged from the tunnel to the sound of a stirring pipe band and that provided a timely lift.

The game began at a frantic pace and more often than not we were on the back foot. They definitely started better and we struggled in the first-half. We were fortunate to trail by just a single goal, scored by Swedish Under-21 star Lennart Nilsson in 15 minutes, as the break approached.

Elfsborg were no shrinking violets and weren't shy at sticking the boot in, although we had a few guys in the team who could look after themselves. Talking of which, Cowboy McCormack got hold of the ball in the middle of the park and played a delightful pass to Dougie Somner, and my strike partner levelled two minutes before half time.

Saints fans in the 4,000 crowd went nuts. We were back in it, and at just the right time.

After the break we were well on top. And then came the moment that annoyed me all the way home. I timed a run to perfection, latched on to a pass and scored a perfectly good goal. What a feeling...until I noticed the linesman had his flag held aloft in some sort of defiant manner. Offside. There was no way it was offside and I was livid.

But the bold Billy Abercromby made amends by firing home a superb volley in the 70th minute to give us a win in our first ever European tie.

It was an incredible feeling and it was a jubilant Saints party that made the short journey back to the hotel. A light meal awaited and we wolfed it down before heading off to find out more about Swedish culture – in the hotel disco.

We enjoyed a few drinks, and a boogie to Abba, but were up a few hours later at the ungodly hour of 4.45am to catch our flight(s) home. It was the same marathon 1000-mile journey, but spirits were incredibly high and we went our separate ways after touching down at Abbotsinch Airport. A job well done.

It may just have been 90 minutes in the eyes of some, but for me I believe the Elfsborg game was a turning point. The gaffer praised me for an 'aggressive display' and was delighted with my overall performance. Music to my ears.

I was well aware that I hadn't really lived up to my price tag, or reputation, but everyone has a turning point in their career, or life, and that might just have been mine.

My first season at St Mirren had been peppered with injuries and a return of just seven league and cup goals in 16 appearances wasn't good enough – not for a guy with the record Scottish price tag on his shoulders. Of course I was concerned. The confidence had gone and, although the gaffer had shown patience, there had to come a point when he would decide to go with someone else. I had to make sure that didn't happen again.

Dundee United visited Love Street the following Saturday and I scored in our 2-1 win. Many hailed it as a candidate for goal of the season. It was a stunning four-man move, which ended with me diving to head a Billy Stark cross past Hamish McAlpine. Mac was back in town.

The scene was set for the second-leg of our Euro tie with the Swedes and not only did we have the rain that we'd had to contend with in Sweden, but in true west of Scotland fashion, the gales had blown in to accompany it. Conditions were atrocious, but we had a job to do and got on with it. Despite home advantage, the game ended goalless and although we progressed 2-1 on aggregate; it would've been nice to win in style. Sometimes though, it's equally as important to grind out a result.

The game provoked a furious backlash from Jim Clunie, although this time his wrath wasn't aimed in the direction of the players…but the fans. The gaffer was raging at what he called, 'the shameful barracking of the team'.

He really whipped up a storm when he stated that the people of Paisley didn't deserve a senior team. He suggested Saints relocate to somewhere like East Kilbride, with a junior team taking over the reigns in Paisley. Controversy was never far from Love Street.

Hang on a minute; I was staying in EK at the time. Honest, guys, I swear I wasn't in on it.

Something was definitely amiss though because whereas we'd enjoyed an average gate of 10,000 the season previous, that figure halved during the 1980-1981 campaign.

But while JC had possibly gone over the top with the criticism of our fans, he was spot on when he blasted a minority for cheering when the Elfsborg goalkeeper was stretchered off with a broken leg following an innocuous challenge by Peter Weir. That was completely out of order. Turned out the poor guy had suffered a triple leg break.

The Saturday after the Elfsborg game, we travelled to Kilmarnock and thumped them 6-1. I don't know whether it was a reaction to all the negative stuff that had gone on in the aftermath of the Euro tie, or whether Killie were just guff. What I do know is that it was our best-ever Premier League result and I scored.

The following Wednesday we had a game with a difference. Tampa Bay Rowdies became the first ever American side to visit Paisley and more than 7,000 fans turned out to greet them.

I say a game with a difference because it was initially supposed to be played under the rules of the North American Soccer League, NASL shoot-outs and all the razzmatazz that goes with it. However, the SFA were having none of it and made us adhere to boring old Scottish rules. But we still had the glamour of the Yankee cheerleaders and the shoot-out before the match started, plus it was a decent game. The Rowdies came into the match on the back of a win over Luton Town and a draw at Birmingham City.

Despite being only six years in existence, they could play a bit, but were still no match for us though. We gubbed them 4-2 and I played most of the game before 'retiring' in the second half.

Next up was Aberdeen at Pittodrie and it was significant for one particular reason. We lost the game 3-2, but there was a watching delegation from St Etienne, our next UEFA Cup opponents, and I was told afterwards that they had picked out myself and Starky as the men to watch. That was a massive compliment.

Prior to the big Euro tie, the gaffer took us down to Largs for a few days to help with our preparations, but once again controversy, and not the big build-up, grabbed the headlines.

Papa Bone was displaced as skipper for supposedly arguing with the gaffer after being dropped the previous week. Apparently he'd refused to go on the bench and was replaced as captain by Jackie Copland.

We had a major task in front of us as St Etienne shared joint top spot in the French First Division with Nantes, but we were handed a major pre-match boost when it was confirmed that Michel Platini was injured and wouldn't play. I suppose there were still Jacques Santini, Johnny Rep, Patrick Battiston and Jean Francois Larios to contend with, as well as a few other French internationalists.

The scene was set and more than 11,000 Buddies, and a few hundred Frenchmen, turned Love Street into the type of atmospheric, European arena that players love to perform in. But once again, torrential rain did its level best to dampen everyone's spirits. It failed miserably though, and supporters got on with making an incredible din in a bid to drive us on to glory against a very good side.

In the first-half it was honours even with both teams creating a few chances. Neither managed to convert any and it was blank at the break. Midway through the second half, I was clean through on goal and had a great chance to put us ahead, but delayed my shot and allowed Castenada, who was a great keeper, to block.

The game finished goalless and it felt like an opportunity lost. The European mindset was far different in those days. Then, if you failed to score a couple of goals in the home leg, your chance had gone. Nowadays, a goalless draw is anything but frowned upon. Many teams have used this thought process to go abroad after a 0-0 and grab a vital away goal.

A couple of days after the first leg, a familiar face arrived in the Love Street dressing room and it was one that cheered me up, and almost everyone else, no end. Like me, Frank McAvennie had started out by plying his trade in the juniors. He had been knocking in the goals for Johnstone Burgh and I'd recommended him to the club. As professionals go, he was a late developer, having just turned 20. I'd never played football with Frank, but knew all about him from my former school, St Augustine's, and the reports were glowing.

Macca was a good lad and we soon struck up a fantastic rapport. He would pick me up in the morning and on most afternoons, after training, we'd head back into Glasgow to the Cue Club, a snooker parlour close to Charing Cross.

On one occasion we'd enjoyed a few frames, and a couple of lagers, and were discussing the finer points of being a soccer star. Macca said to me, 'It's all about image, Frank'. And with that, we decided to pop next door to a trendy hairdressing salon.

'A couple of perms please', we said on walking in and the girls just stared at us. Here I was taking this massive step and changing my long, flowing blonde locks to tight balls of curly perm. It was a massive step helped, no doubt, by the courage-enhancing supplements we'd been sipping next door.

So, perms it was, and once we'd been under the drier for a while, we re-emerged like 'Crockett and Tubbs' from the American hit TV detective show 'Miami Vice.'

In fact, Macca was convinced he was now chumming around with 'Oor Wullie' from the Sunday Post. What a ribbing we took from team-mates at training the following day.

After the crimping session, it was back to the Cue Club and, in between thumping Macca on the green baize, I popped into the toilet. I took one look at my Barnet in the mirror, went back into the main hall and dragged Macca straight into the hairdressers. I said to the girl, 'We'd like the perms out. Can you make our hair straight again?'

Then Macca piped up, 'He might want that, but I'm happy with my new look.'

So Macca kept the perm and I got mine ripped out. At the end of the deal I was £80 down – and my hair was back to the way it had been 24 hours beforehand. Talk about daft footballers.

My hair has been the same since the year dot and I'm sure it'll remain that way till the day I expire.

Macca would go on to make a fantastic impression – on the park – the following season. We both had a great relationship with Saints fans and didn't ever really get any hassle when out and about in the town. They knew we always gave 100 per cent and appreciated our efforts.

Fans would come up and chat about the game and we'd have a drink together, but then we'd move on and just try and enjoy our nights out. We never put ourselves in compromising positions, apart from one night I recall only too well.

On this occasion, we were in our favourite haunt, Toledo Junction in Paisley's New Street, after a particularly memorable game in which we beat Rangers 2-1 at Love Street.

We were having a great night and, being single at the time, I was on the lookout for a pretty girl to share the dance floor with. I wasn't exactly John Travolta, but I was game for a laugh and Macca and I had our fair share of laughs in that place.

I soon got chatting to this 'stunner' and we enjoyed a drink and a dance together. It was approaching the wee small hours and she asked me to see her home. I waved goodbye to Mr Gooseberry and left the club with 'Miss Paisley' on my arm. We jumped in a taxi and she rhymed off the name of some street I'd never heard of.

Before I knew it we were sitting outside this awful looking house, and remember I'd come from a tough housing scheme. The front door had six panes of glass, or rather, it should have had. I think there was only one-and-a-half left. I thought to myself, 'She must live next door.'

Nope, we walked up the path to the front door and she reached inside one of the broken panes and turned the door handle from inside. I was apprehensive to say the least.

It was one of those four-in-a-block houses and when you walk through the front door it leads straight upstairs to the upper flat. She needed the loo, but pointed to her room. Next minute I heard this awful snoring, 'who's that?' I asked.

'Och, that's just my brother, he'll be drunk from the match today. Do you want to go in and say hello?'

I thought it might be the polite thing to do so I gingerly opened the door and peeked in. I couldn't believe the scene that greeted me. He was lying on top of the bed clothes with a can of lager still in his hand.

The room was like a shrine to Rangers, with several Red Hand of Ulster flags on the walls, as well as banners and scarves.

He looked slightly bonkers and I thought to myself, 'time for a sharp exit.' He'll wake up, see me, the guy that scored the winner against his beloved Rangers and want to celebrate by cracking open my skull.

The girl emerged from the toilet just as I quietly closed his door. I made my excuses, as they say, and left.

I couldn't believe I was leaving behind this stunning girl, but she came with a government health warning, not personally, but my health would've been severely compromised had I stayed in that house a moment longer.

I didn't even get her number and was at Gilmour Street train station in record time. I ran all the way from Ferguslie Park without stopping to draw breath.

The Saturday before we were due at the Geoffrey Guichard Stadium, home of St Etienne, we visited Tynecastle for a feisty clash with Hearts. We were desperate for a good 90 minutes before the trip over the Channel.

Not for yours truly though, as I was forced to withdraw from the trip due to 'flu. It had come at such an inconvenient time. I was desperate to play against what was virtually the entire French national side. And I would.

The following Wednesday, more than 20,000 noisy supporters packed the 'Guichard' and I had managed to shake off the viral infection just in time to line up alongside my Buddies. Michel Platini had also won his personal battle with a thigh muscle pull.

We were there that night to try and frustrate the hell out them. We didn't have the armoury to indulge in all out attack, so the game plan was to try and contain for as long as possible. St Mirren were never going to win the competition, but we were squaring up to the big name we'd craved and wanted to enjoy ourselves.

Sure, St Etienne were able to boast the stars, but if Scottish grit and determination, allied to a fair degree of skill, counted for anything then we would give them a run for their money.

Just before kick-off, Jim Clunie sprang one of his legendary surprises, although it was even more of a surprise to Aber. 'You're marking Platini', said the gaffer, "And don't worry about him, he's not as good as everyone makes out.'

Now, Aber was one of those players that would never shirk a challenge. To him, Platini was just another name, although by the end of the night not even the latest SatNav model could've helped him.

He tried following the great Frenchman everywhere, but it just didn't happen and at the end of the game we had to unscrew him from the turf. Aber was a real grafter and a vital player for us with his never-say-die enthusiasm and unstinting determination and I'm sure Platini returned to his chateau that night knowing he'd been in the game.

As expected, it was a tough match and we lost 2-0, but weren't in any way disgraced and although we exited Europe at the second hurdle, the experience had been both enjoyable and invaluable in terms of future participation. In the end, we had been outdone by that tremendous French international, Larios. He scored both St Etienne goals, one in either half, and proved the real difference between the sides.

But if the Portuguese referee Da Silva had given us a fair crack of the whip, things may have finished differently. He gave a free-kick, which led to a goal, to the French side when Johnny Rep had quite clearly fouled Jackie Copland. In fact, the Dutch star actually apologised to big Jackie after the match.

There was also the matter of two penalty kicks that I reckon we should've been awarded. Dougie Somner and Cowboy were both hacked down in the area and both were nailed-on spot kicks. Only Da Silva thought otherwise. But that's European football for you and sometimes the big clubs get the big decisions on home soil.

The one thing that still sticks in my mind about that night actually happened long after the game had ended. The chartered plane, which was due to take us home, had been grounded due to adverse weather and we were put up temporarily in a nearby hotel. An impromptu 'party' was hastily arranged in one of the bedrooms.

The gaffer was in attendance, but was more or less an innocent bystander as the players decided to let their hair down. A few of the directors weren't happy about the racket coming from the room and one in particular, John Corson, the chairman, came along to tell us just that.

The bedroom door flew open and he growled, 'Do you think you've just won the f****** European Cup?'

A few censures were issued before he clocked the gaffer sitting enjoying a beer with the players. Everyone knew that the relationship between manager and directors wasn't the closest, but there wasn't an issue that night, apart from a wee bit of noise, which was toned down at their request.

I got on really well with Jim Clunie. He was a big gentleman, softly spoken on most occasions, but not afraid to dish out the verbals when required. He lost his rag occasionally, but it wasn't in the same way that Fergie would lose his. Jim lost his with a certain amount of dignity, if that makes sense.

I had a lot of time for him and enjoyed listening to his stories about his time as a player, or when he was assistant to Lawrie McMenemy at Southampton, when the south coast side were a real force.

On arriving home from France, we were faced with the prospect of Rangers at home. We were easily the best team on the day, but were once again let down by a poor refereeing decision. Lex Richardson scored a fantastic goal, but it was bizarrely ruled offside and that was that. One point dropped, rather than one gained.

A couple of weeks later we were due at Tannadice and once again I missed out because of 'flu. I was back seven days later to help the team to a 2-1 win at Celtic Park, courtesy of a last-minute goal by Alex Beckett, a real unsung hero at Love Street.

Just three weeks after the match in France we learned that the gaffer and directors were to part company. Unfortunately though, we were left with the directors.

I don't know what went on in the days after St Etienne, whether or not it was down to that little party, because players simply aren't privy to that sort of information. Boardroom meetings and battles are off-limits, but it must have been serious for Jim to get the shove.

I found out through the local paper. It reported that Jim had been summoned to a garage in Paisley, owned by Corson, and it was there that he was handed his jotters. The ins and outs, I'm not sure of.

I didn't know who half the directors were at St Mirren. There was no interaction between players and board members, which, in a way, was pretty sad. We were all fighting a common cause, but there was a definite distance between us.

At Clydebank, Jack Steedman would come into the dressing room before games and wish us good luck, try and gee us up and occasionally offer an extra £25 if we won the game. I didn't mind that type of intervention.

It was similar at Aberdeen. The chairman Dick Donald was a lovely man, as was his deputy, Chris Anderson. They would both be waiting with a pat on the back as we emerged from the dressing room and would wish us good luck.

At both these clubs, although the directors got involved, there was never any attempt to try and undermine the manager. Their involvement was minimal, but appreciated.

We were absolutely gutted for Jim. It was a major shock and, to a man, we were sad to see him go.

Ricky McFarlane took over the reigns on a temporary basis and he was a great lad. He had a tremendous knowledge of football, although his primary job had been that of physiotherapist, and he was one of the best I'd ever worked with.

When he took over as caretaker boss it was a bit of a shock because we all knew Ricky as the physio and big Jim's assistant. Nevertheless, he had the full backing of the players and, while we were missing JC, life had to go on. At least Ricky would bring stability to the club.

And he had been with us every day as a coach so the transition proved seamless and we continued to work hard.

But just like Jim Clunie, Ricky could be tough when required. He wasn't afraid to dole out the occasional boot up the backside. It must be difficult being one of the lads one day and the gaffer the next, but he managed it as well as anyone.

Of course, the papers were full of speculation as to who would get the job on a full-time basis. Ricky wasn't quoted.

Names such as ex-Manchester United manager Tommy Docherty, former Lisbon Lion Tommy Gemmell, Hibs legend Pat Stanton, former Rangers players Davy Wilson and Davie Provan (who had been Fergie's assistant at Love Street) and even Ally MacLeod were all in the frame.

The salary was estimated at around £15,000 a year, which wasn't a great deal more than the players were getting at that time, so I immediately ruled out myself as player/manager, I didn't need the hassle.

The job in hand was made all the more difficult due to boardroom in-fighting. It's often suggested that this doesn't affect players, who just get on with playing, but when boardroom unrest is splashed all over the papers, and it's visibly affecting the manager, then that's bound to be passed on to the dressing room.

Ricky enjoyed a great start to his managerial career, although I wasn't really given the opportunity to play much of a part in it. I was finding myself on the bench week in, week out and my appearances were curtailed to the last ten or 15 minutes as a sub.

But the team was winning and all I could do was mark time and do my bit when called upon. This was often with the reserves in midweek games and I scored in just about them all.

A couple of weeks before Christmas, Saints were once again making the headlines for all the wrong reasons. John Corson was sacked and the boardroom was again in upheaval. It was like a soap opera being played out in front of an enthralled public.

Just before the chairman was axed I recall Ricky saying that he didn't want the job on a permanent basis, which was a surprise, because he seemed to be enjoying it. At the same time, he appealed for calm at the club, in a bid to repair Saints' tarnished image.

I suppose, in a way, our good run of results was taking the focus off the boardroom and Ricky's infectious personality was one of the more positive aspects of being a St Mirren employee at that time.

The week before Christmas we were whisked off to Stirling University for a couple of days to 'get away from it all'. We took part in a couple of training sessions, sigh, and played a bounce match against the University side. We stayed at a local hotel and it was a welcome break. It was also great to be able to train with Dougie Somner because he was part-time and we only got to see him now and again.

A couple of days after indulging in turkey and all the trimmings, Ricky was surprisingly announced as the new St Mirren manager. He had been at the club in various capacities for six years. He was due it and we were delighted.

It was rapidly approaching 1981 and my New Year resolution was simple – to make more of an impact on the team. I was facing a real challenge, having been in and out of the team. I wanted a sustained berth to see what I could achieve, but there was only one person that could make it happen and that was me.

I remember sitting at home that New Year, sipping on a can of lager and reflecting on my year-and-a-half in Paisley. Moving up to play in the Premier League had been exciting but overall, I don't think things had panned out the way I'd have liked. Whether I had underachieved, or just taken longer to settle in at the higher level was up for debate.

I spoke to Ricky just after the New Year and told him I was unhappy at being left out so much. I was well aware that the exceptional form of Bone and Somner was the reason I had been benched more often than not, but I was still hurting. He knew I wanted to play every week. In fact, I would've played every day of the week, such was my enthusiasm for the game. I continued to work hard on the training pitch and in reserve games so that I would be ready to answer the call when it arrived, and it would arrive.

The traditional Ne'erday game with Morton was scheduled for Cappielow and former gaffers, Alex Ferguson and Jim Clunie, watched from the stand as the teams ground out a 1-1 draw.

Once again I was left warming the bench. The former Rangers goalkeeper Erik Sorensen was appointed as Ricky's assistant just before the match. The weather was atrocious and we had to train on a red ash pitch at Ralston, a leafy suburb of Paisley, which took me back to my childhood days when I played every day on the blaes surface at Cadder School.

A turning point for me was a game against Kilmarnock at Rugby Park – and I wasn't even playing. We lost 2-0 to Killie, who were bottom of the league, and they had just sacked their manager. We were pushing for a European place and had been expected to win. I was on the bench.

That midweek, I was gearing up to play alongside the other reserves and fringe players in the Renfrewshire Cup final against Morton when Ricky told me I wasn't in the starting eleven.

That was the final straw. I was furious. I may have been less than halfway through a five-year contract, but what chance did I have of ever getting back into the first team if I couldn't even make a glorified reserve match?

I went to see him and he explained, calmly, that he wasn't about to take a risk, as he wanted me fit and healthy for the weekend league clash with Celtic. Oops.

Joy soon turned to despair though, when the match was cancelled with the Love Street pitch under several inches of snow.

The second leg of the Renfrewshire Cup final was played a few days later and this time I was risked. We needed game time and Ricky played a few first team players. We won 4-0 and I scored the first – and set up the other three.

I'll always remember the Paisley Daily Express naming me as man-of-the-match and suggesting that a 'superb one-man-show' had destroyed Morton.

It didn't help me win a starting place in the side for the Scottish Cup third round game against minnows Dumbarton a couple of days later though. Before the match, the Sons announced that they'd tried to sign Johann Cruyff, and that raised a chuckle in our dressing room.

Unfortunately, we were laughing on the other side of our face at the final whistle after a shock 2-0 defeat. I came on as a late sub for Peter Weir but the tie was gone by then and it was a red-faced group of players that trouped disconsolately back to the dressing room.

Ricky's response was to try to sign Stevie Nicol, from Ayr United, but the £200,000 price tag scared him off. It didn't scare Liverpool, though, and the classy defender headed for Anfield.

Our untimely Scottish Cup exit led to Saints directors fixing up a game against a top English side to fill the free Saturday. Imagine our joy when it was announced that the mighty Arsenal would be heading to Paisley.

However, Morton were scheduled to play Aberdeen in the Scottish Cup fourth round that day and complained to the SFA that our glamour clash could affect their gate. We were forced to switch to the Sunday and, as it turned out, Morton drew a paltry gate anyway.

We had a couple of matches before the London giants arrived in town. Jimmy Bone was suspended for the league match at Airdrie and I was due to take his place, but once again the match was postponed.

I was then named in the line-up for a midweek friendly at Hamilton, but picked up the 'flu and was forced to withdraw. On the Friday night I had recovered sufficiently to play for the reserves against Airdrie and bagged a hat-trick. I was back on song.

A crowd of 10,000 turned up to watch us play Arsenal less than 48 hours later and, although we led 2-0 at half-time, they roared back to win 3-2. At least I managed to score, despite suffering terrible toothache. It was a joy playing against Graham Rix, Frank Stapleton and Paul Davis.

From toothache to a neck injury. The season was ending on another low note as injury again took hold, but my despair proved a turning point for plucky Saints. We trailed Partick Thistle 2-0 at half-time in a match we simply had to win, even though victory wouldn't guarantee European football.

I picked up a neck injury a few minutes after the break and was forced to leave the field. Young Alan Logan came on and scored a hat-trick in a pulsating 3-2 win.

I was back in the side for our trip to Tynecastle – a ground I loved – seven days later and scored, along with Alan, to clinch a 2-1 win.

We then beat Morton before hosting Celtic in another must-win match. And we did. Thankfully Celtic had clinched the title and we took full advantage to post a 3-1 win. I managed a couple of goals, although I suppose my second could've been described as 'ungentlemanly'.

As Lex Richardson swung over a corner, I just knew that Pat Bonner wasn't getting it. I told him so, stood at the back post and nodded home before thanking the big man. I don't think he appreciated the comment though.

That was our last game of the campaign and, unfortunately, even a decent win over the champions didn't prove enough to grab a Euro spot. We lost out to Rangers on goal difference and that was that – for another season.

In reality, it hadn't been a bad effort. Celtic were crowned champions, seven points ahead of Aberdeen, and we finished on the same points total as Rangers, in joint third spot.

It showed how far Saints had come as a club and we really were firmly established as a top four Premier League side. We took great satisfaction from that. We now had a pre-season trip to Denmark to look forward to...or did we?

AVOIDING AN INTERNATIONAL INCIDENT

UNFORTUNATELY, the pre-season tour of Denmark, which had been arranged by Erik Sorensen, failed to materialise. Games against a Danish Select and Odense had already been pencilled in, but the club had encountered difficulties fixing up a third match, which, like our Brazilian jaunt, was necessary to make the trip viable. So, we swapped the beauties of Copenhagen for Paisley's Gleniffer Braes, where we trained initially, before heading to the sandy dunes of Erskine. Already I was regretting the indisciplines of my close season.

And the moment we arrived back from our six-week break we were caught up in an international storm. The club had arranged a prestigious pre-season friendly with Spanish big guns, Atletico Madrid - a match that caught the imagination of the Paisley public. The opportunity to pit our wits against the likes of Brazilian superstar, Dirceu was keenly anticipated.

We were then told the match was off and, on digging a little deeper, it seemed the Spaniards had snubbed us to court favour with Spain's King Juan Carlos because of the dispute with Great Britain about Gibraltar. The Spanish club insisted the cancellation was down to travel difficulties. They were apparently on a tour of Russia and were having trouble getting from Moscow to Paisley.

Earlier, King Juan Carlos had refused to attend the wedding of Prince Charles and Lady Diana Spencer because they had chosen to spend part of their honeymoon on the hotly-disputed island. St Mirren received a telegram from the Spaniards to say they wouldn't be able to come to Paisley, and that was it. International incident avoided, we simply got on with preparing for the new season. Instead of facing Dirceu, we headed for the Highlands to play in the Keith tournament. Not much difference, huh.

The club then hosted an open day for fans to meet the players. We arranged a match involving the first and second team players and guess what? I suffered a knee injury. Thankfully, it didn't keep me out of the opening League Cup match at Celtic Park. And what a way to start the new term.

We gubbed the champions 3-1 thanks to unfortunate Celtic defender, Willie Garner scoring twice - for St Mirren. He deflected my shot into the net for our first goal and by 4.45pm he was our top scorer having scored a second own goal.

A draw at home to Hibs was followed by a trip to Perth, where St Johnstone's new kid on the block was attracting bags of headlines. Everyone wanted to see how good Ally McCoist was and although he scored a goal, I managed two. Anything you can do Ally…

That game is memorable for another incident. We were 3-2 up with a few minutes to go and the home side were pumping high balls into our box. Jackie Copland made a superb clearance and they rather bizarrely started screaming for a penalty claiming Jackie had touched the ball with his hand.

Play was stopped and one of their players grabbed the ball and plonked it on the penalty spot. I was having none of it and sprinted all of 30 yards to boot the ball as far away as I could. I knew it hadn't struck Jackie's hand. My team-mates stared at me in disbelief. The referee waltzed across and I thought, 'Here we go, I'm in trouble'. No way, thank goodness. He merely pointed out that the linesman had flagged for offside. I was a relieved man and happy that my little rush of blood hadn't resulted in anything more than our free-kick.

I was enjoying the League Cup and grabbed the winner against Hibs at Easter Road, a ground I would continue to enjoy playing at after moving to Aberdeen. And, because it was the winner, I milked it for all it was worth directly in front of Hibs boss, Bertie Auld, the guy that had callously dismissed me during my brief spell at Partick Thistle. It was a sweet moment.

We qualified for the quarter-finals then opened our league campaign with a win over rivals Morton. At that time I was mixing my sports during leisure time. I still enjoyed a couple of games of snooker, but the bulk of the players were now playing golf.

Our second Premier League game, a visit to Broomfield, Airdrie, was significant for more than just the two points we gained as a result of an exciting 4-3 win. It marked the debut of Frank McAvennie, and what an impact he made. He played extremely well and scored two goals. Macca had arrived.

A couple of weeks beforehand, during a training session, I got involved in an altercation with Billy Abercromby. Aber trained the way he played, but took it too far, in my opinion, during one particular session. Macca was just a lad, but that didn't stop Aber going right through him that day. It was bang out of order and I told him so. Macca copped a nasty one and was lucky that it didn't force him to miss a few games.

After two games we were joint top with Celtic and on the back of that, Ricky McFarlane was appointed part-time boss of the Scotland Under-21 side. A couple of months into the season, news broke in the press of St Mirren's precarious financial situation. The club was apparently in real trouble and there was talk of Saints going to the wall.

The first we heard about it was when we read it in the papers. We were sheltered from that sort of thing, although I'm sure Ricky was being kept abreast of developments. There was nothing else for us to do, but continue to do our best and hopefully that would add a few more to the gates and help alleviate any worries.

San Jose Earthquakes were in the United Kingdom around this period on a 'George Best Farewell Tour', as the great man had decided to hang up his boots. Representatives contacted Saints about a challenge match, but the board turned it down.

We met Forfar in the League Cup quarter-final second leg. After a 1-1 draw at their place, we were under pressure to get our pride back. I think the 6-0 score line did just that.

I'll always remember picking up the local paper the following day and seeing one of my goals that night described as one of the best-ever scored at Love Street. It was a real beauty, mind you. A 30-yard curler that nestled proudly in the top corner, and it helped set up a semi-final showdown with Rangers.

One of the best goalkeepers I ever came up against was Alan Rough. He was superb. And he was at it again when we played Thistle, at Firhill. The Jags were leading 1-0 when I found myself in a fantastic position to level, but Rough defied logic by saving a shot he had no right to get to and then leapt off the ground to save the follow up. He had no right to get to that one either. I had the last laugh though when I scored with a minute or so to go, even if I was a yard offside. It was the only way I could get the better of him.

The downside to that match, however, was that I suffered a twisted knee. I played on and it made me doubtful for the semi-final against Rangers. I was desperate to play in that game. I worked hard with our physio and coaches in the days leading up to the first leg and was passed fit a few hours before kick-off.

Looking back though, I wish I hadn't made it. During the match, I tangled with Tom Forsyth and down I went in agony. There was no way I could play on and our trainer helped me from the field. Our supporters were booing Forsyth, but the injury was nothing to do with big Tam. When I turned to try and get away from him, my studs caught in the turf and I felt it go there and then. I had damaged my cartilage and would require an operation.

I left the stadium on crutches and my worst fears were confirmed when the club sent me to see a specialist the following day. I was looking at up to ten weeks on the sidelines. I had targeted the League Cup final in November as my comeback date, but that was dead in the water when we lost 2-1 to Rangers in the quarter-final second leg at Ibrox.

During my time out, the club targeted Sandy Clark as a replacement, but the Airdrie striker turned down the opportunity to play at Love Street. I hated training, but was delighted when given the all-clear by the physio to resume light work at the start of November. Hopefully I would be back playing soon. I missed nine matches and that was more than enough. Ricky McFarlane told me he was hoping to have me back in the team for our trip to Celtic Park at the beginning of December. Nice easy game to ease myself back into action. But I never made that game as I had a bad reaction to the injury when I played a few reserve games.

I played a few reserve games beforehand and there was a slight reaction. The gaffer refused to risk me and told me to report to Love Street for the reserve match on the same day. As I was walking away from the stadium he said, 'Remember Frank, it's a 2pm kick-off, not three.'

This, I believe, was to save cash by not using the floodlights. It was only then that I realised the club was in dire straits. In any case, the match was cancelled due to a frozen pitch.

I must admit I wasn't in the slightest bit disappointed to see the back of 1981. What's that they say about a new year and a chance to wipe the slate clean? I had endured more than my fair share of injuries and I was hoping, no, make that praying, for an even break in '82. I was back for our New Year derby match with Morton and came off the bench to play my part in a 2-1 win. It felt good.

Next up was a clash with Rangers at our place. Playing against the Old Firm always seemed to bring out the best in me. Ironically, my nemesis was also due to make his comeback in this match. Ally Dawson, ironically from Renfrewshire, had been out for a while and we were set to renew hostilities…or were we?

The weather had been shocking and a fresh wave of snow hit Paisley on the week of the big game. A postponement looked the only option, but no one would make the call, and that indecision cost us a short trip to either Spain or Italy. Ricky was desperate for 90 minutes ahead of our Scottish Cup tie with Morton and had pushed the powers-that-be to make a decision on the pitch, which was frozen solid.

We had been invited to play Roma in the Olympic Stadium, with a match in Seville another option. However, the Scottish football authorities dragged their heels and, finally, the club were forced to write off plans to play on exotic terrain. In the end, we faced our great county rivals without a game under our belts, but beat them 2-0.

But disaster struck - once again - in our next game though. The only New Year resolution I'd made was for an injury-free year, but that came unstuck at the end of January in a league match at Dundee. We won 2-0 at Dens Park, but I limped off with a calf strain and was badly winded after a clash with one of the Dark Blues. 'Here we go again', I thought, and I missed out on the next few games. It was doubly disappointing because we were playing well and I was desperate to be a part of it. A decent run had taken us into third place in the league, just a couple of points behind Celtic and Rangers.

I was soon back in the side scoring goals and when we held Dundee United to a draw at Tannadice, courtesy of a 'brilliant' McDougall header, we leapfrogged Rangers into second spot, just four points behind Celtic. Despite being sidelined frequently with a string of injuries, I had still managed 13 goals, just one behind Macca.

It was the middle of March before we lost our first game of the year, against Rangers, and while we were disappointed to slip back to third, we were devastated to read in the papers that the club would have to sell players to survive. It simply wasn't what you wanted to hear while chasing the league championship and, believe me, that's exactly what we were doing.

Whether that devastating news had a bearing on our next game, I'll never know. We were up against Celtic at Love Street and if this was a test of our title credentials, we failed miserably. I was on the bench and sat there in agony as we lost four goals before the break.

'Okay, Frank, on you go and see what you can rescue', said Ricky as we sat shell-shocked in the dressing room at half-time. Within four minutes of the re-start I'd clawed one back. Bang - Celtic ran up the park and scored a fifth straight from centre. I scored again on the hour, but by that time we were a well-beaten side.

The new kids on the block had been taught a harsh lesson by the old masters. It was a warning. Remember your place and respect the establishment. But would we listen? No way, we wanted a piece of the cake and were determined to get it. We didn't want to be known as the perennial nearly-men of Scottish football.

Macca and I continued to score and we continued to hang on in there. We were still in the Scottish Cup and due to play Fergie's Aberdeen in the semi-finals at Hampden. The game duly came along, but it was filled with controversy.

With an hour on the clock, I chased a hopeful ball into the box. Jim Leighton caught it cleanly, but my momentum carried me straight into him. He dropped the ball and it trundled behind the goal line. To my surprise, referee Hugh Alexander awarded us a corner kick. Leighton was furious, and I can understand why. Lex Richardson swung over the ball and Cowboy nodded it in my direction. I wheeled and hooked it high into the net. The Dons players went ballistic, but we were 1-0 up with half-an-hour to hold on if we wanted to play Rangers in the final.

Seven minutes later though, Mark McGhee went down in the box after tangling with Billy Thomson and Alexander pointed to the spot. Was this a case of the referee trying to even it up? It mattered not because Gordon Strachan smashed home the kick and that remained the final score. We lost the toss for replay venue and the match was played at Dens Park. Least said about this one, the better. We didn't play particularly well and lost 3-2.

The hangover continued through to the following Saturday and, surprisingly, we lost 1-0 at home to Dundee. It was a significant game for me because after this I was dropped for 'not trying hard enough.' Ricky assured me I wasn't being made a scapegoat for the surprise defeat and, anyway, I missed out on a 4-1 thumping by Aberdeen as well as the next few games. In fact, my next game was against Aberdeen in the 2nd XI Cup semi-final.

The dandy Dons were rapidly becoming the bane of my life. We lost 7-2, and in a double dose of disappointment, Macca scored a brace at Airdrie to overhaul me at the top of the goalscoring charts. I wasn't a happy bunny. It wasn't just me that had a stinker against Dundee.

I returned to the first team for a league match at Parkhead and Ricky praised me afterwards for my industry. We got a 0-0 draw, but then lost eight goals to Aberdeen and Rangers within the space of four days. Our season was unravelling before our very eyes.

The spectre of Saints having to sell to survive raised its ugly head again, although this time I was actually named alongside Dougie Somner as two players who would most likely be moving on in a bid to balance the books. It wasn't a nice feeling. It was yet another negative newspaper headline. Apparently, the club were 'desperate for cash.'

I missed out on our penultimate league game, against Aberdeen at Love Street, and the 2-0 reverse meant our European dream was officially over. God knows how we managed to completely mess up our title challenge.

We had been doing so well, but ended up missing out on a UEFA Cup place as well. It wasn't what you would term an 'awful' season, more of a frustration. We were so close to achieving something good, but ended up with nothing for our efforts. We weren't in the least bit surprised when the club announced they couldn't afford to send us on a pre-season tour of Europe, and that we would instead be going to the Isle of Man.

One pre-season event I did enjoy was the annual charity bowls tournament at Ralston, in Paisley. It always attracted some big names and that year was no different.

There were lots of celebrities present, including Rangers pair Tom Forsyth and Colin Jackson, but I was lumped in with Lex Richardson, plus two directors - Jack Gilmour and 'bowling expert' Fraser McIntosh. The event was organised as a fundraiser for the war veteran's home at Erskine and my team won the tournament. I enjoyed a game of bowls, as did the bold Lex. At least we ended the season with some silverware.

With the formalities officially over, I was invited to speak at a sportsman's dinner. I refused point blank. Macca, Cowboy and the rest of the gang may laugh at this, but I'm actually quite shy.

Macca could speak all night long at these events, but it's simply not me. I'd need ten pints just to get up and face an audience. At a push, I would maybe get up there and answer a few questions, although I couldn't take the lead with 100 pairs of eyes gawking at me. The thought of all those people thinking, 'he's just awful' really does drive me to despair.

Maybe I'm lacking in confidence in that way, but as a footballer it's a different type of confidence needed to run out onto the pitch in front of 50,000 people. There are always nerves when you take to the turf but once the game kicks-off, they disappear. That's not the case in a hall full of prying eyes though.

CONTROVERSY 'RAINS' SUPREME AT HAMPDEN

MY fourth season at Saints began with a trip to the land of the tail-less cat and the birch (which I would no doubt have been given a few times if it was still in use in Scotland). I'd never been to the Isle of Man before so it was another new experience, courtesy of the strapped-for-cash Saints board. But the facilities on the Manx island were faultless and the entire trip was more than worthwhile.

We were based at Port Erin, which the Isle of Man tourist board had apparently arranged for us. Nothing but the best for the Buddies. Our first match was against a local Island XI, which, at first glance, sounds as though we were tackling a bunch of butchers, bakers and candlestick makers. However, throw in former Liverpool captain and hardman Tommy Smith plus Manchester City star Mike Summerbee and it'll give you a better idea of the standard of opposition. Regardless, we won 5-0 and I helped myself to a couple of goals. I also managed to stay off Mr Smith's radar.

We ended our mini-tour by beating Sunderland before heading home to face the mighty Leeds United at Love Street. We won handsomely, but I missed out because I was due to serve a one-match suspension in our opening sectional League Cup match against Ayr (which we won), so Ricky went with the 11 who were scheduled to start that game.

I was on the bench for our next game, a trip to Dumfries to play Queen of the South. We were expected to win comfortably, but struggled somewhat and I was delighted when Ricky told me to get stripped on the hour mark. The goal that eventually won the tie was an absolute cracker. And I don't just say that because I scored it.

This was, arguably, the best of my entire career.

Pouncing on a loose ball about 35 yards out, I let fly with this unstoppable shot. The goalkeeper watched it whiz straight past him and into the top corner. I loved scoring goals, but this one gave me particular pleasure.

As the league campaign edged ever closer, we were quoted at 20/1 for the title. I was a betting man, but even I wouldn't have touched those odds with a bargepole. We were a decent team, but nowhere near genuine title contenders. We didn't have the staying power.

We were still in August and, although it was a new season, it was the same old story as far as the club were concerned. It wasn't a surprise to pick up the paper and see that St Mirren were considering calling in the Receivers. The timing was awful, but thankfully the report was like a Cowboy McCormack shot - wide of the mark. We responded by putting six past Queen of the South at Love Street and Macca, Starky and I bagged doubles.

We lost our next match at Ayr and the post-mortem included Ricky allegedly saying he wouldn't suffer 'posers' in the team. Naturally, my mind wandered to Macca and me in Toledo Junction in our cool 'Miami Vice' suits. Hopefully he meant a different type of poser.

We duly qualified for the quarter-finals of the League Cup before heading for Easter Road for our opening Premier League match of the season. It was a 0-0 draw and memorable only for a disgruntled fan hitting Ricky on the head with a pie.

To say we didn't enjoy the greatest of starts to our league campaign would be an understatement. We picked up just two points from our first four games and suddenly the decision to keep my pennies in my pocket, regarding a bet on St Mirren to win the title, was already looking good.

We were dumped out of the League Cup by Hearts on an aggregate of 3-2, before finally managing our first league win in a five-goal thriller at home to Kilmarnock. I was named man-of-the-match, but, for me, the best moment of the game came on the hour mark when Macca scored the winner. It was a goal of exceptional quality and put my opener to shame.

The boy from the Milton was an excellent player and his rise to prominence was one of whirlwind proportions. We showed we were back on song in a classic encounter with Rangers a few weeks later. Jim Bett scored first for Rangers, but we fought back and equalised before half-time. I was clean through and rounded keeper Jim Stewart, but he hauled me down. Penalty. I always fancied my chances from 12 yards, but our regular taker, Ian Scanlon, was having none of it and duly converted.

I managed to score on the hour mark and thought it might end up being the winner, but Rangers full-back Davie MacKinnon popped up in 70 minutes to crash home the leveller. It was a good point in a game we might just have lost earlier in the season.

Another couple of draws followed and while we'd turned the corner, we had still won just one game in 13. It wasn't anywhere near good enough and we took out those frustrations on Hibs in a 3-0 gubbing. That was as good as it got though. We lost our next three games, conceding 11 goals and registering zero in return.

Once again, I was in and out of the team like a yo-yo. There didn't seem any rhyme or reason to it. We were leaking goals like a sieve and any signs of improvement were a distance away. Our fans were becoming increasingly disillusioned, and no wonder. We beat Motherwell 3-0 and drew with Killie. Big deal.

It was approaching Christmas and frustration at a lack of first team opportunities had really set in. I was sub one week, playing the next, not listed the next, and so on. It was an awful time. We were given Christmas Day off and told to report for training 24 hours later to prepare for a match against Dundee on December 27. It was one we had to win.

For some reason I was optimistic about playing - and also winning the game convincingly. I was wrong on both counts. I turned up at Love Street bright and breezy and was disappointed the moment I looked at the team sheet. Scanning the one to 11, the name McDougall was definitely absent. Not another game on the bench, I thought. Nope, not even that.

I trundled off to the stand to watch the game and, for tuppence, I could so easily have walked straight out the stadium and into the pub. It was a rotten feeling. The game was equally as bad and ended 0-0.

Once again, New Year, new hope, was my philosophy and we were scheduled at Easter Road on January 2nd. I was back in favour and played the whole game. We got a credible 1-1 draw, although the game was also notable for the St Mirren debut of one Chic Charnley.

Chic was an exceptional footballer, although I don't think he ever received the credit he deserved for his undoubted talents. Might just have been something to do with his questionable disciplinary record. How many red cards was it Chic? Think I lost count at a dozen.

A couple of days later, we played Morton at Love Street and I was back on the bench. It was extremely disappointing, although poor Chic wasn't even in the 13.

Ricky was chopping and changing at every turn, so with little continuity around, there was no chance of building up a head of steam.

The following week we played Celtic at our place and lost 1-0, although it should've been 1-1. With just seconds remaining, I rounded Paddy Bonner and stroked the ball towards the empty net...until my nemesis, Danny McGrain, came from nowhere to clear the ball off the line. I was absolutely flabbergasted. After the game, Ricky failed in a bid to land Gordon Dalziel from Rangers. Did my miss annoy Ricky that much?

Our next game was at home to Aberdeen, and boy did we owe them one after they'd mauled us 4-0 at Pittodrie. The game ended 1-1 but we suffered a severe injustice.

Scan put us 1-0 up and we were playing well. I then got on the end of a cross and flicked it past keeper Jim Leighton. They couldn't possibly come back from 2-0 down, although I didn't get the chance find out.

Willie Miller stuck out a hand and prevented a certain goal. For some strange reason, referee Andrew Waddell didn't see it that way and waved play on. It was a dreadful, dreadful decision by the ref and cost us the points. Moments later, Leighton pulled off an unbelievable save from my shot and I just knew it wasn't going to be our day. I was right - they went on to score two and equalised later on.

A trip to face Dundee United was next on the agenda and we soon found ourselves 3-0 down. We showed tremendous character to nip a couple of goals back, but lost 3-2. We got our revenge the following Saturday though when we knocked them out of the Scottish Cup.

Big Dougie Somner scored the only goal of the match and, it was reported, West Ham and Manchester United were watching Frank. Unfortunately, it was the McAvennie variety and not me.

We followed that up with a trip to Rugby Park and yours truly proved he could've played in a bygone era. Keeper Billy Thomson had a great goal kick on him and this particular one travelled the length of the park before ending up in the arms of the Kilmarnock keeper.

I followed in though and bundled keeper and ball over the line. It was a good old-fashioned shoulder charge, although the poor guy would've ended up on the terracing had it not been for the 'safety' net. Of course, it was a foul, but the barge had rendered him useless and I cracked a 30-yarder past him moments later. Starky completed the job. The win took us five points clear of the drop zone and for the first time in the season, we had a bit of breathing space.

We were due at Cappielow for the fourth round of the Scottish Cup, as if a derby match needed an extra edge. It was an eventful afternoon for me and, apart from scoring our goals in a good 2-0 win, I picked up a stupid booking for kicking the ball away, which meant a suspension was looming. I couldn't really blame referee Brian McGinlay for that one.

I landed a two-game ban, which meant missing a league game at Dundee and the next round of the Scottish Cup at Airdrie, which, in turn, meant missing out on the opportunity to renew old acquaintances with Bill Munro and Blair Miller, who'd moved to Broomfield from Clydebank.

Before that though, we went on something of a run, beating Rangers and drawing at Motherwell. It was then time for my suspension to kick in and we headed for Dens Park. We thrashed them 5-2 and then put another five past Airdrie in the cup.

I didn't know whether to laugh or cry. Naturally, I was delighted for my mates, but it meant I was eyeing another spell on the sidelines, and it was all my own stupid fault. Kicking the ball away, or mouthing at a referee, is one of the most foolhardy things a player can get booked for. Needless to say I learned my lesson.

I had to chuckle though at a poem a talented supporter sent in to the local paper on the eve of the Airdrie match. It read; 'McDougall's two at Morton, made him the hero of the land. He willnae play at Airdrie, 'cos the stupid eejit's banned.' That just about said it all.

Billy Stark had been rattling in the goals and, by mid-March, he was sitting on 11, one ahead of me, with Macca a further goal behind.

Next up was Celtic at Parkhead. I was in the team and trained like mad, but the day before the game, I pulled up during a run. It was a disappointed striker that trekked slowly back to the changing rooms.

Two minutes later, the door opened and in limped Lex Richardson, closely followed by Ian Scanlon. The three of us missed the Celtic match, although the lads managed a good draw.

We knew we had an outside chance of qualifying for the UEFA Cup and the dream moved a little closer when we went up to Pittodrie and won 1-0. That win took us up to fifth, just a point behind Rangers. Whether or not the Dons had one eye on their European Cup Winners' Cup semi-final tie with Waterschei I'll never know, but it was a vital two points nevertheless.

I played the last half hour of the game, despite not having fully recovered from the leg injury I'd picked up in training, although I was fit to face Rangers in the semi-finals of the Scottish Cup.

It was played at Hampden on a wet Tuesday night and is arguably one of the most controversial games I have ever been involved in. We had acquitted ourselves very well indeed and were probably the better team over the piece.

After 90 minutes, the tie was still goalless and it looked as though we were heading for penalties when Rangers scored a hotly-disputed goal. There was something like 118 minutes on the clock when an innocuous looking cross came into our box. We had been the best team in extra time, but it was all hands to the pumps with so little time left. Even I was back defending.

Jim Bett headed on the cross to Sandy Clark, who flicked it goalwards. There was an almighty scramble on the goalline before Lex thumped it clear. Phew, that was close, I thought, as we moved out en masse. Next thing I knew, referee Brian McGinlay had blown his whistle and was running towards the centre circle. Even the Rangers players looked bemused. And it was a few moments before even they realised it was time to celebrate.

I was in the box when Clark flicked the ball towards goal and was in a great position - far better than McGinlay - to see that the ball definitely did NOT cross the line. In fact, it was a good foot away from the line. There was no way it was a goal. What angered me most was McGinlay's arrogance. Despite the obvious dubiety over the goal, he wouldn't even consult his linesman. We swamped him and continued to protest long after he'd blown the whistle to signal the end of the game. We were all around him as the Rangers players made for their supporters behind the goal.

Next thing, Ricky pushed his way through everyone and started pulling players away from the harangued official. At first I thought he was showing an incredible sense of dignity, but later learned he'd just wanted to get to McGinlay himself. It was all the more difficult to accept because we'd already been on the wrong end of one awful decision during the match. Lex had been illegally upended in the box just as he was about to pull the trigger. Stonewall penalty? Don't be daft; it's Rangers we were playing.

In the final minutes of normal time, big Peter McCloy had pulled off a brilliant save from my 18-yard shot. I still don't know how he kept that one out. Big 'Gas Meter' was much maligned, but I rated him highly.

We had little time to feel sorry for ourselves as we were still challenging Rangers for a Euro spot. Four days after the massive disappointment at Hampden, we mauled Motherwell 4-0.

Macca bagged a treble, although I somehow managed to convince him in the dressing room after the match that my lob had been the best of the game. Macca nodded his head, but didn't for a moment agree.

The deadly duo were on the scoresheet again the following midweek in a 2-2 draw at Killie, in a game we really had to win to keep the pressure on Rangers. However, we lost 4-0 at Ibrox the following Saturday and the Euro dream was ever further away, but not completely gone.

A win against Dundee, at Love Street was an absolute necessity. It wasn't going too well, though, when Cammy Fraser put the visitors in front. We were lethargic and going nowhere when the heavens opened and it poured. Someone up there liked us. We were led of the park for ten minutes but the rain became heavier and the referee abandoned the game.

We played the game again on the Monday night, this time with far more success. Alan Logan put us in front early on, but Dundee equalised with just ten minutes to go. We needed a spark of inspiration from somewhere and thankfully I managed to score in the dying seconds. It was such an important goal, although it soon became bitter-sweet. Just after the game I learned that Dougie Somner had been freed. We had joined the club at the same time and helped each other through the early days. He had become a good mate and I was sad to see him go.

Two days later, Aberdeen beat Real Madrid in the final of the Cup Winners' Cup in Gothenburg and while that result didn't really have any great impact on me at the time, it soon would.

But we had our own battle to fight, and what a battle it was. We had to go to Morton and win to secure a place in Europe. And win we did. I kept up my good record at Cappielow by again scoring both goals in a 2-0 win. Cowboy's 50-yard run and pass set me up for the first and a Macca cross, which the keeper dropped, provided me with a tap-in for the second. Thank you very much.

It was a great feeling to be back in Europe and gave us all something to look forward to during the close season break, which began with a team trip to Spain.

First up though, we could reflect on a fantastic season that saw us recover from a disastrous start. To clinch a UEFA Cup spot, when we were second bottom for so long, was an incredible achievement. We could rightly be proud of the second-half of the campaign, if not the first.

On the trip to Magaluf, we met up with players from Derby County, Aston Villa and Everton. It was a real busman's holiday and we swapped football tales with our counterparts from south of the border. We had a great time and on our return I became obsessed with my usual strict regime of not looking after my body during the close season.

THE END OF A L**O**VE STREET AFFAIR

I WAS happy at St Mirren and the prospect of leaving had never entered my thoughts. This, though, would be my last season at the club. It was number five and began with a touch of controversy.

I agreed to play in a pre-season benefit match for long-serving Arthurlie player Bobby Picken. My team-mates, in the rather grandly titled International Select, would include Barrhead boy Alex McLeish, Frank McGarvey and Lex Richardson. Junior giants Pollok would provide the opposition. As far as I was concerned, it was a light-hearted way to start the season, and there would be a bit of banter up for grabs. It was also a nice way to recognise a long-serving junior.

The match was scheduled for July, not long after we had arrived back from Magaluf, but no sooner had we agreed to take part, than we were banned from doing so. Apparently SFA chief Ernie Walker refused permission on the grounds that contracted players weren't allowed to turn out as guests during the close season. What a load of cobblers. I mean, what are the chances of getting the likes of McLeish, McGarvey and the others to be available at a certain time during a busy football season? It was red tape gone mad as far as I was concerned. We were all happy enough to play, so what was the problem? And I reckon we should be rewarding loyalty instead of treating it with disdain.

A few days later my Saints team-mate Billy Stark was on his way to Aberdeen for £70,000: another shrewd piece of business by Fergie. However, the club knocked back a six-figure bid for Macca from English first division side Luton Town. The Hatters were a top side at the time. I was disappointed for him, but delighted that we would remain team-mates for another season, although I knew he would inevitably move on at some point.

Ricky did make one addition to the squad during that close season. A young lad by the name of Rowan Alexander joined from Queen of the South. The fee was around the £25,000-£30,000 mark and the lad was apparently a natural goalscorer. But did I see him as a threat? No, because I had confidence in my own ability. I did see him as a good addition to the squad though.

On the eve of our pre-season trip to the Isle of Man, we were drawn against Feyenoord in the first round of the UEFA Cup. The Dutch side contained such luminaries as Johann Cruyff, Wim Van Hanegen and a certain young lad called Ruud Gullit. They would be fearsome opponents but, for the moment, they would keep.

We were dealt a blow, of sorts, on hearing that Manchester City had withdrawn from the Isle of Man Cup. They had appointed a new manager and he had decided against participating. Who was their manager? Some chap by the name of Billy McNeill. So, we wouldn't be renewing old acquaintances then.

We had a couple of challenge matches lined-up before heading south and Rowan managed to score in both. This lad certainly knew where the goal was. But after such a great start to his Saints career, tragedy struck in the opening match on the Isle of Man.

We lost 2-1 to Burnley and Rowan was carried off with a serious ankle injury. I got our goal and then scored a couple in our next match, a 3-0 win over the local select. At least I had hit the ground running.

As soon as we returned from the Isle of Man we were pressed straight into action - on the bowling green. The Ralston charity competition for Erskine Hospital was becoming one of the best known on the circuit and continued to attract a host of sporting celebrities. My team included referee Douglas Hope, (thankfully it wasn't Brian McGinlay) former Rangers player turned journalist Doug Baillie, and skip, Maxie Gray. Others taking part were Jock Stein, Rangers chairman, Rae Simpson, refereeing giant (literally), Tom 'Tiny' Wharton and, well, McGinlay.

A couple of days later we squared up to Queens Park Rangers - Simon Stainrod, Clive Allen et al - in a friendly at Love Street and, despite beating them 3-2, I suffered a nasty ankle knock.

With just 15 minutes on the clock, I challenged goalkeeper Peter Hucker for a loose ball. He was quite clearly getting there before me, so I jumped over him, as you do a thousand times in your career, but landed awkwardly on my ankle and it was game over. It was agony and was soon diagnosed as the same injury as Rowan suffered.

The season was scheduled to start a week later and we were down to play Rangers at Ibrox. Miraculously though, I recovered sufficiently to grab a place on the bench. Thankfully, the injury hadn't been as bad as first feared.

Macca put us ahead moments before half-time, but Rangers were awarded a dodgy penalty just after the break. The foul on Davie Cooper was quite clearly committed outside the box, but referee George Smith thought otherwise and pointed straight to the spot. Ian Scanlon was furious and was red carded for his over-zealous protests.

Robert Prytz scored from the kick and it looked as though we'd toil with just ten men. That shouldn't have been a problem, as about ten minutes later when Ally Dawson went straight through Tommy Wilson - who was stretchered off - and I was convinced we were about to go head-to-head for the remainder of the game with ten apiece. How wrong could I be? Dawson escaped without even a warning. I often wondered how Smith could look at himself in the mirror after that match.

We got a point though and it was a decent start to the campaign, but then struggled to take care of tiny Forfar in the League Cup and just scraped though by the odd goal in five after two very tough games.

In the next round we were drawn against Hearts and played the first leg at Love Street. It ended 2-2, but once again we were on the receiving end of an incredibly poor decision by Brian McGinlay. Phil McAveety put in a brilliant tackle on Hearts legend, Donald Ford and McGinlay pointed to the spot. That man was the bane of my life. We were toiling though and it was a real worry, especially with Feyenoord looming large.

Once again I was in and out of the team and missed out on our home match with Dundee just four days before the UEFA cup-tie at Love Street. In fact, I was sitting just a couple of rows behind Wim Van Hanegen in the stand and I'm sure he went home rubbing his hands with glee after watching us struggle to a poor no-score draw.

It was the Paisley monsoon season when the talented Dutch squad arrived in town for the first leg. The former European Cup winners were no doubt used to playing in far more glamorous surroundings, but one thing was guaranteed, they would know they had been in a game by 9.30pm.

Personally, I was gutted. I failed to make the game because of an ankle injury and it was something of a double blow to learn that I wouldn't be lining up against one of the finest players the world had ever seen - the great Johann Cruyff. It might have been bad news all round for me, although I'm sure the Paisley public lapped up seeing the great man in the flesh and forgot all about me for 90 minutes!

A crowd of 10,000 turned up on an awful night and in just four minutes, they saw Macca head inches over the bar. But on the half hour they witnessed a Ruud Gullit shot heading straight for the safety of Billy Thomson's arms, before it struck the unfortunate Cowboy and deflected into the corner of the net. An uphill struggle had just become a mountain to climb (although Cowboy could claim to have scored from a Gullit assist).

In the second-half, Billy Thomson kept us in the tie by producing a wonder save to deny Gullit a second goal, although realistically it would take a monumental effort in Rotterdam to give us any chance whatsoever. We received a little crumb of comfort the following Saturday. We lost to Hearts at Love Street, but discovered that Ajax had thumped Feyenoord 8-2. Could we take heart from that?

Our date with destiny arrived and we headed over to play Feyenoord on their patch. The atmosphere was electric. The fans were so close to the pitch and you felt that one wrong move and they would be right on to sort you out.

We managed to defy them for around an hour and realised that if we could nick one, we had every chance of claiming one of the biggest scalps in Europe. Up popped Van Til though to unleash a ferocious drive from 30 yards - 1-0.

Like Johan Cruyff, I had passed a fitness test. The fates brought us together, probably the only time I got close to him, and I was booked for being just a tad late. Something to tell the grandkids, maybe.

In the 77th minute, Jeliazkov, a substitute, grabbed the second and it was game over. It was also game over for me a few moments later. I got involved with this man mountain of a guy called Van De Korput. He was absolutely huge and Feyenoord had just paid Torino £3 million for his services.

Late on, he came right through the back of me and I was in agony.

He raked his studs right down the back of my calf and the gaping wound would eventually require several stitches. I bounced straight up from the challenge and squared up to, well, his naval.

He accused me of spitting on him, which I didn't do, but the referee, who hadn't seen the incident, went over to consult his linesman and sent off both of us on his say so. I reckon the linesman may have spotted me giving the big guy a Cadder slap. But he deserved it.

He may have been twice my size and build, but I wasn't letting him bully me. I would dine out on my tales of going toe-to-toe with this giant and well, socking it to him, for months afterwards. What I wouldn't dine out on, though, was the immediate aftermath of my red card. For years now I've tried to forget it, although certain ex-team-mates delight in bringing it up.

There were two tunnels at the Feyenoord Stadium. One for the home team and the other for visiting sides. I rather foolishly made my way down the wrong one and the moment I did, I heard this loud panting sound. When I looked round, this giant of a man was coming straight for me.

I got off my mark and ran as fast as I could - there was no way Van De Korput was getting his grubby mitts on me. It was like the London underground system and I didn't have a clue where I was, or where I was going. I eventually shook him off though and next thing, I was back out on the pitch.

The home fans in the crowd noticed and began to cheer. Thankfully I found the right tunnel this time (well, there were only two) and took sanctuary in our dressing room.

Cowboy was handed the unenviable task of marking Cruyff that night and that's partly the reason he's got a new knee. The amount of times he was turned inside out.

There was one moment of Cruyff magic in the game and Cowboy will be glad that it was Macca who was closest to him on this occasion. The keeper rolled the ball out to the Dutch master and he seemed to have all the space in the world. I bawled at Macca to close him down, which he did. Now, Macca was quick, but one little shimmy from Cruyff and he was away.

Macca watched him disappear into the distance, looked at me and we just shrugged our shoulders. I said to Macca after the game, 'Johann Cruyff's some player, and he has the right initials.'

It was hardly the perfect end to what had been shaping up as a good night. 1-0 down from the home leg, we'd held out for an hour but the majesty of Cruyff and the guile of his 'apprentice', Ruud Gullit, proved too much in the end.

To be fair, I had a few chances that night, but I think the occasion was maybe too big and I passed them up. Cruyff was the daddy of them all at the time and was virtually untouchable. You couldn't get near him - his aura was far too big for a start. I suppose a 0-3 aggregate sounds like a bit of a tanking, but it genuinely wasn't. We'd more than held our own against a great side.

And big Van De Korput? He may have played in a star-studded Dutch international side at the 1980 European Championships, but he wasn't really that fast, or maybe I was just quicker on the night. It's amazing how quickly you can run when needs must.

On the eve of the match, Ricky McFarlane took a few of the senior players aside and told us he was quitting the hot seat. We were devastated, but the guy had made up his mind and that was that. Nine years was a long time at the one club. Erik Sorensen was put in temporary charge until a permanent replacement could be found. And, as fate would have it, our next game was at Celtic Park. Just what a rudderless side needs after being dumped out of Europe.

Celtic had a 100 per cent league record, but we gave a good account of ourselves and I managed to head home the opener. Celtic equalised, but it was another good result.

Inevitably a list of candidates for the vacant manager's post was drawn up. Benny Rooney, Mike Jackson, John Clark, Jackie Copland, Peter Cormack and, of course, Erik Sorensen. Erik had the advantage of being at the club and knew the place inside out. We wanted him to get the job. Just days after throwing his hat into the ring though, he was axed.

It was a sad day and he left Love Street in tears. In a brief statement, Erik branded the departure of Ricky 'stupid and unnecessary', hinting that the exodus wasn't all down to Mr McFarlane. The following day, it was announced that Alex Miller was the new boss.

At the time he was player/coach of our great rivals Morton and, at the age of 34, he became the youngest manager in the Premier League. It was an interesting appointment, one that we hadn't seen coming and the players kept an open mind. We were employed by St

Mirren and would work with whoever was in charge. And as fate would again decree his first game in charge would be at Ibrox, his home of 17 years, in a League Cup tie.

It was a huge game for the club, as we hadn't started too well in the league and the League Cup, at this moment, represented a decent chance of glory. What happened that Wednesday night though was both shambolic and embarrassing.

There we were, running out onto the pitch at Ibrox to tackle one of the biggest teams in the country - with no manager in the dug out to lead or advise us. The gaffer had arrived at Love Street a couple of hours before the game, introduced himself and gave some sort of pep talk ahead of the game. He then travelled down the M8 to Greenock where he played for Morton in the same competition. Unbelievable.

With little leadership, we crumbled, and lost the game 5-0. In all my time in football I had never seen anything like it, or haven't since. It was farcical and the Saints board should never have allowed such a situation to occur.

Alex Miller brought in Martin Ferguson, brother of Sir Alex, as his right hand man, and Drew Jarvie was also introduced to the coaching staff. Our next game was at Pittodrie and we lost 5-0.

Instead of backing the players and trying to unite the dressing room in the face of such adversity, our esteemed leader declared that he would sell the club's star players to finance re-building. How about that for a vote of confidence? He followed up by announcing that any players who were unhappy could go. He said, 'I'll sell anyone - if I can sell one player to buy three then I'll do it'.

We finally notched our first win of the season on the last Saturday of October. And what a victory it was. Rangers were the visitors to Love Street and we thumped them 3-0. John Greig had resigned as manager of the 'Gers 24 hours before the game, but that didn't concern me one bit and I started the 'rout' with the only goal of the first-half.

A fortnight later, I had an 'interesting' game at Tynecastle. I got us off to a flyer with a decent volley then talked myself into an early bath. It was a remark over an innocuous incident and I should've known better.

Miller had me in to his office to discuss my disciplinary 'issues' and told me he was introducing fines for on-field misdemeanours. I was well aware that my actions hadn't helped the team in the slightest, but let's just say I wasn't too impressed by what he had to say to me.

Miller was a strict disciplinarian, a teetotaller and a fitness fanatic. That's all fine and well, but don't try to ram your views down the throats of players who have their own routines and opinions. Okay, we all know that my dietary arrangements could've been better, but I trained hard and was never anything less than 100 per cent ready come three o'clock on a Saturday afternoon.

Toledo Junction in Paisley's New Street was our venue of choice for the player's night out on a Wednesday. He banned the night out, but we were having none of it. Macca and I loved our dancing and this may come as a shock to many, but I was a far better mover on the dance floor than my curly-haired team-mate.

The first time he enforced the ban, we ignored it. We were up at the bar when I looked in the mirror and saw Miller and Martin Ferguson walk in. I said to Macca, 'They're in'.

Up they marched like a couple of coppers from The Sweeney. Miller told us to hand back our drinks and get out. Macca pretended not to hear and asked what he wanted to drink. Miller was fuming. He about turned and stormed out. They were like the fun police; although I did get on really well with Martin, he was a nice guy. I remember Fergie stopping Wednesday nights out at Aberdeen, but that was different as we were more often than not playing European ties.

It was around this time that Macca and I were invited to open a bar in Yoker, called Jarvie's. Imagine our surprise, and delight, when it turned out there would be three of us performing the opening ceremony. And 'celebrity' number three was none other than the funniest man I've ever heard – Mr Billy Connolly.

We were only supposed to be there half-an-hour, but it turned into a bit of a session and we sat with the Big Yin supping away to our wee hearts' content. He was great, as he's just such a funny guy. It wasn't long before big Billy started to pick on Macca though. But he deserved it because who drinks Pernod and blackcurrant in Yoker? Billy gave him pelters and, if I remember correctly, Macca soon switched to pints of lager.

Following our little tete a tete with Miller, word came through from UEFA that I had received a four-game suspension from European games for the sending-off in Rotterdam.

We then beat Hibs 2-1 at Love Street and Miller gave me his backing by telling the press, 'McDougall's a good player and if he's fit and available, I'll play him'. I was back for the next game - Celtic at home - and we pummelled them 4-2.

Celtic were 2-0 up and looked unbeatable. We hit them with four goals though and ran out worthy winners. I scored one and made a couple and was named man-of-the-match in the local paper. They claimed I'd given the Celtic defence a 'torrid time'. It was all good.

The reigning Premier League champs, Dundee United, were next to fall - 4-0. We were looking like a different team from the one that had started the season. After such a decent victory, I thought we'd at least have the next day off. No chance. We were in bright and breezy on the Thursday morning for some conditioning work.

The gaffer believed it beneficial to come in the following morning to do some fitness work, in a bid to stop stiffness setting in. Personally I would rather have done my 'conditioning' on the green baize.

Our final League Cup tie against Rangers was listed in the 'meaningless' category and I was rested. I would much rather have taken part. As it was, my replacement, coach Drew Jarvie, shouldn't have played because he was cup-tied with Airdrie. It meant little I suppose because we lost 1-0 and were already out the cup.

We had mixed results in the lead-up to the festive season and had a decent 1-1 draw at Ibrox. Again I managed a goal against one of the big two. My goal-scoring record against the Old Firm was comparable with anyone. The big games seemed to bring the best out in me.

I then scored a pretty spectacular effort against Motherwell on January 3, and Cowboy hit the winner. We were a good double act. We then suffered a twice-postponed match with Celtic, due on both occasions to heavy snow, then an 'iced-off' match with Hearts. The winter weather really had taken its grip on Paisley.

I wasn't normally chosen for the seasonal indoor six-a-side tournaments in venues such as the Kelvin Hall or Coasters, in Falkirk, and I'm glad I missed out on one in the latter venue at the end of January.

I was enjoying a beer and watching on from the packed gallery as the lads played Motherwell. But my heart went out to team-mate Tony Fitzpatrick when he was barged from the back and went flying into the glass partition. Ouch. He suffered a suspected broken nose.

Suddenly I felt a great deal safer sitting in among supporters.

If my last season at Saints was memorable for anything in particular, it was our rather 'interesting' Scottish Cup campaign - and we didn't even make the final. It started off in the capital against Meadowbank Thistle, a re-incarnation of works side, Ferranti Thistle. They played at Meadowbank Stadium in Edinburgh, the Commonwealth Games venue and I was looking forward to seeing it for the first time.

Meadowbank were small time and we were expected to brush them aside with ease. With just six minutes on the clock, their keeper pulled off an amazing save from a shot, which, from the moment it left my boot, looked a homer all the way.

It soon became apparent that a cricket score against the minnows wasn't on the cards and in the end the heroics of big Billy Thomson kept us in the cup. Jags winger Adrian Sprott, who would later find fame at Hamilton for scoring the goal that knocked Rangers out of the Scottish Cup, at Ibrox, sprinted clear of our defence and only Billy's outstretched leg prevented us suffering a fate similar to Graeme Souness's Rangers. In the end it was 0-0.

But everyone had been surprised that the game had even been on at all. Right up until kick-off, snow looked like winning the day and the game was only given the go-ahead an hour before kick-off. In fact, Macca and I had been so confident that the match would be off that we booked up a short break to Majorca to top up our tans. The gaffer caught us just as we were about to jet off to Palma Nova. We had initially been given permission to miss training at the start off the following week, and weren't due back until the Tuesday.

I was raging (again) after the game when I was substituted a few minutes into the second half. We were all absolute mince and I didn't like the idea of being made scapegoat for a woeful performance. I told the manager this as I walked dejectedly past the dugout on my way to the dressing room. After the game he denied I had been made a scapegoat and insisted he could've taken off any one of ten players. So why didn't he? At least there was always a chance I could pinch a goal.

Our first attempt at a replay was cancelled due to frost. Paisley still hadn't thawed out. We finally got the replay on and some of us wished we hadn't bothered. Again we were woefully inept and the Jags raised their game. The match finished 1-1 after 90 minutes and 2-2 after an extra half-an-hour.

In fact, Adrian Sprott had put the visitors 2-1 up in extra time. We were three minutes from an infamous exit when Neil Cooper popped up to score his second of the game. He saved our bacon.

While we were sitting in the relative calm of the dressing room, a verbal battle was taking place in a corner of the stadium over the venue for the second replay. A second replay against Meadowbank. It was just so wrong. We lost the toss and the game was played in Edinburgh. Sprott put Meadowbank 1-0 up early on and it took us an hour to level, through an Ian Scanlon penalty. Thankfully Macca scored late on to put us through, but it had taken five HOURS to see off the plucky part timers.

A few days later it was back to league duty and in the 4-0 thrashing of Dundee, I lived up to my nickname, Zico, by smashing home a 20-yard free-kick. In the next round of the Scottish, we were drawn at home to Hamilton Accies. Mark Fulton and I looked to have put the Saints on easy street, but they scored with six minutes to go to set up another nervy ending. By that time I had limped off with a nasty leg injury and it was agony sitting there watching us almost press the self-destruct button again.

The following day, a few of us gathered in the pub to watch the draw for the quarter-finals being made live on television. The draw threw up an interesting derby match against Morton, at Love Street. At least we had home advantage, which would surely count for something.

I had managed to shrug off my leg injury by the time the match came round and it was an absolutely enthralling cup-tie. We shared seven goals and thankfully we scored four. Morton missed a penalty while trailing 2-1, but we had enough in the tank to hang on for a 4-3 win. Our opponents were furious though and had initially asked the SFA to cancel the game due to an injury and illness crisis.

At 2-2, I remember colliding with their goalkeeper in the box. The referee pointed straight to the spot and their players went berserk. Scan scored the penalty, as he normally did and that put us ahead for the second time of the afternoon.

The draw for the semi-finals pitted us against Celtic and Aberdeen would face Rangers in the other last-four tie. Before the big Hampden match we had five make-or-break league matches which would decide whether or not we qualified for Europe again. I was suspended for the first of these, against Hearts at Love Street, and all we could muster was a disappointing draw.

I then missed our next two games and was hurting like hell sitting in the stand. For once, I agreed with something that Alex Miller said. 'I know McDougall has been training hard, but it's up to him to fight his way back into the team'.

A three-match suspension was no good to neither man nor beast at this stage of the season, and I knew that more than most. I was prepared to work like never before to make it up to my team-mates. To my great surprise, I was in the team the moment the suspension was up. I scored on the day we signed John McGregor from Liverpool, but it wasn't enough to prevent St Johnstone winning 4-2.

But we handed out a thumping of our own in our next match; a 5-2 success at Dens Park, Dundee. They were no match and I scored a couple early on. For my second, I ran 50 yards and outpaced Dundee's Jim Smith. I don't think I could outrun anyone now. John McGregor was also on the scoresheet. Mind you, so was Aber, so Dundee couldn't have been up to much.

It was time to face our date with destiny. We were so desperate to reach a Scottish Cup final and were determined that this would be our year. Hampden was packed to the rafters, but Brian McClair opened the scoring for Celtic on the half hour. We battled back and I equalised five minutes before the break, thanks to great work by Macca and Cowboy.

We were very much holding our own and the tie looked like petering out in a draw, until fate dealt Saints yet another Hampden heartbreak. Tommy Burns hit the post with a thumping shot. It rebounded out to the penalty spot where Mark Fulton and Celtic captain, Paul McStay challenged for the loose ball. The howling wind carried it straight over the head of Billy Thomson, who was left stranded, and into the net.

In that instant, our hopes of being involved on cup final day bit the dust. McStay, Burns and Murdo MacLeod ran the show from midfield, but Celtic hadn't turned their superiority into goals, which had meant we were always in with a chance.

Yet another Scottish Cup semi-final defeat had taken its toll and we played three league matches in the ensuing ten days with just a solitary point to show for our efforts. Alex Miller denied there was a dressing room crisis, but I can tell you, it wasn't a happy place to be. We then lost 2-0 to Dundee United at their place and our European dream was over.

The following day, Macca was linked with a move to Pittodrie and Miller issued a 'hands-off' warning to The Dons. We had just two league games left in which to restore some pride and we did just that. A 2-2 draw at Tannadice, with all the goals coming in a titanic first half, gave United a fright.

Paul Sturrock scored first for United and I managed to equalise with a header, after outjumping Richard Gough. Drew Jarvie then put us in front before Dave Narey levelled. In the second half, Hamish McAlpine pulled off a tremendous save to deny me the winner. How he got to that header I'll never know.

Our final match of the season was against Aberdeen, who had just been crowned Premier League champs. We were mid-table, but still beat the Dons 3-2; although Fergie rung the changes with a Scottish Cup final against Celtic coming up, which they won.

Macca ran the show and played me in for our first goal, which beat Leighton and went in off the post. It was a commanding performance and I wonder if Fergie saw something he liked. It was to be my last ever game for Saints and, thankfully, I signed off with a goal. Further counters from Aber and Macca secured the points.

A few days after the cup final, Fergie was in the market for a striker. He was losing Mark McGhee, while Gordon Strachan was rumoured to be heading for Old Trafford. At this moment, a move to the Dons hadn't crossed my mind.

Meanwhile, Spurs boss Keith Burkinshaw had told the club he was standing down after the FA Cup final and the London giants targeted Fergie, offering him a King's Ransom to up sticks and leave. He politely declined as he had initially signed a five-year contract and still had time to see out.

Fergie targeted Celtic's want-away forward Frank McGarvey and Hibs' striker Willie Irvine as replacements for Hamburg-bound McGhee. Macca was also in the frame. No sooner had the final whistle blown in the St Mirren-Aberdeen game, than a war of words was breaking out, mostly from the manager's office, over the out-of-contract players.

At that time, there were a lot of unhappy players at Love Street. It was known as the 'summer of discontent' by the Press, as myself, Billy

HERE'S THE BURDZ!: Me, aged five, with my Uncle Robert. It wasn't just McAvennie who was always surrounded by birds!

HAPPY COUPLE: I doted on my Gran and Grandad.

SOMETHING TO SMILE ABOUT: Dad and I share a moment.

ANOTHER TROPHY: But I appreciated every single one.

BUDDIE BOY : A Saint not a sinner at Love Street. (Photo courtesy of the Paisley Daily Express)

MY NEMESIS AND ME: I shared a couple of 'moments' with Rangers star Ally Dawson. (Photo courtesy of the Paisley Daily Express)

TRAINING WAS NEVER MY THING: Can you spot me at the back? (Photo courtesy of the Paisley Daily Express)

WHAT A FEELING: Just scored the European Cup winner against Servette. (Photo courtesy of the Aberdeen Evening Express)

ANOTHER TROPHY: And Fergie joins in the celebrations. (Photo courtesy of the Aberdeen Evening Express)

PICK IT OUT: One of my 'famous four' against Celtic. Paul McStay and Roy Aitken look on helpless. (Photo courtesy of the Aberdeen Evening Express)

DANDY DON: in action for Aberdeen.

NIGHT OUT: Mum and I enjoying a drink or two.

DREAMS ARE MADE OF THIS: At home with my coveted Bronze Boot.

I SHOULD'VE GIVEN HIM A START: Former world snooker champion Rocket Ronnie O'Sullivan and me.

WHAT A DOUBLE ACT: Eric Cantona and me at United's Cliff training ground.

THE NEXT GENERATION: With my daughters, Kelly, left and Deanna at Kelly's 30th.

SERVING UP SUCCESS: I pour more than I down now!

Thomson, Ian Scanlon, Mark Fulton and Tony Fitzpatrick had all refused to sign new contracts. From a personal point of view, I genuinely felt I deserved a rise. I had been on the same money since signing in 1979 and we were now five years down the line.

I told the Press that I'd rather go back to work as a scaffolder than sign what was on offer, and they made the most of it. It was true, though, and I would've stuck to my guns. Miller fired the opening salvo in the local paper by suggesting we would all be better off staying at Love Street and that we would be just as well off, cash wise, than anywhere else in Scotland. Somehow I didn't share his view on the matter.

We were then treated to some more of Mr Miller's wisdom when he suggested that our financial demands could lead to the break up of the team. He pointed out that as the team had won nothing, the players didn't deserve a rise. That was fine and he was entitled to his opinion, but did he have to rub it in by suggesting that there would be no big rush to sign any of the out-of-contract players?

He then jetted off to the USA on a family holiday and the following day Cowboy joined Dundee in a swap deal for Peter Mackie. Billy Thomson and Mark Fulton then went public by telling the Press they wanted to quit Saints and the rumour mill swung into action.

In Miller's absence, Martin Ferguson insisted the club could close if they gave into player's demands. I don't know whether Martin had been told to say that by the board, or whether there really was a chance of St Mirren going to the wall.

Miller was no sooner back from his holiday than he disciplined Billy Thomson for speaking to the Press about his state of contractual limbo. Billy was raging and was soon on the move to Dundee United for a giveaway fee of £75,000.

Fair play to the big man as he'd signed a five-year deal, but he was worth far more than the fee paid by the Tannadice club, which made us think that Saints' financial situation couldn't have been as perilous as was being made out.

The manager called a Press conference in a bid to clear the air on his want-away players. He insisted we were as well paid as any in Scotland, which I would soon discover wasn't true. The next move in this demoralising game of human chess was for our esteemed manager to announce a ban on salary increases, but that more lucrative bonuses would be on offer.

The next statement announced the beginning of double training sessions. More work for the same money. It just didn't make sense. My contract expired on the last day of June and there was no way it was going to be settled by then. In fact, come mid-July, I was still no nearer being sorted and started pre-season training with Saints in a bid to keep fit.

Then, all of a sudden, I was off to pastures new.

On Monday, July 22, the local paper insisted my departure had stunned Saints fans. They weren't the only ones. The paper also carried the following quote from Miller, 'I am sorry to lose McDougall because he was a player of great ability, but we could not turn down what Aberdeen offered'.

Despite the fact that I was probably a better player than when I'd arrived for £80,000 more than Aberdeen paid for me. I couldn't work it out.

Looking back, I'm thankful that Miller and I shared just part of a season at Love Street, although it felt like a great deal more. I found it difficult working for someone who I had absolutely no respect for, professional or otherwise.

Drew Jarvie, a striker of some repute, was his assistant and he also had that 'I'm the boss' attitude, which players don't really like. I know that managers and coaches have to distance themselves from players, but surely there still has to be some sort of relationship there. To a certain extent I suppose I had been spoiled by having gaffers such as Bill Munro, Jim Clunie and Ricky McFarlane. All three commanded my full respect.

There was conflict from the moment Alex Miller arrived till the day I left. That was no good. We had always enjoyed a tremendous team spirit at Love Street under both Jim and Ricky, but I'm afraid that spirit followed Ricky out the dressing room door. We had a job to do though, which was tested to the limit one day when Macca turned up for training with a black leather suit on. It would've looked ridiculous on anyone else, but for some reason the Milton 'man about town' got away with it.

Unfortunately, for Macca though, it wasn't just any morning, but a Thursday morning and as we were banned from going out on a

Wednesday, Miller was onto him in a flash. 'Enjoy yourself last night Macca?'

It was quite obvious to everyone and their granny that Macca hadn't been home. But he just nodded and started to get changed. Miller reminded him that going out on a Wednesday night was forbidden and Macca assured him that he'd stayed in.

We all waited for the explosion, but it never came. Miller just turned and walked out, and that famous Macca grin flashed from one side of his face to the other. Macca was at it again the following Thursday morning. We were all hanging around the dressing rooms before training and just one guy was missing. Miller came in, had a quick look around and said, simply, 'Where is he Frank?'

I told him I didn't know, and he said, 'Okay, let's go'.

We jumped into his car and headed straight for Macca's house in Summerston, which is just at the back of Maryhill. When we arrived, the curtains were drawn and there was no sign of life, never mind a Premier League footballer. I knocked on the door - no answer. I looked at the gaffer. 'Keep knocking', he instructed.

Eventually this excuse for a human being opened the door, starkers. 'Come on', I urged.

'I'm not coming in today', was all he said before slamming the door in my face.

I jumped back in the car and told him Macca was ill. He went nuts. We drove back to Paisley in abject silence. It was the journey from hell.

When I moved to Aberdeen I soon forgot all about the final six months or so in Paisley. I had enjoyed four-and-a-half seasons at a great club, with some great people and they had given me my first shot at the Premier League, and for that I was eternally grateful.

I had shared some fantastic moments with my team-mates and we had almost reached the Scottish Cup final on so many occasions. I would never forget my time at Saints but there was a new challenge on the horizon and it was one I was desperate to embrace. It was goodbye to Scotland's most prominent town, and hello Granite City.

AN OFFER I CAN'T REFUSE

FIVE years at the same club is a long time and I enjoyed every single one. I loved Saints and it was only the last few months that the wow factor began to evaporate. I had a great bond with Saints fans until, that is, I returned as an Aberdeen player. We won the match 2-0 and I set up one of our goals.

Unfortunately the evening was peppered with chants of 'Frank McDougall, you're a w*****, you're a w*****'. What was that all about? I had never done anything to tarnish my standing with the Paisley public and was disappointed to hear that. I'm sure it was just a small section of fans that were involved.

My first instinct was to give them the fingers, but you can't do that. I thought the best way to shut them up was to score goals. And listen, 20 minutes of grief could never undo five brilliant years.

Whenever I bumped into Buddies away from the football they were fantastic and that was a relationship I was keen to continue. There will always be some folk that hold it against you when you move on, but there's nothing you can do about that. To this day though, when Saints fans come into my pub before games at Pittodrie, we have some great banter.

Love Street was a fantastic ground - St Mirren's spiritual home - and I'm glad to report that there's a big photograph me at the new stadium, so that makes me happy. But all good things come to an end and I knew it was time to move on. Well, if I didn't at first, I certainly did when I knocked on Alex Miller's office door and asked for a wage rise.

The look on his face said it all, and he mumbled, 'There's no rise.

You'll get the same, like it or lump it'. That was enough for me and I told him there and then that I wouldn't play for the club again unless he upped my pay. I even contemplated quitting football altogether. I was just so fed up with the money I was on. I hadn't received a wage rise in five years.

Of course, that was nothing to do with Miller, as this was the first time my contract had come up for renewal, but I was determined to make a stand and my future was in the hands of our esteemed board. Everyone pushes for, or gets, a wage rise at some time during their working life and I was no different. The cost of living goes up year on year and you need a rise to counter that.

You know, even if they'd offered me another tenner a week it would've been something. I might not have accepted it, but it would at least have told me they valued my contribution and felt I had progressed sufficiently to be worth a bit more cash. But nothing was forthcoming and discussions hadn't just reached stalemate, they had stalled altogether.

I don't know if everyone at the club was on the same money, or if other players were getting more than me. That wasn't my concern. I didn't ever shout about someone getting this or that. I was only interested in me. I felt as if I'd done the business for the club and wanted more than the £220 a week I had been on since first signing for the club. I didn't, and still don't, think that was unreasonable.

So, Mr Miller's door was closed and I soon realised my only option was to move on. I hadn't heard anything by the time my contract came to an end on June 30, but I continued to train with the club.

No one wants a half-fit player and I couldn't afford not to train, so I had to keep fit and the killing sands of Erskine certainly helped me do just that.

I was ready to report back as normal the following day when the phone rang on the Sunday afternoon. It was Alex Miller and he told me, totally out of the blue, that Coventry, Lokeren and Aberdeen were interested in signing me.

He said simply, 'Take your pick'.

I was lying unshaven on the sofa at my gran's home in Cadder and was slightly taken aback.

I reckon he wanted me out and, by now, I wanted to go. These were my options - the 'lengthy' list of clubs keen to sign me. I'm still convinced that Miller wanted my goals, but not me. Unfortunately, we came as a package.

The thought of playing abroad didn't excite me in the slightest. I didn't want to live outside Scotland. I was flattered that a club like Lokeren, who would eventually sign Jim Bett, were interested, but when they were mentioned in the same breath as Aberdeen - no contest.

Since the moment I made the decision, I never once regretted it. Some folk dwell on what might have been, but I made the correct choice. There was only ever one place I wanted to go.

I told Miller, 'I'll go to Aberdeen'.

He said, 'Okay, meet Alex Ferguson at Scone Palace tomorrow'.

And that was that - an inglorious end to half a decade at Love Street. But you can't stay at a club if you're unhappy. My relationship with the manager had been festering for a while. I didn't hate Alex Miller, but just didn't enjoy working with him.

I totally understood what he was trying to achieve. He had been at Rangers all those years, didn't smoke or drink, and that's the way he wanted his players to be. It just wasn't me though. Do I bear Alex Miller any grudges? Absolutely none.

But this was it, a new beginning and I've always been one who prefers to move forward rather than regress. It was a chance to work with Alex Ferguson, a man who had been achieving great things up north and who had single-handedly managed to break the Old Firm stranglehold on Scottish football. You could do nothing but admire Fergie - sorry boss, I mean Sir Alex.

I was up bright and breezy next morning and headed up to Scone Palace on the train and in my best suit. I walked into the building and he stood up to greet me. His reputation preceded him and he lived up to every inch of it. There was just the two of us there and that was the way I preferred it. No fuss, just Fergie, me, a pen and a contract.

'This is what's on offer. There's nothing more. If you want it, sign there and if you don't, I'll see you later, son'.

Those were Fergie's exact words; the beginning, middle and end of his speech. Eat your heart out Aristotle. Short and to the point. No messing around with Fergie.

Approaches like that didn't always work with me, but it did this time. Even then, Fergie had a tremendous standing in the game and to this day, I reckon he was the only manager in the world who could have won the league for Aberdeen at that precise moment.

After signing a contract that would guarantee me at least £300 a week, plus bonuses, for the next three years, he congratulated me and told me to get my arse up to Pittodrie the following day for a run-of-the-mill medical. Like he'd requested, I hadn't messed around. I had signed the contract and that was that. Fergie was no nonsense and I like to think I'm quite similar.

It was a great contract, but I later discovered there had been a bit of wrangling going on behind the scenes regarding my signature. Fergie wasn't sure he wanted me and had sought advice from three people.

First of all he spoke to Alex McLeish and asked him who he thought was the best striker he'd played against. Back came the reply, 'Frank McDougall'.

For all that Fergie is one of the game's major players and, allegedly, a very single-minded person, he still values the opinions of those in his confidence and is never afraid to change his mind.

He then had a chat with a guy called Tam Young, a former Petershill player and the Pollok Juniors manager at the time. He respected Tam's opinion on the game. He also spoke to his brother, Martin. I had a lot of time for him as he was a genuine guy and well respected at Love Street.

The story went that Fergie didn't want to sign me because of my 'reputation' as a party animal. He knew I could score goals, but was apparently a bit put off by my love of discos and the fact I enjoyed a night out with the boys.

But Martin convinced him I was worth taking a chance on and that if anyone could 'tame' me, it was his brother. Fergie listened and I was on my way north for £100,000. But while it was a lot of money, I got the impression that Fergie believed I was a 'high risk' sort of player. I was only 26-years-old though and the best was yet to come.

Fergie had been a successful centre forward in his playing days and had once moved for a record transfer fee between two Scottish clubs (£65,000 from Falkirk to Rangers). I like to think he saw something of himself in me. He had also been brought up in a tough part of Glasgow, although in his case it had been Govan.

Fergie was also keen to sign Frank McAvennie at that time, and

Macca knew it. I think the gaffer wanted him over me, but in the end he listened to those in his confidence and plumped for me. I was so glad he did.

Don't get me wrong, I felt for Macca. He was a good mate, but you have to look after yourself and I was delighted to land a big move. Macca read about it in the papers and while he called to congratulate me, you could tell he was gutted. He was perhaps a bit jealous. I know I would've been had the boot been on the other foot. Regardless of that, he was still big enough to call and I appreciated that. But it wasn't too long before he got his move and boy was it a cracker.

West Ham United, bossed by John Lyall, lured him away from Love Street and he proved a smash hit at Upton Park. Frank and I have remained good friends to this day and it's a friendship I value.

But it was pastures new for yours truly and I was going to a team that had already started to dominate Scottish football. Pittodrie was a great place to be and the quality of player there was incredible.

Throughout the team, from Jim Leighton in goals, to Miller and McLeish, Billy Stark and Neil Simpson, Peter Weir and Eric Black, quality oozed from every pore.

I signed for the Dons the season after they won the European Cup Winners' Cup and everyone in the city was on a high. I soon realised I was joining a club who were bang in the middle of dominating the 1980s.

I left Fergie at Scone Palace and headed straight down the road to Glasgow to collect a few bits and pieces. Fergie had told me to report to Pittodrie at 8.30 the next morning and I couldn't be late. However, my news called for a slight celebration and I made for a little pub in Possilpark called Rockefellers.

I was sitting there having a beer and had told only a handful of people, when the guy selling the next morning's papers came into the pub just after 10pm. There it was, splashed all over the back page, 'McDougall signs for Dons'.

They hadn't wasted any time in announcing the transfer. But just seeing it on the back page gave me goosebumps. I knew then that I was heading for the big time. It was up to me whether or not I would make it.

My good fortune continued and I accompanied a young lady home from the pub that night, and despite having a good time, I still managed to get up bright and breezy the next morning to head up on the 'cattle' train to the north east of Scotland.

I was a heady mix of anticipation and excitement, with a little trepidation thrown in for good measure. First things first, and I was introduced to my new team mates; Miller, McLeish, Leighton...it was like meeting the Scottish international team. Fergie had assembled a squad to be proud of and I was now an integral part of it.

Fergie was a real hands-on gaffer. He took training along with Teddy Scott, a Dons legend, and he knew all the dodges. He was a hard man and never once let his guard slip. But, although my introduction had been smooth enough, the coming days were like a roller coaster. The Press attention was massive and I was the subject of countless interviews for newspapers, television and radio. Then, a couple of days after my medical, the brown stuff really hit the fan.

When I signed for Dons I'd had a slight problem with my groin. It was anything but a career-threatening injury, but something I'd picked up in my last match with St Mirren. I'd taken it easy in training with Saints because naturally I didn't want it to scupper my chances of a move. It was the first time I'd ever suffered a groin injury.

Before signing for Aberdeen, I'd taken a Cortizone injection in a bid to get through the early days - it was my little insurance policy. I could just picture the Dons doctor pressing it during the medical and me hitting the roof. 'Ah, so you're injured son'. That wouldn't have gone down too well, and I was desperate for this move to go through.

I didn't think for a moment I was being deceptive and still don't. It was never an operation job, just a pull on the groin. What it needed was rest, but that was something I just didn't have time for. When I knew I was heading up to Scone for talks with Fergie, I called the St Mirren doctor and asked him to give me the injection. He agreed and off I went.

I had duly signed my contract and turned up for pre-season training. We were doing a bit of running one day when I felt the groin go. Obviously the effects of the jag had worn off, although I thought I was the only person who noticed the wince, but unfortunately your man spotted everything. I still believe Fergie had more than one pair of eyes. Fergie was no surgeon, but he was a wise man.

'McDougall', came the cry. It was no doubt audible on the other side of our training ground, and probably throughout the entire city of Aberdeen.

He wanted a word in my ear and I knew exactly what that word, or words, would consist of. He went berserk. 'You were injured when we met at Scone, weren't you?'

I don't imagine the injury would've prevented him from signing me, but the man demanded transparency and he was quite right to demand it. After all, he was paying out a large chunk of money from the club's coffers, so the least he deserved was the truth.

That was Fergie all over though. In charge of everything to do with the club and he ran the place with an iron fist, although I still believe he's one of the fairest people I've ever met.

Despite all that, I would become used to Fergie's war cry of 'McDougall', during our two-and-a-half year relationship, and I'm afraid to say I brought a heck of a lot of them upon myself.

Like getting caught having a fly puff in the bushes at our training ground. Fergie had me sussed and I took that as a challenge and tried to stay one step ahead - a futile exercise. To this day, he probably still has a few grand of mine in fines.

It was quite often a psychological thing - he was the boss and would go to great lengths to make sure we knew it. He would say to me, 'I will put you on the dole McDougall, you'll be signing on if you don't get your act together.'

If anyone turned in a below par performance, or threw strops which Fergie believed had compromised the team's performance, he would be waiting for you in the dressing room. It wouldn't be the first time I'd seen £1 million players sing Baa-Baa Black Sheep in the corner of the dressing room.

He'd scream, 'If you're going to f****** play like children then you can act like children all the time, now sing a f****** nursery rhyme.'

It definitely scared a lot of people and while I like to think these tactics didn't frighten me, I'd be lying if I didn't admit to being apprehensive on a number of occasions. He was a fierce man - make no mistake about that - but I was looking forward to working with him.

I knew he could make me a better player, once we had both got over my pesky groin strain.

MY GRANITE CITY DREAM

SIGNING for Aberdeen was fantastic, but I knew I'd be judged on how many goals I scored. The Dons have had their fair share of top strikers, such as Joe Harper and it was my aim to join him as a club great. It may sound a bit grand, but that was my goal.

My presence may have had a positive effect on the squad because days later, John Hewitt and Willie Miller penned new deals to follow Alex McLeish and John McMaster, who had re-signed the day before. The McDougall influence was immediate.

Seriously though, it was something positive for fans to feast on, because the Dons had become embroiled in a controversial transfer triangle with German side, FC Cologne, who insisted that they, and not Man United, had signed Gordon Strachan. It was a bizarre situation.

Regardless, pre-season training had come and gone, and I'd worked through it despite the injury scare. It was then off to West Germany for a five-match tour, but it didn't get off to the best start with my old St Mirren team-mate Peter Weir being sent home with a recurring ankle problem the day before our first game.

We started off with a low-key challenge against lower league side, Victoria Gogh, and won 2-0. Then a 2-0 loss to Bayer Leverkusen followed and the groin injury dictated that I missed both. At that point, it looked like I'd be heading home to the Granite City still waiting to make my Aberdeen debut.

Good news was just around the corner, though and I played the full 90 minutes against BW Berlin the following night. We lost 1-0, but it was a great feeling to finally pull on the famous red jersey. A bit low key perhaps, but a debut's a debut and I'm sure at least one of my fellow strikers was happy I'd been passed fit, as we were in the middle of an energy-sapping 'five games in five days' schedule.

It may be more than 25 years since that game, but I recall sweating buckets due to the awful humidity. For posterity, the team was: Leighton, Mitchell, McKimmie, Bell, McLeish, Miller, Stark, Simpson, McDougall, Hewitt and Black. Good times.

We moved on to Stuttgart and an Eric Black goal was the difference between the sides. I was once again handed a starting jersey, but suffered a slight reaction to the groin and missed the final match against Fromlach.

Despite playing in just one and a bit matches, the German trip was still a good exercise from my point of view, as it helped me bed in with my new team-mates. Unfortunately, there wasn't scope for much jiggery-pokery with Fergie on the prowl.

I had been rooming with Peter Weir before he'd unfortunately had to head back home and we got on well. I enjoyed the odd cigarette though and Peter wasn't for allowing it in the bedroom. I suddenly developed this chronic snoring problem and Peter soon found another place to bed down for the night. No one else wanted to share a room because of the din.

We returned to the UK and the gaffer had arranged a friendly against Leicester City. I missed out and was a major doubt for our Premier League opener against Dundee. I was nowhere near ready and watched from the stand as the lads won 3-2. Naturally I was keen to get playing domestically and it looked as though my Premier League debut would come at, you guessed it, St Mirren.

In a bid to prove my fitness, I played for the reserves in a midweek match at Alloa and set up a goal for Brian Grant. Wee Joe Miller also scored and my performance appeared to make up the gaffer's mind for the Saturday trip to Love Street.

It was strange returning to my old haunt in a different-coloured jersey, while changing in the away dressing room was surreal.

Returning to the place I'd enjoyed five great years was a big thing for me. Of course, it was great to see a lot of my old mates, but I was determined to put in a good performance and leave with all three points, just to get right up the nose of my former gaffer. I reckon I achieved both.

We won the match 2-0 and while I didn't score, or last the full 90 minutes, I did make a telling contribution, crossing for Willie Falconer to bullet home the clinching goal with a fine header. I reckon I had been pressed into playing against Saints, which I certainly didn't mind. Eric Black suffered an injury in training two days before the match and all in all, we were more or less down to the bare bones.

My 'welcome' back to Paisley arrived a few minutes before half-time. Mark Fulton crocked me from behind and I eventually limped off. I wasn't too happy about that. As a guy, I liked Mark, but the following season, when we played Hibs in the League Cup final at Hampden, he was all over me like a rash. He had obviously wanted to impress his new employers and was pulling my jersey and noising me up at every opportunity. In short, he was a pest.

I was never one to get wound up by nuisance defenders and try as he might, he just couldn't get the better of me. As we were walking off at the end, after beating them 3-0, I shook hands with him and said, 'No luck Mark, mind and check your bonus'. He just looked at me and I gave him a wink. Players could hassle me all day, but I enjoyed having the last laugh, and if I could do it with a big smile on my face then all the better.

It's never easy going back to your old club, but on the whole my former team mates were brilliant and we shared a laugh and a joke - and a post-match Coca-Cola – before I was spirited onto the team bus for the three-hour journey home.

Before the game, I was worried about how the Saints fans would receive me. The majority were great and no doubt realised I had given everything for the club while there. There were others who decided to wreck the homecoming by giving me abuse. That was up to them, but I was now at a bigger club and one where I could realistically achieve success.

I had always felt a bit inferior while at St Mirren, especially if we'd been playing the likes of Aberdeen, Celtic or Rangers and were sharing a dressing room corridor with players such as Miller, McNeill or Forsyth.

But now I was with guys of similar stature and you walked into opposing grounds with your head held high. You were part of the top team in Scotland, one that was ruling the roost and you had every right to walk tall.

The Love Street injury kept me out of a shock 3-1 League Cup defeat at Airdrie the following midweek. I learned a little more about Fergie as we sat in the Broomfield dressing room, moments after losing to the Diamonds. Fergie had just been named as Jock Stein's assistant for Scotland's forthcoming World Cup campaign, but was in no mood for celebrating.

He went absolutely berserk and no one escaped his wrath. Not even me, and I hadn't even been playing. I was soon wondering what I'd let myself in for. Suddenly, working under Alex Miller felt quite appealing.

Tam McQueen, who had just signed from Clyde, hadn't played that night either. We were both injured, but he looked over at us and started shouting, 'If you's b******* don't want to play football on a Wednesday night that's fine by me, but you won't be going out. You will sit in your digs and watch Coronation Street'.

Naturally, neither of us felt the time was right to exercise our right to free speech. We all trudged miserably out the dressing room and onto the team bus. It was a wretched journey back to Aberdeen. And sure enough, the following Wednesday we're in our digs and the phone rings at 7.30pm – on the dot.

Kitty, our landlady, went out into the hall to answer it. We could hear her say, 'Yes, Mr Ferguson, the lads are sitting watching television. Do you want a quick word? No, well okay, speak to you soon'.

As she was replacing the receiver, the door was closing behind me and I was off down the harbour for a game of snooker. I wasn't just disobeying orders for the hell of it - I needed to get out of that house.

Kitty was great, but I felt like a caged animal and had never before, at any time in my life, been 'grounded', except when I'd been caught drinking while at primary school. On this occasion, my only crime was being injured.

I got the impression Fergie felt I was at it, but I was the type of player who wanted to take part in every game. I hated sitting on the sidelines, so no one could ever accuse me of feigning injury. I reckon the boss thought everyone was at it though.

The club had digs all over the city and Fergie was constantly checking up on his players. I'm sure a lot of it was well-intentioned, but I hated the thought of being shackled. I couldn't cope with it. And when I was sneaking out to play snooker, I wasn't drinking. Just a fresh orange and lemonade and a frame or two of snooker. No big deal, boss.

The following Saturday we won up at Tannadice and seven days later I made my home debut in a 4-1 success over Hibs, in which I grabbed my first goal for the club. It's a great feeling to score in front of your own fans and for me, it was a special day.

We had started our league campaign with three wins from three and a comfortable victory at Morton the following Saturday had us oozing confidence. Fergie was once again working his magic.

Rangers then held us to a 0-0 draw at Pittodrie and it felt like a moral defeat. But we were soon back on track and I managed two goals in a great 4-0 win over Hearts. Fergie had us believing in ourselves and we felt we were good enough to take on anyone.

The double against Hearts was particularly significant because it signalled the start of an incredible run in which I scored in eight successive league games. This included goals against Celtic and Rangers, and a couple of doubles against St Mirren. It really was a purple patch and confidence was sky high.

I still had a lot of pals from my St Mirren days, but was able to cast friendship aside whenever we came face-to-face. On one such occasion, I was up against Billy Thomson at Tannadice. Billy pulled me down for a penalty, which helped us win 2-0. I thought it was a nailed-on spot-kick, but others may have disagreed. Regardless, Billy and I shared a refreshment after the game. There were no hard feelings.

When I scored my first goal at Pittodrie, the gaffer almost missed it. We had a European Cup first round tie with Dynamo Berlin looming and Fergie was desperate to watch them in action beforehand. That meant flying out to East Germany on the Friday night and missing our game against Hibs.

Saturday was the regular day for East German league fixtures, but due to the country's biggest marathon that weekend, games were put back 24 hours. He was able to fly out straight after watching us demolish Hibs.

Berlin were a good side so it was important to see them in the flesh.

They had just clinched their sixth successive league championship and had scalped both Aston Villa and Nottingham Forest away from home. It had the makings of an excellent two-legged tie, but, of course, I would be observing from the stand, having been handed a four-match European ban for my misdemeanours in Rotterdam.

I scored many goals at different levels throughout my career, but the one on Saturday, September 1, against Hibs, will live long in the memory. When you move to a club the size of Aberdeen, you're desperate to get off the mark as quickly as possible.

Almost 15,000 fans witnessed my first Pittodrie goal, a flashing header, which gave me enormous satisfaction. Around 70 minutes had elapsed when Tam McQueen sent John Hewitt on a wide run. John stuck in a great ball and I got across my marker to head home. I'll never forget that goal.

I was playing up front with Eric Black and while we were doing well together, we both reckoned a little extra practice wouldn't go amiss. You've probably gathered by now that I wasn't too fond of training, but I was super keen to make an impact at Aberdeen and a first for yours truly was on the horizon.

The team were given the Monday off, but Eric and I were in as normal, working on our fitness and trying to enhance our already blossoming partnership. And you know what, I actually enjoyed the extra work.

I missed a number of chances during a couple of my early matches and Fergie hauled me into his office for a 'chat'.

'Have you lost your confidence son?'

I was worried about a few personal things back in Glasgow and told him so.

He replied, 'Sort out your personal issues and don't worry about the goals. One will go in off your bum and that will be that'.

And he was so right. We were due to play Hearts at home, a few days before the second leg of the tie with Berlin (we'd won the first leg 2-1), but I didn't think I'd be listed. I reckoned Fergie would go with his 'Berlin' strikers. I was wrong, well sort of. Eric limped off at half-time and I was sent on to replace him.

During the game, a cross hit me on the side and went in. I scored another and then I couldn't stop scoring. Fergie was right, again. He was so good at giving players a confidence boost. He was certainly the master at getting inside your head.

It was the game that started my run of scoring in ten successive matches, which, as I'd mentioned, included eight league games. The run included a couple of challenge matches and it's something I'm still immensely proud of. We crashed out of Europe in Berlin, but that just made the pursuit of another Premier League title our main priority.

I scored against Celtic and then again at Dundee. In that game though, my old Buddie, Cowboy, came right through me and I ended up limping off before the end. I'm so glad he was my mate.

I then grabbed a double in a 4-0 win over St Mirren. That afternoon marked something of a personal achievement because I managed to halt the 'Pittodrie penalty hoodoo' by netting from the spot. It had been quite a while since we'd converted a spot kick at home. The goals were coming thick and fast and I was on something of a roll.

The team were doing well and Fergie won the manager of the month title for September. I couldn't help but think he might have shared a drop of the firkin of beer he received from the sponsors. I never got a sniff.

Things were rolling along smoothly in the league and a welcome break, in the shape of a friendly with Coventry City, was used a fixture filler. It was a decent enough game with the Sky Blues naming the likes of Bob Latchford, Cyrille Regis, Peter Barnes and Paul McGrath in their side. Martin Jol, who would become manager of Tottenham Hotspur a couple of decades later, also played.

A crowd of 10,000 turned out on a cold Tuesday night to see the match, which proved just how well-supported the club was. We won an entertaining match 4-2 and I kept up my record with a double.

You wouldn't think a 3-1 win over Morton at Pittodrie would rank as one of the most memorable games in my life. It was all about what happened after the game though. Most people like praise, there's no getting away from that, but when Fergie mentioned at the post-match Press conference, 'There's no doubt McDougall is currently the best finisher in Scottish football. He's worked hard since he came here and we've still to see the best of him', I was made up.

It was mid-November and I was leading the Premier League goal charts by one from Celtic's Brian McClair, with Macca also up there. Happy days. And they were about to get even better.

Any time I'd gone to Ibrox as a St Mirren player, we hadn't been allowed on the pitch for a pre-match kick-about. Fergie was about to change all that. While at Saints, we had to train on a specially constructed red ash patch of ground under the main stand. The first glimpse of the lush grass surface came when the teams ran out at five to three.

I'm sure it was a psychological tool on the part of Rangers and it seemed to work more often than not. Just imagine visiting players running out onto the park for the first time moments before kick-off and 50,000 fans baying for their blood. That could get to some people.

My first game at Ibrox as an Aberdeen player was in the November of 1984 and I arrived on the south side of Glasgow in the middle of that fantastic scoring run. We changed into our training kit and Fergie told us to get out onto the park to stretch our legs. A sign proclaiming 'Keep Off the Grass' awaited and was accompanied by a heavy stare from a chap I assumed was the head groundsman.

I jogged back into the dressing room and told Fergie we weren't allowed on the pitch, and that we were being forced to stretch our legs in that dimly lit area under the stand.

'Like f*** you are', he screamed, and off we went up the tunnel and on to the edge of the grass, where this defiant looking groundsman stood.

'What's the f****** problem?' shrieked a purple-faced Fergie.

'No one's allowed on the grass until kick-off, that's the rules', he replied.

'F*** your rules', he barked and with that he booted the sign straight up in the air and told us to get on the park.

We sort of hesitated, waiting to be told otherwise by this 'defeated' 'Gers official. He didn't respond, we ran onto the pitch and Fergie stood guard, arms folded, as Teddy Scott put us through our paces.

It may sound like just another little Fergie moment, but it was hugely significant and showed that when Aberdeen came to Glasgow, they would not be bossed around by the Old Firm.

We took that confidence into the game and beat Rangers 2-1 and I managed to score the winner. From that moment on, I realised that I was part of the biggest football club in Scotland. Anything was achievable.

Alex Ferguson hadn't just turned the Dons into a brilliant football side - he had also made sure that when his club came to town, they wouldn't be pushed around.

Celtic and Rangers were still massive institutions, but by constructing a team that could more than hold its own on the park, Fergie was able to gain the upper hand on the big two and suddenly coming down to Glasgow didn't hold the same fear that it once had.

Before I started playing football, I knew how big the Old Firm were, how much power they wielded and that was the same for all of the smaller teams visiting Parkhead or Ibrox.

But in eight Premier League games in my two full seasons at Aberdeen, I was never once on the losing side against Rangers (five wins, three draws) and we also gave Celtic a real run for their money.

A few days after the Ibrox encounter I was lifting my first trophy as a Don. It's not one that many people will remember, mind you. We made the short trip to Station Park on a cold November night to help Forfar Athletic celebrate 100 years in existence. It was 1-1 and Forfar were playing well when a McDougall diving header helped seal a 2-1 win - and we lifted the Forfar Centenary Cup.

At the end of November, we beat Dumbarton 1-0 and I scored the only goal. It was the eighth successive league match in which I'd netted. When you're in the midst of your career, there are lots of things you don't take in. You set little records and move on. It's only when you finish playing and have the time to reflect that you realise exactly what you have achieved.

The following month, we were due to host Celtic and even by this stage it was turning out to be a straight fight between 'them and us' for the league championship. And this is where Fergie came into his own.

He got a hold of me on the Monday morning prior to the game and said to me, 'Frank, you're injured'.

I assured him I was fine and he shook his head, telling me once more that I was injured.

This baffled me because I'd just played two days beforehand in a good 2-1 win at Tynecastle and, to my knowledge, I hadn't picked up an injury in that game. Okay, it was the first time in ages that I hadn't scored, although I did come up with an assist.

Anyway, I listened to the great man and wasn't surprised the next morning when I picked up the papers and the headline screamed, 'McDougall to miss vital clash with Celts after picking up injury against Hearts'.

I was starting to believe it myself, but had a word with Fergie and he simply asked me to trust him and if anyone asked, yes, I was injured, which was a pity because the match had been billed as the battle of the strikers.

Aberdeen's Frank McDougall and Eric Black versus Frank McGarvey and Mo Johnston of Celtic. The papers had been predicting 'goals galore'.

All week the story was the same, but with a different twist. McDougall was by now struggling to make the clash and it looked as though I would be watching with the punters. On the day of the match, Fergie read out the team and, sure enough, my name was missing. I was absolutely gutted. Packed house, Old Firm in town, biggest day of your life…

I was standing reading the team list, trying to make sense of it, when Fergie walked up. I was just about to let him know how I felt when he put his finger to his lips. I knew he was up to something. But when he said, 'you're playing', I didn't know what to say.

At 20 minutes to three, as the players came out to limber up, I was standing at the tunnel with my shirt and club tie on. Fergie then walked up to me and said, quietly, 'go in and get changed, and do your stretching in the dressing room'.

I was dumbfounded, but did as I was told and sneaked into the dressing room to get changed.

When we took to the pitch I could see all the Celtic lads looking at one another and shaking their heads. They were obviously as confused as me, but you could say the plan worked because we won the game 4-2 and took a significant step towards the title. It was our fourth successive win over Celtic at 'fortress' Pittodrie.

I scored the fourth goal that day, not bad for someone carrying a nasty 'injury', and it came about when Peter Weir sent over a delightful cross. Celtic keeper Pat Bonner came out to claim the ball, but missed it completely and I nodded in unchallenged at the back post. The perfect end to the perfect day and all made possible by Fergie's incredible mind games.

A few weeks later, just after Christmas, we played St Mirren at Love Street and I scored both our goals. Thankfully, legendary manager, Jock Stein, who was boss of Scotland at the time, picked that game to run the rule over me.

When I heard that big Jock had been at the game I was delighted. Playing for Scotland would've been a dream come true because they don't come more patriotic than me. And big Jock was an absolute legend.

I awaited the announcement of the squad with eager anticipation and was gutted when my name wasn't on the list. What could I do but continue doing my best in the hope of getting the nod.

When Jock Stein died tragically in Cardiff, Alex Ferguson was handed the job of getting Scotland through the World Cup play offs against Australia. After just missing out on a cap previously, I felt I was in with a chance of gaining international recognition this time round because I was still scoring for Aberdeen.

Fergie knew exactly what I was capable of, but when it came down to the nitty gritty, he plumped for Macca to lead the line alongside Kenny Dalglish and Davie Cooper. The latter two were Gods in my eyes and there were no complaints there, but I thought I might've got the nod over Macca.

I was in the pool, but my old Saints team-mate was called upon to get Scotland through and he didn't let anyone down. He worked his socks off and didn't mind tracking back and closing down defenders, so I suppose that's why Fergie picked him. Failing to win a cap for my country is a low point, but not something I dwell on.

Anyway, 1984 had been a good year for me and 1985 was set to be even better. January, though, was a strange month. Not bad, just strange. We started off the New Year on a low note with a 2-1 defeat at Dundee United, in front of almost 22,000 people, but that was all forgotten a fortnight later when Rangers visited.

The build-up to the game was something special and media interest was incredible. We went into it on the back of 2-0 and 5-0 league wins over Hibs and Morton respectively. The latter had proved another Fergie masterstroke.

The game had been scheduled for Cappielow, but when it was frozen off our wily gaffer suggested playing the match at our place. That win helped us open up a five-point lead over Celtic and with it came a huge psychological boost, even if I picked up a groin strain.

The Rangers game was a big test of our title credentials though and a sell-out crowd of 23,000 packed Pittodrie in the hope of seeing something special - and how they got their wish. Well, the home fans at least.

We thrashed them 5-1 and I scored my first ever Dons hat-trick. It was a magical feeling and I was on cloud nine as I travelled back down the road to Glasgow with team-mate Alex McLeish's dad, Alex senior. He travelled up for every Dons match to watch his son and I was soon hitching a lift home, regardless of where we'd been playing that day. I would be heading down the road to see my daughter, Kelly, who lived in Glasgow, and with Alex based in Barrhead, it was the ideal set-up.

After the Rangers game, we held our own post-mortem and despite being a big 'Gers fan, you could tell Alex Snr. was delighted that we had won the match so convincingly. He was incredibly supportive of his boy and enjoyed coming up to watch us play on a Saturday.

The fact that he was happy about us beating Rangers didn't surprise me. I was a big Celtic fan, but it didn't stop me being over the moon when I scored four against them.

Our preparation for the Rangers match had been a bit bizarre. We headed off to Cairo to take on Egyptian First Division side, Ismaili and it also provided me with my one and only look at one of the world's greatest landmarks.

The game was played on a bumpy pitch (with most of our lads wearing training shoes) in terrible humidity. As a fair-haired player, I toiled. It was 130 degrees and I was substituted three times. But it wasn't hot enough to stop me scoring both our goals in a 2-2 draw. I reckon I went through two-dozen salt tablets in a bid to stave off dehydration.

It was a worthwhile exercise though and was watched by around 11,000 supporters - and a massive TV audience, who tuned in to live coverage. I was a TV star in Egypt.

The day after the match, we had some free time and headed off to the Pyramids. It was the most incredible experience and one that has lived with me to this day.

But I wasn't as impressed with the River Nile. We went on a boat cruise down the famous river and it reminded me of the Forth and Clyde Canal, at least the section that ran through Cadder. It was filthy and littered with dead animals. I suppose it has all changed now with the country enjoying a tourism boom.

Back home, the race to be crowned top scorer in the Premier League was heating up and I had pulled four clear of Celtic's Brian McClair.

Our next game was against Alloa in the Scottish Cup and we won 5-0. I missed the game because of 'flu and was in and out of the team over the next few weeks as the groin problem reared its ugly head again.

I did manage to grab the goals that helped us beat Raith Rovers in the fourth round of the Scottish Cup to set up a quarter-final clash with Hearts at Tynecastle and that would prove to be a low point in my Dons career.

Back to Stark's Park though, and my first goal against Rovers is one that will live long in the memory. It was an overhead kick - from the edge of the 18-yard box. Unfortunately, I aggravated the groin and missed the next couple of games - a 2-0 loss at Parkhead and a home win over St Mirren.

Next up was that Scottish Cup quarter-final tie against Hearts. It was scheduled for Tynecastle and was one match I was desperate not to miss. We were on £1,500 a man to progress and I declared myself fit to play. Of course, I wasn't 100 per cent due to the groin, but thought I'd get through the game. The extra cash was also an incentive.

The match was only a few minutes old when we were awarded a free-kick in a pretty dangerous area. I was taking the free-kicks at the time and as I shaped up to strike it, the injury was the furthest thing from my mind.

The moment I hit the ball, there was a grimace on my face and Fergie pounced on it in a flash. He hauled me off and went through me like a dose of salts, before turning his attention back to the game. I didn't know where to look. I had tried to work a flanker and had been caught.

We may have escaped with a 1-1 draw and lived to fight another day, but my personal fight would arrive the following morning. After the game, I was sitting in the dressing room when Fergie came steaming in. He was furious. He went on and on about everything - the injury, the performance, the fact that we hadn't progressed. I just sat there quiet as a mouse.

We were in Edinburgh, so I was keen to get home to see Kelly. We were only an hour away and I was eager to take advantage of that. I eventually plucked up the courage to ask, but he was having none of it.

He screamed, 'You won't go to Glasgow. You'll come up to Aberdeen with the rest of us and get a train back down to Glasgow, but you better be up for training first thing tomorrow morning - at 7am'.

He continued, 'And you can forget the f****n' bonus, you're getting nothing if we get through the replay'.

For the record, I eventually got half.

I decided to head back up to Aberdeen and stay there, but I was fuming inside. I had a few beers and tried to relax, but I knew training, which was by now just a few hours away, would be anything but fun.

We were at the training ground bright and breezy, just after 7am and while it may have been a beautiful sunny morning, there was a cloud of gloom hovering menacingly above the complex. The mood was one of apprehension among the players. Fergie had left the squad - and me in particular - in no doubt whatsoever how he felt about our failure to see off Hearts the previous day. My team-mates were in for a tough day, but I knew only too well that I would be the main focus of the gaffer's wrath following my 'injury' shenanigans. I wasn't frightened of Fergie, no way, but I was certainly wary of him. He was no shrinking violet and had been brought up in the school of hard knocks.

We were sitting around in the changing room, stripped for action and indulging in a bit of light-hearted banter. I always sat next to Alex McLeish and this time was no different. In fact, when the door burst open and the gaffer marched in, I had half-hoped it was Big Eck he was eyeing. Nope - Fergie's face seemed redder than normal - and that spelled big trouble for yours truly.

'Here we go,' I thought, and started blabbering a load of codswollop to Eck, who returned a bemused look. The gaffer was already walking towards me at a frighteningly quick pace and when he let out his familiar war cry of 'McDooougal!', it reverberated around the room, which had now fallen silent. He screamed, 'Ah've seen a f*****g snail move quicker than you. We're gonna work you on that training ground today. Still injured, McDougall?'

For a split second it seemed as though it was just the two of us in the dressing room. No one else mattered. I started to worry in case he would catch a sniff of alcohol from my breath, so I chewed harder on my gum. He was only a few feet away when it appeared he was walking in slow motion. It was a weird feeling.

The fact I was chewing gum seemed to annoy him even more. He was scowling like a rottweiler and he was getting closer. Within seconds he was right in my face. It wasn't possible to get any closer. I was for it. I had a lot of respect for Fergie, but I had learned a long time ago that in a situation like this, you lash out first and ask questions later. Only problem was, I wasn't on the mean streets of Cadder, I was at my 'work' and it was the boss that was in my face. But he had completely lost the plot and I wasn't for waiting to see what he was about to do.

I lashed out with my right fist. It was far from a bout-winning punch and more a 'half-dig' since I was sitting down at the time, but I caught Fergie on the side of the face and he went down like a ton of bricks. Of all the stupid things I had done in my life, putting Fergie on his arse had just stormed straight into the charts at number one. Although I was acting on my nerves, I still knew I had the capacity to hurt Fergie and I didn't want to do that, regardless of what he did, or didn't have on his mind.

I gazed at my hand, and then down at my boss. It was as though he'd fallen to the floor in slow motion. But he bounced straight back up as though on a trampoline and began screaming at the top of his voice. He was looking at Teddy Scott, but shouting at me. 'F**k off McDougall, get to f**k back to Glasgow'. Then he told Teddy, 'Get him out of here, he's f****n' finished'.

And I didn't doubt him for a moment.

It may have been 13 or 14 years since I'd last boxed, but I hadn't lost the speed or accuracy and that would be my downfall, I was sure of it. I'd been in dozens of fights - legal and illegal - before that day, but I felt sick to the pit of my stomach. Beads of perspiration dripped from my brow and I was 100 per cent sure that I'd blown it.

Fergie stormed off and it was Teddy who came over and herded me out the dressing room and into an adjoining room. I could still feel the stares of team mates drilling holes into the back of my head. Teddy didn't say much, he didn't have to, but his look of despondency said it all. I was going through the whole gamut of emotions: anger, at myself and at Fergie, for treating me in such a degrading manner in front of my team-mates embarrassment, frustration and stupidity.

We sat for a moment and few words were spoken. I eventually said to Teddy, 'I've blown it, haven't I? My big chance and I've f****n' blown it. That self-destruct button.'

He shook his head and said, 'I'll speak to the gaffer. You go home and get a good night's kip. Train with the reserves tomorrow'.

I nodded. Teddy fetched my clothes and I changed before sneaking out the dressing room. The lads had started training and for once in my life I felt completely isolated. I should've been with them. I hated training with a passion, but for once in my life, I sorely wanted to join in. I had a quick look round before heading off and they were just getting on with the routines. I was still imagining pockets of players discussing the morning's entertainment. I headed straight home and the journey was a lengthy one. Just me, alone with my thoughts in an Aberdeen taxi. Thankfully the driver didn't want to talk.

'Had I just landed one on the gaffer?' I'm afraid I had.

I was pottering around in the house, running the whole thing over and over again in my head. Why did I lash out? Was there really any need? Surely the gaffer wasn't about to thump me, so why did I feel the need to 'get in there first'? That night was one of the longest of my life. So many times I decided that the best course of action would be to drown my thoughts in litres of alcohol. Thankfully I resisted the temptation.

The following morning I was at the training ground early. I had decided that the moment I saw the gaffer I would apologise profusely. It didn't happen that way. I spent the day - no, make that the entire week - dodging Fergie. I checked every corridor and every room before I entered to make sure they were Fergie-free zones.

It was fully seven days before I next clapped eyes on him at close hand. There was no avoiding him this time. I crept round a corner in Pittodrie and literally banged into him. He looked me straight in the eye and I mumbled what represented an apology. 'Sorry gaffer, I don't know what else to say'.

He didn't once break his stare and said, simply: 'You can make it up to me on the pitch. I want you back in the team'.

I thanked him from the bottom of my heart and he nodded and walked off. I was happier than Larry has ever been. Teddy had once again worked his magic and while my crazy actions had cost me a fine of two week's wages, at least I still had a job.

But that whole incident sums up Fergie and he's still the same to this day. He refuses to loosen his grip on Manchester United and you can see that he is still bigger than the very biggest. A few have tried to flex their muscles and failed. Beckham, Stam - the list is long and illustrious.

Welcome relief came in the shape of the Player of the Month award for January. This time I was the one getting the cheque for £250 and the firkin of beer. I was given the award on my 27th birthday, which made for a great double celebration. Oh, and guess who won the manager's award? That's right, Fergie.

I missed our next eight games - including the replay with Hearts - due to a combination of injury and being dropped. During that time my team-mates won five Premier League games on the bounce to set up a nerve-tingling title showdown with Celtic, at Pittodrie.

A fortnight before that though, we'd been turfed out the Scottish Cup by our old adversaries, Dundee United. We lost 2-1 in a midweek replay after drawing 0-0 on the Saturday. A colleague overheard Fergie saying we would've won had McDougall been fit. He liked me again.

I'd only managed a couple of reserve games in the lead up to the Celtic match and the day before the title decider Fergie took me into his office. 'I want you to play against Celtic, Frank'.

I was surprised he'd asked me to play. I know his reasons, but it was such an important match and I certainly didn't want to let anyone down. I was always ready to play for the gaffer though and agreed without a second's hesitation.

We more or less needed just a point to win the title, but, as usual, that wasn't good enough for Fergie. He wanted us to win it in style.

I wasn't 100 per cent fit, but you get your fitness by playing and if he wanted me to play, I was ready. I wasn't the type of guy who could afford to miss training. If I missed a day it felt like a week, whereas guys like Billy Stark could miss a couple of days and be neither up nor down. I was 'big boned' and had to work hard just to stay on an even keel.

For a game of such magnitude, the build up was pretty low-key and that suited me down to the ground. Maybe I'd just been burying my head in the sand and keeping out of the way, but that's the way it felt to me.

When we took to the park though, that all changed, because the 23,000 fans crammed into Pittodrie were making one hell of a din. As usual, though, the moment the match kicked off, the nerves disappeared.

I didn't have the best of games and was subbed midway through the second half, but I still got a pat on the head from the gaffer as I pulled the tracksuit top over my sweat-filled red jersey. I had run my guts out for the cause.

It was an unusual scenario that day, especially for Celtic, as I'm quite sure they weren't at all used to going into games as underdogs. But they were pushing us hard for the title that year and there wasn't much between the sides.

Celtic had thrown down the gauntlet by taking the lead. They may have had the bit between the teeth, but we had the confidence and ability to beat any team in the Premier League at Pittodrie and we eventually got our equaliser when skipper supreme, Willie Miller, came up for a corner and scored at the King Street end.

There was unbridled joy at the final whistle as the people of Aberdeen celebrated in unison. It was my first ever senior league championship and it felt fantastic. And to win the title in my first season at Pittodrie was extra special. I thought back to my time at St Mirren, and the fact that I'd played in five semi-finals. Always the nearly men, but now I was a winner and it felt great.

You gain so much confidence from playing in a title-winning side and start to believe that you can go on and achieve anything in the sport. And we fully deserved it because we were quite simply the best team in the country without a shadow of a doubt.

Technically speaking, we weren't actually champions as a result of drawing with Celtic. Four days later at Parkhead, there was the small issue of an Old Firm game to be played, and if Celtic failed to win that, we couldn't be caught. As a result, a bad tempered match finished 1-1, with Rangers having two men sent-off, although an Ally McCoist strike meant we were 'officially' crowned Kings of Scotland - for the third time in five years.

The following week we travelled through to Tynecastle for our first game as champions and I knocked in a hat-trick in the first 12 minutes as we won 3-0.

It was a sweltering hot day in Edinburgh and I was completely knackered. I later joked to Fergie that I was happy to have scored my goals in the first part of the game because by half-time I could hardly walk.

I remember running straight up to Willie Miller when I scored my first and telling him that I was back...he agreed. Craig Levein was Hearts' centre-half that day and I gave him a torrid time.

The following day, we were asked to take part in a light-hearted 'Question of Sport' type event as part of the Aberdeen Supporters' Association's annual meeting and celebrations. It was held at the Beach Ballroom and there were more than 1000 fans present. As you can imagine, there was an incredible atmosphere in the place. The teams were made up of current Aberdeen players and ex-Dons stars. Wee Joe Harper was in the latter and they beat us 34-27. For the record, and so you can see that it wasn't all my fault, I was accompanied by Billy Stark, Alex McLeish and Bryan Gunn.

The following Saturday it was back to the football and I scored in our last league game at Morton, which had always been a happy hunting ground. Another ground I enjoyed visiting was Easter Road, although I would always plead with Willie to shoot up 'murder hill' in the first-half, if he won the coin toss, while the energy tank was full. He normally obliged.

We ended up winning the title by seven points from Celtic, with Rangers a further 14 adrift. In doing so we qualified for the European Cup, which would be the first time I'd played in the continent's premier competition, assuming we could successfully negotiate the first round.

I bagged 22 league goals in my debut season at Pittodrie, which was enough to make me top scorer in Scotland, but I sometimes wonder how many I would've scored had I featured in the eight league games I missed. As a reward for our success, we were packed off to Majorca for a week's holiday. It was a fitting reward for our season's endeavours.

But even though we were presented with an ideal opportunity to let our hair down, you still got the impression Fergie had eyes and ears in the largest of the two Balearic Islands.

Just before heading off to sunnier climes, I was thrilled to be shortlisted for the Scottish Professional Footballers' Player of the Year award along with Davie Cooper, Paul McStay and Jim Duffy. Exalted company indeed. I was unsuccessful on this front and the accolade went to Jim. He was a worthy recipient and it had still been a great season for me.

And you know what, I was even looking forward to getting back for the new season, which just wasn't like me at all. Frank McDougall and pre-season training? A bit like fried bread and caviar.

FRANKIE GETS THE BOOT (LA BOTTE DE BRONZE)

THAT first season at Pittodrie was everything I could've dreamed of…and more. It was as though everything I touched turned to gold, or bronze, to be more accurate. It may have been the perfect introduction to life at Scottish football's summit, but one goal not on the radar at the start of the campaign was the European Golden Boot.

The very thought was absurd. As a genuine football fan I knew all about it - who didn't? But Frank McDougall in contention to win the trophy? Give yourself a break.

As a team, we had achieved a lot and I was happy to have played my part. Throughout my career I never once tried to hog the headlines, but had no problems whatsoever with players who liked a bit of the limelight. It just wasn't me though. Football is very much a team game and I'm well aware that sounds rather tired and cliched, but there is a squad of around 20 players in that dressing-room and if you don't fight for one another then it's more or less a lost cause. At Aberdeen we were tight – and I don't mean with our cash.

Being in contention for the Golden Boot was an incredible feeling, though, and once I discovered I was in with a chance of winning it, I was made up. Mind you, it wasn't until a club official mentioned it, with just a few weeks of the season to go, that I realised I was in the running.

The rules are quite different these days and players in the so-called lesser leagues are awarded a percentage for every goal scored.

Organisers reckon it's harder to score in the likes of the English Premiership, or Spain's La Liga, so a Scottish striker would have to score more goals just to keep up with a Wayne Rooney or a Lionel Messi, which, I suppose, is fair enough.

I missed around eight league games that season and reckon that if I had managed to stay fit it may have been the Golden Boot instead of the Bronze, which was awarded for third place, that I would have been collecting. Still, it was an incredible feat and another string to my bow. This lad from Cadder really was going places.

Paris was one place I was going, to collect my award, and it was just the most incredible experience. Normally, things like this didn't happen to guys like me. But this was real, although I had to pinch myself when I clocked who was handing out the prizes. West German football legends, and I don't use that term loosely, Franz Beckenbauer and Paul Breitner, were standing ten feet tall on stage and I could feel my limbs shake when they announced that I'd secured third spot in the race for the 1985 European Golden Boot. Wow. What a feeling.

For the life of me, I can't remember a word of what was said during the presentation. I'm sure we exchanged a few pleasantries, but for all I know we could've been talking global warming, or the world economy. I was certainly in another world.

The event was held in a local circus, which merely added to the fantasy atmosphere, especially where I was concerned. For goodness sake, I had just beaten Gary Lineker and Kerry Dixon (joint fourth) in the race for one of the biggest individual football prizes in Europe. I was having difficulty in registering that fact on my own personal Richter scale .

Porto striker Fernando Gomez was a worthy recipient, but just to be mentioned in the same breath was awesome. From a patch of barren grass in Cadder to the bright lights of Paris. I received my trophy, made an incredibly short speech, even by my standards, and left the stage.

On returning to my seat, I almost fainted. Who was sitting directly behind me, but none other than Eusebio - the Portuguese footballing great. The only guy missing from the party was Edson Arantes di Nascimento. Pele, to you and I. And who was next to Eusebio? Why, Mr Sepp Maier, one of the best goalkeepers ever to strut his stuff on the world stage. It just got better and better.

I had always admired Eusebio though, and as the ceremony drew to a close, with the presentation of European Team of the Year to Everton, which was gratefully received by gaffer Howard Kendall, I immediately sought out the Benfica star and veteran of many an engrossing World Cup campaign. It didn't take too long, but I was shaking like a leaf as I approached him.

'Excuse me, sir,' I said, standing a matter of inches from this God-like figure, and acting like a ten-year-old fan asking for his first signature. 'Can I have your autograph please?'

His reply knocked me for six. 'Sure, Frank, it would be my pleasure.'

'He knows my name,' I said to myself. 'This guy is class'.

He handed me back my signed invitation and I stood there, looking at him like a starstruck wee boy. We chatted for a while and it was among the greatest moments of my life - Eusebio and Frankie boy having a wee natter about all things footie.

After a few drinks, which I needed, a luxury team bus took us back to our hotel.

What a team that would've been...Maier, Beckenbauer, Breitner, Eusebio, Lineker, Dixon, Fernando Gomez, Jose Torres and well, McDougall. And managed by Howard Kendall. I reckon we may just have won more than our fair share of trophies, although we might have been a little lightweight at the back.

It was such a proud moment and once I'd managed to get my head round the whole evening, it helped me accept the fact that I'd earned my place at football's top table.

I was sponsored by Adidas at the time and would regularly head south to their main factory to choose from their extensive range...free gratis, of course.

I had a wee problem with Adidas boots though, and it's something I haven't been able to reveal, until now.

They hurt like hell and I struggled wearing them. I was more comfortable with my old Puma boots, but I couldn't exactly take money from Adidas and wear a rival brand on the park. So, I came up with a novel way of overcoming this minor difficulty.

I carefully peeled off the broad white flash from the sides of my Pumas, grabbed a pair of Adidas boots and carefully stripped off the three white stripes from my sponsored footwear and stuck them on to the now unbranded Pumas. The massive German company was none the wiser, it was far comfier on my feet and everyone was happy. I used extra-strong glue to make sure the stripes didn't work their way loose during a match.

Adidas were all the rage at the time and everyone in Cadder was cutting around in three-stripe trainers and tracksuits, but I was getting 'paid' to wear this up-to-the-minute gear.

It was another fantastic perk, but something I could never quite work out. They gave you the gear…and money…as worn by Frank McDougall…if only they'd known it was Puma I'd been knocking in the goals with.

I hadn't always lived the life of a footballer though and when I was travelling over to Paisley from Cadder on the number 54 bus, the fast-paced life of Bentleys and WAGs seemed a million miles away.

I didn't need all that superficial nonsense though. I was at my happiest when kicking a ball around and certainly hadn't tried to be a professional footballer just for the trappings.

This was never better illustrated than by the manner in which I transported the Bronze Boot back to Aberdeen - in a supermarket carrier bag. Oh, and if I remember correctly, it was the same bag I'd used to take my boots back and forward to Love Street in.

Winning the Bronze Boot was yet another chapter in my incredible story, and one I'm still proud of to this day. I may not physically have the trophy on the mantelpiece, but it's recorded at UEFA HQ and etched in my memory, where it'll remain till the day I die.

THE B⚽SS

FERGIE was the boss, no doubt about it.

As long as you accepted that, you were okay. So, why did I feel the need to challenge his authority from time to time? Maybe it was mischief-making more than anything else.

We trained at Seton Hill, a ten-minute mini-bus ride from Pittodrie. On one occasion we'd just finished a punishing session and were making our weary way back to the bus when Fergie stood on the front step, barring our way. We were only a few yards from the bus when he suddenly shouted, 'You can all f****n' run back to the stadium', and, with that, the door slammed shut and the coach moved off.

'B*****d!, I thought. It wasn't the first time he'd pulled a stunt like this, but on this particular occasion it was around 90 degrees. The sweat was pouring off me and now he expected us to run all the way back to Pittodrie. He wasn't on.

The lads started jogging, but I was having none of it. I jumped a bus and asked the driver to get me to the stadium as quickly as possible. He was a bit bemused, but when I explained the situation, he thought it hilarious and didn't ask for a fare. He was a big Dons fan, which was just as well, as I didn't have any cash.

I beat Fergie back to the ground and made straight for the shower. Moments later, the door came crashing in and there before me stood a furious looking gaffer.

'How did you get back so quick?' he fumed.

'I'm fast', was all I said. He was absolutely livid and hated the fact that I may just have got one over on him.

'You're fined a week's wages, ya smart b*****d'.

'I'll ask ye once again, how did you get here so quick?'

'Bus', I replied. He just looked at me and growled, 'You're still fined a week's wages', and with that he stormed out the dressing room.

I genuinely thought he was joking about fining me a week's wages, but he wasn't, although it wasn't the first time I'd incurred his financial wrath.

Fergie was a genius, as well as an extremely ruthless man. He was a fantastic coach and a superb motivator, but he was a bad loser and on one particular occasion after we'd lost, he was walking along the track at Pittodrie and I was heading in his direction with a couple of my team-mates.

'All right boss?' I said to him, but he looked straight through me and kept on walking. We all sort of looked at him thinking, 'did that just happen?' We didn't lose very often, but when we did it put him in a foul mood.

When you won he was great and, if you did the business for him, he was the type of gaffer who would look after you till the cows came home. No one enjoys losing, but he really hated it.

I had lots of moments with Fergie. Of all my contemporaries, I had the most run-ins with him and I normally stood my ground. I'm not saying the other guys were scared of him, but it seemed to be me more than anyone else who would talk up. Maybe they just didn't need the hassle.

His team talks were legendary and he had us believing we were world-beaters, regardless of the opposition. Although, I wasn't usually singing his praises when we'd report back for pre-season.

Most of the guys looked after themselves during the summer break - I didn't. I wouldn't be looking forward to hearing the words, 'McDougall, on the scales', because inevitably I'd be a good bit over my target weight.

'8lbs over McDougall, you'll get that off in a week. Here me, a week I said'.

And I'd get it off in a week. It was hard work, but the close season was over and we had a job to do. I would make sure I had enjoyed my six-week break and to be honest, it doesn't matter what you drink, or eat during that period, you're going to be sick on your first day back anyway, so that was the 'motivation' for letting my hair down.

It's also amazing how much muscle can be lost in that spell, but it soon comes back when Fergie gets you out on that training ground. I'm convinced that man had spies all over the world. He'd say to me, 'Enjoy your drinking sessions in Benson's Bar during the break?'

I'd be thinking, 'How the hell does he know that?' He was in Aberdeen and I was in Possil. How does he do it?

If you had a quiet drink with Eskimos in Alaska that man would know about it. Quite how he managed it I'll never know, but he did. He had eyes and ears everywhere and I'm sure he kept tabs on us all, or maybe it was just me.

When I was forced out the game in 1987, Fergie was brilliant with me and that has continued to this day.

I know I make him sound like an ogre at times, but he isn't. I wouldn't hear a bad word against the guy. We had our issues, but they were forgotten almost as quickly as they happened. Neither of us is into grudges. He was great for me and I'd like to think I did my very best for him. I'm sure there was a mutual admiration there. At least I'd like to think so. He was my boss and there's a line you don't cross, but we definitely got on well.

He once told me that when he first went to Manchester United, he said to chairman Martin Edwards, 'I need you to get rid of five players'. Bryan Robson, Paul McGrath and Norman Whiteside were among them, three of United's biggest stars.

Edwards told him he couldn't do that if he wanted to win the league. But he was adamant, and eventually got his way. Many commentators reckon that after a pretty disastrous start to his United career he was close to getting the sack and that Mark Robins saved his bacon with his FA Cup equalising goal against Nottingham Forest.

According to Fergie, it was a lot of old tosh, although he admits he did struggle in his new environment for a couple of seasons. Maybe the Robins goal won him a stay of execution, but I don't think it saved his job. Fair play to the directors though, for sticking with him.

I would often travel through to The Cliff to watch United train while I was living in Bury. You had to fight your way through thousands of supporters just to get close. It's undoubtedly the biggest club in the world and with that comes a tremendous level of responsibility for the manager, but Fergie handles the pressure - well, most of the time.

We used to sit and chat about the old days, although the subject of whether or not McDougall may have followed Fergie to Manchester, had injury not struck, never raised its ugly head.

On one occasion though, Fergie's assistant was putting the first team squad through their paces. The strikers were practicing free-kicks. The great Eric Cantona stepped forward to try his luck from 20 yards and put the ball in the stand. That was the cue for Fergie to shout, 'Oi Cantona, come over here a minute'.

And with that, the talented Frenchman ambled casually over. He looked at Fergie and shrugged his shoulders, 'What is it boss?'

'Come and have a look at what a real striker looks like', and he pointed at me.

My face went the colour of Cantona's red training top. He just laughed, said hello, and strolled back to the hub of the action, collar bolt upright as usual. Fergie looked at me and laughed. He was an awful man.

Looking back, I reckon I may have been in the frame to follow the great man south to Old Trafford. I was in the prime of my career; 28-years-old, and United needed a proven goalscorer.

Obviously there are no guarantees how it'll go once you're there, but I always had belief in my ability. I haven't spent too much time dwelling on the past, but I suppose everyone has those 'what if' moments from time to time.

When the Stretford End was being rebuilt, a mate of mine, Colin Dunne, who owned a double-glazing company, wanted to buy a corporate box. He asked me to speak to Fergie and he ended up with first pick. He still had to pay £33,000 for the privilege though.

Fergie's teams were always packed full of strong characters and one player I hit it off with straight away at Pittodrie was Alex McLeish. I got on with everyone, but big Eck and I were good mates.

In fact, when I got the pub in Aberdeen he offered to open it for me and I was more than happy for him to do so. It wasn't an issue for him at all, even though he was a busy guy at the time. I'm not surprised he's followed Fergie into management, and at the very highest level. He had a great teacher.

Fergie is the type of guy who will argue and argue with you, but if come up with the goods for him he will always back you 100 per cent

- in everything. He knew all about my so-called 'reputation' before signing me, but was confident he could get the best out me and he did.

I reckon my game improved 60 per cent through working with him. He was meticulous in everything he did and he expected you to be the same. It was a great mindset to get into. All he ever thinks about is results. Everything he does from Monday to Friday is geared up to that result on a Saturday afternoon.

I reckon there was a mutual respect between us, but after my career ended I reckon he felt sorry for me and tried all he could to help out and that speaks volumes for him, because he is a busy, busy man. I'm sure there was a great deal of sympathy for someone at the peak of their career being forced to throw in the towel.

He had moved on to Manchester, but I was still 'his' player. He was the first person I phoned when I got the dreadful news and he was great with me. At the end of the call he said, 'If I can ever do anything for you Frank, just ask.' I did and he was a man of his word.

I've mentioned elsewhere that Willie Miller was such a fantastic team leader and would lead the revolt whenever a borderline decision went against us. Fergie also demanded we contest every decision and he's still doing it today.

He has a tremendous influence on a lot of things. In fact, I don't know for the life of me how Rabbie Burns managed to waltz off with that Great Scot title having never won a European Cup in his lifetime.

Fergie definitely made me a better player, of that there's no doubt. He constantly demanded improvement. If you scored 30 goals one season, he'd want 40 the next. He wanted you to be the best, but I could handle that pressure - it was in my make-up.

We've talked about the boss being a great motivator and how he helped mould me into the type of player that feared no one. After playing for Fergie reputations meant absolutely nothing. He would say to me, 'Frank, you're up against Michel Ronkin today. He's got 140 caps for Belgium, outstanding defender, reads the game like no other'.

I'd say, 'So what?' and he'd love that.

'You're up against (Tom) Forsyth and (Colin) Jackson, Frank'.

'So what boss?'

It was a challenge to me and I knew he was 100 per cent behind me.

It was a game we played. He would gee me up, I would give him the answer he wanted and we would bounce off one another.

For me, there was no difference between playing for Scotland Boys Club at Cadder pitches, with the big mesh fence behind it and facing up to either half of the Old Firm at Pittodrie, or their place. They were massive, but I was bigger, and there was no inferiority complex. Fergie made sure of that.

I just wanted to score every time I kicked a ball and whether or not it was between Hampden goalposts or a couple of jackets was immaterial. Scoring goals genuinely is a better feeling than sex. But while scoring four against Celtic, plus hat-tricks against Rangers and Hearts, were among the greatest days of my life, missing a penalty against Hamish McAlpine and Dundee United - and getting hooked – was the worst.

Football is a whole series of individual highs and lows. I had a tough start at Aberdeen and went six weeks without scoring, but Fergie was right behind me, despite Dons fans quite rightly asking, 'Who's this duffer you've bought?'

Maybe a lesser manager would've hit the panic button and sold off the mis-firing player to keep the fans happy. Not Fergie though, he protected his players fiercely. But it happens to the best of them and I went on to set a record of scoring in eight successive league games.

I remember, a few years later, sitting in a pub in Manchester and watching Rangers' Marco Negri come within a whisker of beating my record, but he missed a penalty against Celtic. I was never one for stats and records. It's nice to have them, but if he had beaten it I really wouldn't have lost any sleep.

Naturally it's a regret that I didn't train harder in those days, but my culture was football-beer-snooker, in that order, and if it held me back then so be it. There's nothing I can do about it now, but sometimes you sit there and wonder what would've happened had you applied yourself a bit more. A Scotland cap perhaps?

But, especially at St Mirren, most of my team-mates were no fitter than me. When you do pre-season training, everyone does the same thing. Of course, there's always the scope to stay back afterwards and put in an extra shift and I did that occasionally.

At Aberdeen, Peter Weir would cross in 200 balls after training and

I'd practice heading and kicking them past Jim Leighton. That wasn't about fitness, but helped with accuracy.

Very seldom did I miss the target though. It's a bit like putting. If you're short of the hole, then the ball will never drop. In football you just have to give it that bit extra and that's usually enough.

You hear ex-players constantly banging on about having to hit the target, making the goalkeeper work and they are 100 per cent right. Sure, there will be times when you miss, but if your concentration is total then nine times out of ten you will either score, or make the keeper earn his corn.

You will also get the breaks if you stick you're head in where it hurts. I've had more than my fair share of kicks in the face, but they never stopped me putting my head on the line again and again. You inevitably get your rewards.

I reckon I was fortunate enough to be blessed with talent. I learned a lot kicking a ball against the wall in the back garden, but if you haven't at least got a decent level of fitness then it'll prevent you reaching the very top. A lack of fitness won't stop you scoring goals, because instinct will on more occasions than not get you into decent positions, but obviously the fitter you are the better it is for your all-round well-being. I like to think I was lightning over 10 to 20 yards. Any more and I was out of my comfort zone.

For me, it was all about playing on the last defender. They ball watch and that's normally all you need to get in there, nick the ball and race in on goal. It all happens in the click of a finger and once you're away, they're struggling to recover. And I never once had to look and see where the goal was. If I had my back to goal I could feel where it was.

One of my strong points was bearing down on goal with just the keeper to beat. I loved that scenario. Just him against me. It soon becomes a battle of wills with the striker trying to con the keeper into diving. And 90 per cent of the time he will go down, but if he stays on his feet you start thinking, 's***, this has just become that bit harder.' All you want to do though is ripple the back of the net - it's the only thing on your mind. These days though, it seems like some players are thinking more about Bentleys and Ferraris.

Joe Harper was an incredible finisher and on one occasion while we were chatting, I told him that if I had stayed at Aberdeen till the end of my career, I reckon I could've overtaken his record as Dons all-time top scorer. He didn't disagree, but we were out a similar mould - both natural predators with an eye for goal.

Every time Joe and I get together the conversation inevitably turns to goals and Aberdeen have certainly had their problems sticking the ball in the back of the net in the last season or two, but you'll never catch me slagging off any of their players. A reporter called me up just before Jimmy Calderwood was sacked and tried to get me to have a go at a couple of the Dons front men. No chance. It has never been in my nature to criticise other players and I'm not about to start now.

It's always hard to compare eras, but when I was playing, I reckon there were better defenders doing the rounds than there are today. It was also a tougher era for forwards. I don't see too many McLeishs, Millers, Nareys or Hegartys on goal patrol these days.

F⚽UR PLAY DEMORALISES CELTIC

I WAS proud as punch as I arrived back for pre-season with my first ever championship medal in my pocket. I'm not saying I skipped through training, but there was definitely a spring in the old step in the run up to the new campaign.

We headed off to sunny Switzerland for a few challenge matches, five in all, and yet 'more' training. We won three of the five and the gaffer had arranged another three on our return.

We were certainly ready to defend our title and started off with a great 3-0 win over Hibs at Pittodrie - and I scored twice. I had a good feeling about the term ahead. We negotiated the opening rounds of the League Cup against Ayr United and St Johnstone and I scored in both.

Disaster struck though when I picked up a niggling injury, although that wasn't the reason for missing out on both legs of our European Cup tie with Akranes of Iceland - I was still suspended. However, we safely negotiated that hurdle though.

Despite winning our opening three league matches, we dropped some daft points and were soon lagging behind Celtic. So, we headed for Ibrox knowing we had to win. Fergie was furious at our indifferent run of form and it's fair to say we weren't too happy either.

We had an incredible first-half and went in 3-0 up at the break. Surely the gaffer would be pleased with our efforts? We should've known better. We sat there listening to Fergie's assistant, Archie Knox, heap praise upon us for the manner in which we'd dismantled the 'Gers in the first 45 minutes.

'Let's just take things a bit easier in the second period', Archie said. 'You've earned it'.

Next thing the dressing room door was almost taken clean off its hinges and the great man, followed by his even greater presence, stormed in.

'You'll take f*** all easier', he blasted.

He was shouting and bawling like a man possessed and throwing things around.

'I want quick free-kicks and quick corners. I want you to hassle Rangers at every opportunity and every time they have the ball. If I so much as see anyone slacking they will be taken off straight away – you're feet won't touch the ground. Understood?'

Perfectly.

I can still see the look of embarrassment on Archie's face as Fergie was moving around the dressing room like a demented demon.

Of course, once again it was Fergie playing mind games. There was no way on this earth he wanted to court disaster by allowing us to take our feet off the gas. We would protect our lead by attacking and the man was 100 per cent right. Complacency wasn't in Fergie's vocabulary.

In the second round of the European Cup we drew Servette, which meant a return journey to Switzerland following our pre-season tour. I had a decent game, but Michelle Ronkin, the big Belgian, kept a close eye on me.

Reputations didn't mean a great deal to me and I played my normal game. I'd like to think I gave him as many problems as he gave me. I loved playing against the big boys and revelled in it. I respected these guys, but certainly didn't fear them.

Servette were a good side and in the first leg, at their place, the two teams were evenly matched and the contest finished goalless. The draw set us up for, what I thought, would be a relatively painless night at Pittodrie.

How wrong could I be? They pounded us at our place in front of a full house and, while I managed to score the game's only goal with a diving header, we were pretty fortunate to get through. I also 'scored' a second, but a Willie Miller foul on their keeper meant it was ruled out. It was a great feeling bagging my first European goal though.

Servette may have taught us a soccer lesson that night, but our name was in the hat for the quarter-finals. In between the ties with the Swiss side, we had the not-so-insignificant matter of the League Cup final against Hibs at Hampden.

It was played just four days after the European Cup first leg tie, but there was no sign of jet lag as we walked the vast Hampden pitch prior to kick-off. It was my first League Cup final, although I was surprised to learn that it was a competition in which Fergie had yet to taste success. We were determined to help him achieve a clean sweep of domestic trophies.

And we did so in some style by thumping Hibs 3-0. It was a performance that incorporated just about everything, apart from a McDougall goal, although I almost capped it off by adding a fourth. John Hewitt played a beautiful through pass to me and I chipped Alan Rough, but, unfortunately, the ball cleared the bar as well as big Roughy.

After the game, I witnessed something I'd never before seen, or have done since, and that was the great man shedding far more than just a single tear. It was his ninth domestic honour with the Dons and I'm sure we won't begrudge him just a solitary slip of his normally watertight exterior.

It was also the first time I'd played in a live televised final. My first biggie and I was determined to make sure I would enjoy it for years to come. I did and it's a memory I'll treasure forever.

Four days before the second-leg against Servette, we tackled league leaders, Celtic at Pittodrie. It was an incredible afternoon for yours truly. As far as I know, I'm the only player ever to achieve ten out of ten in the Sunday Mail star ratings.

It was the first Saturday in November and, as I said, Celtic were in town. Despite a lacklustre start to the season and the small matter of being only a few months into the campaign, it was already being billed as a vital match in terms of the championship. We'd lost 1-0 to Hearts the previous weekend and were under a bit of pressure to get back to winning ways.

The Old Firm didn't like coming to Pittodrie in the 1980s and we did all we could do take advantage of that situation. Fergie tried every trick in the book to enhance Pittodrie's reputation as a fortress and I helped that particular day.

We hammered Celtic 4-1 and I helped myself to all four goals.

It was an unforgettable afternoon, but that very night, I remember people asking if I was in any way disappointed at demolishing my boyhood idols. I can answer that question quickly and easily. It was one of the greatest days of my life. I loved scoring goals, but to score four in one game against the team that went on to win the championship, well, does it get any better?

After that day, no one could ever accuse me of not trying against Celtic, even though I had a good scoring record against them beforehand. For some reason, there was always that question at the back of some people's minds. To many, there are only two teams in Scotland that matter.

My motivation was simple. We were desperate to win every game we played and we were playing for that all-important bonus. But my silver cloud had a murky lining. I was gutted to discover that TV technicians had gone on strike just two hours before kick-off and the game hadn't been covered. To say I was disappointed that such a fantastic individual scoring feat hadn't been captured for posterity would be a major understatement.

I remember sitting later on that night talking to a couple of friends - over a celebratory beer or two - and saying that if I'd known how the day would pan out, I may even have considered paying the technicians the rise they wanted myself, if indeed that was the reason for the strike.

But at least I received two match balls as mementoes. Celtic scored first that day and then I equalised at the King Street end just before half-time.

Snow was teaming down as we emerged after the break and the pitch had changed from green to white. The referee insisted in using an orange ball and I scored three times with it. After the game, Fergie came straight over and gave me the warmest hug.

But he then grabbed the orange ball from me and said, 'You're not getting that one McDougall, I think you enjoyed kicking f*** out of it too much.'

To my knowledge, only one other Aberdeen player has scored four against Celtic in the same match. The legendary George Hamilton managed it in 1947 at Celtic Park. And, I couldn't believe it when such a Dons great congratulated me on my feat a couple of weeks after the game and it made me feel great. To be in a select band of just two is an incredible achievement. I accomplished a lot in my eight-year pro career, but that performance is up there with the best.

However, midway through the season came the call that everyone dreads. 'You're dad is ill and in hospital'.

I hopped on a flight straight away and was down at the hospital in Bury within a few hours. He was just hanging on, but we still managed to have a chat and that meant the world to me. He passed away the following day.

It was as though the half hour I had with him was meant to be.

We talked about everything that had happened in our lives and he told me he was proud of my achievements. It was fantastic to hear him say that. I held his hand and it was a poignant moment. When he died the following day I was devastated, but it was easier to take knowing that I'd had the opportunity to speak with him one last time. I took it hard, even though my grandparents had brought me up. He was still my dad and I never, ever forgot that.

It was strange, because he wasn't into football at all. He only ever saw me play once and it was for St Mirren against Celtic in a cup semi-final at Hampden. We lost 2-1, but I scored that day and I can still remember the pride etched all over his face when we met up after the match.

His passion was fishing and I liked that about as much as my dad liked football. It just wasn't for me. He was a crane driver and tended to work a lot of nights and would go straight to his fishing in the morning.

My dad's death hit me hard, but I knew I had to get straight back into playing again and an old adversary lay in wait. We were up against Dundee and I was in direct competition to my former Buddie, John 'Cowboy' McCormack. He was playing alongside big Bobby Glennie and I must admit, I ripped them apart, but only after Cowboy had been giving me grief, pulling my jersey and stuff like that. I was determined to make him pay. We won the match and I scored twice in the last five minutes.

Dundee were fighting for their lives and desperately needed the points, but we were also hot on the title trail and were equally as keen to nab all three. It was 0-0 up until late on and when Cowboy was clattering into the back of me, it was as though we'd never met. Thankfully though I managed to escape his evil clutches late on and he was left chasing shadows.

Cowboy and I were still great friends at the time, but business was business, and once again there was the not-so-insignificant matter of a £300 win bonus at stake. That was all the incentive I needed to ensure Cowboy and his new mates were on the receiving end of my wrath. We both had our own agendas - he's Dundee and I'm Aberdeen. Supporters have paid a lot of money to watch us battle for the points and the last thing they want to see is a couple of old pals going through the motions.

That said, there was one occasion during the game when Cowboy tackled me inside the box and down I went. The referee didn't award a penalty, but there was no chance of me getting a yellow card because I genuinely went down in the challenge. I absolutely despise players who throw themselves around in the box, looking for penalties and trying to get opposition players into trouble. They should be banned and fined.

In those days, matches between Aberdeen and Dundee United were huge affairs and these 'New Firm' derbies attracted massive crowds. Of all the defenders I came up against, my toughest opponent was undoubtedly Paul Hegarty. The Dundee United pivot was such a fit lad, very quick and hard as nails. There weren't many fitter players around than Hegs and it was so hard to shake him off. He was never more than a few inches from you all through the match. Don't get me wrong, I scored my fair share of goals against United, but it was always a difficult task.

Rangers defender Tom Forsyth was another formidable opponent and while he was extremely physical, he wasn't dirty. Big Tam was such a growler though, you'd hear him before you saw him. You definitely knew when he was around and your heart would be going ten to the dozen. There would be this huge growling sound coming from behind and, crunch, big Tam had left his mark.

Playing against Alex McLeish, while I was at St Mirren, was also challenging. He was all over you like a rash. He would be in your face and winding you up and he used to get on my nerves.

Willie Miller is probably one of the best players I've played alongside. He was such an intelligent player and read the game like no other. He was also a master at getting decisions from referees. As soon as something contentious happened in a match, Willie would lead the protest charge at the match officials and more often than not it would go our way. Listen, the Old Firm got away with it for 100 years so why not Aberdeen? A lot of folk thought Fergie was the instigator-in-chief of such moves, but it was Willie who orchestrated most of it. It goes without saying that Fergie wasn't against us capitalising on such a tactic.

Peter Weir was a smashing player as well, equally at home on either his right or left foot. He ghosted past defenders as if they weren't there. I had a lot of time for Peter both on and off the park. Starky was another great player, and friend.

Naturally I was at my happiest on the football pitch, but it wasn't my only passion. I've always been a keen snooker player and played regularly while at the Dons. On one occasion I made it to the final of a big tournament in Aberdeen and was desperate to take part. We were banned from going out on a Thursday night though, and guess which night the final fell on?

It was a fantastic standard so I was chuffed at making it so far and didn't want to miss out. I had a big decision to make. When we had a game on a Saturday, Fergie didn't like us socialising after a Wednesday, but as I hadn't planned on boozing, I didn't think there would be a problem. I decided to go for it, although it wasn't easy keeping a low profile in a city like Aberdeen, where the citizens thought so highly of their footballers.

While on the green baize, all thoughts of Fergie's furious face were left behind. I thoroughly enjoyed the experience, but despite being 5-3 up at one point, I lost the match 6-5. Reaching the final was still a fantastic achievement and I'd had a good night out without my grumpy boss knowing anything about it.

Until those bloody journalists spoiled my plan. The match was covered in the local press and, as always, Fergie clocked it, even though it was tucked away in the inside sports pages, close to the obituaries. I was almost reading of my own demise.

I was a week's wages lighter despite assuring him that not a glass of beer had passed my lips. He no doubt thought, 'Frank McDougall in a pub all night and he doesn't have a drink. Yeah, right.'

It was the same with golf. There was a great links course directly across from Pittodrie and the players had an open invitation to play whenever we wanted.

Only problem was, Fergie could see right onto the first tee from his office.

That didn't stop us, though - we would start at the second tee. To this day, I've played that course 101 times and have yet to complete 18 holes. Old habits die hard.

We all liked to think we had put one over on the boss. He probably knew fine well what we were up to. I suppose I refused to fully conform and by my actions made a rod for my own back. He knew I could score goals though and that was normally my route straight back into his good books.

The switch to Aberdeen had been a great one for me personally and I was playing at the top level in Scotland. In the 1980s it didn't get any better than being a Dons player. To take my career a step further I would have needed to move south or abroad, but not to just any club, because outwith the top four or five clubs in England, the remainder would've been a backward step. It's certainly something I would've welcomed, but maybe not after just two seasons at Pittodrie because life was so enjoyable. Why change a good thing?

I don't think the game down south differed too much from Scotland in those days. Of course, it's a hell of a lot faster now, but back in the 80s there wasn't a great deal of difference between the top leagues. Scots were the dominant force down south in the 1980s and we more than held our own.

But, there's always a huge gap between the second round of the European Cup and the quarter-finals. After scoring the winner against Servette, I was desperate to see who we'd get in the last eight.

It was Gothenburg, which was obviously a somewhat poignant draw, given the club's famous Cup Winners' Cup victory over Real Madrid in that very city. I was looking forward to it, but things hadn't exactly been going well on the injury front and there was no guarantee I would make the game.

The Saturday before the first leg, we beat Hibs 1-0 at Easter Road but I wasn't listed. My back had been playing up and I would've been about as useful as a chocolate fireman. I was devastated. I watched the first leg from the Pittodrie stand and it wasn't a happy place to be. Not because we only managed a 2-2 draw, to leave us with only a slim hope of qualifying, but because the injury was really starting to play on my mind and foul moods were becoming the order of the day.

I was never a good spectator. I played football because I loved it, and because it provided me with a good standard of living. One thing I was never comfortable with though was watching the team struggle. Who knows if my inclusion would've made a difference, but I wanted to get out there and find out.

We had good strikers at Aberdeen and no matter who played we always felt we could win. That's why the Gothenburg result wasn't a complete disaster; we still had 90 minutes to put it right. I missed our next three games and before I knew it, the second leg of the European Cup in Sweden was upon us. I didn't think I had a hope in hell of playing.

The match was on the Wednesday night and we had planned to fly out to Gothenburg late on the Monday. Fergie called me into his office first thing on the Monday morning and said, 'Frank, I've arranged for you to fly down to Glasgow to see one of the country's top chiropractors. I want you ready for Wednesday's game. If we don't score, we're out'.

I was delighted. My spirits were up and I headed for Aberdeen Airport, where I caught a flight to my home city. This was just the boost I'd needed to release me from the doldrums. Off I went with a spring in my step, but part of the treatment involved this guy standing on a box behind me and giving me some sort of bear hug. I heard much cracking and crunching of bones and then I was told I could go.

I flew straight back up the road feeling a million dollars. I breezed back into Pittodrie like a new man - and a foot taller - and made straight for the gaffer's office. He asked me how I was and I told him I felt great. With these three words, a huge smile enveloped his face. We were off and trotting.

We headed to the airport to catch the flight to Sweden. I was like a little boy in a sweet shop. On the Wednesday afternoon, we had our usual Euro team talk at the hotel and, horror of horrors, I wasn't mentioned. I couldn't believe it. I sat there quiet as a mouse, listening intently, just in case I'd missed 'McDougall' being mentioned. Nope, I got it right the first time. Frank McDougall wasn't in the team and Frank McDougall wasn't too chuffed.

I started thinking, 'why did he send me down to Glasgow and back up again on the same day if he wasn't going to play me?' I couldn't work it out. Of course, I thought I would be playing from the start, why wouldn't I? Wasn't that the whole point of the chiropractic exercise? He still hadn't said a word as we hit the dressing room and as I was listed as a sub, started to get changed like everyone else. We then trooped out onto the magnificent playing surface at the Ullevi Stadium for a warm-up.

The first-half ended 0-0. We desperately needed a goal. Gothenburg were happy to sit in because as things stood, they were through. With just ten minutes remaining, Fergie said, 'Okay, Frank, get stripped, you're going on to rescue this tie'.

'Fat chance of that', I thought, but did as I was told.

It's nigh on impossible to make an impact in the last ten minutes of any game, far less a European Cup quarter-final. That's what happened and the game petered out at 0-0 - we were out. I was subdued as we headed back to Scotland and still couldn't quite work out why I hadn't played from the start, after all the hassle to get me fit.

Things weren't exactly going according to plan in the league either and we were in grave danger of losing our title. Immediately after Sweden, we failed to beat Dundee, at Pittodrie and the two lost points left us trailing Celtic and Hearts. I missed that game and the narrow win at Motherwell the following Saturday. Fergie brought me back for the Scottish Cup semi-final against Hibs at Dens Park and we thumped them 3-0 in front of almost 20,000 fans. We were desperate to salvage something from the season and at least we had a cup final to look forward to. Our opponents would be Hearts and they were involved in a two-way fight for the championship.

The Wednesday after the Hibs match, we scraped a 3-2 win at home to Motherwell, but the next four matches were the main reason why the title race had become a two-horse race. We lost at home by the narrowest of margins to both Celtic and Dundee United within the space of five days and followed that up by drawing against Hearts and Rangers. Four league games and just two points to show for it. Hardly the stuff of champions.

We had lost some stupid points over the course of the season and that had put paid to any hopes we had of retaining the title. I certainly wouldn't say we were inferior to the other top clubs in the division, so Fergie had every right to be furious. He knew, as much as we did, that the players and infrastructure were in place at Pittodrie to make us perennial challengers, but on this occasion we hadn't stepped up to the plate and had been punished.

The week before the cup final we travelled to New Kilbowie, home of the Bankies, and beat them 6-0. I played the full match, scored a couple of goals and put in a decent all-round performance. I reckoned I was in line for a cup final starting place. With Fergie, though, nothing was ever guaranteed. We would have to wait and see. Despite winning the League Cup earlier in the campaign, the Scottish Cup represented our only chance of ending the campaign on a high.

MY FINAL RECK⚽NING

IT'S meant to be the pinnacle of every player's career but the Scottish Cup Final of 1986 holds bitter-sweet memories for me. We went into the match against Hearts on the back of a crushing 6-0 win over Clydebank, although, in terms of league positions, the game had been meaningless, because we'd already resigned ourselves to finishing fourth in the Premier League.

In terms of preparation for the big match against Hearts though, it was invaluable and provided a timely confidence boost. Personally, I was delighted to play against the Bankies as I'd missed the four league games previous - and we hadn't won a single one. The build up to the cup final was just incredible though.

We arrived at our luxury hotel, near Glasgow Airport, the evening before the game and rested overnight. I'd taken a couple of sleeping pills in a bid to get some shuteye, but it didn't work and I tossed and turned the entire night. Once again I was by myself as my team-mates refused to share a room because of my 'snoring'. But that was fine.

I got nervous before any game, regardless of whether it was Alloa at home or Celtic away; the nerves were always there. But the night before the cup final I was a wreck. I suffered a double dose of the jitters. With no sleep at all, I awoke for breakfast a little bleary eyed, although most of the lads were the same.

I had also been having a terrible time with my back and had been in excruciating pain for most of the night, which no doubt contributed to any lack of sleep more than the butterflies. I spoke to the boss on the QT before his official get together at the hotel for his team talk. I told him I didn't think I could play. It was one of the biggest days of my life and I was desperate to play, but knew it wouldn't be right to blag my way into the team.

We had a serious heart-to-heart and he asked me to play. I agreed and immediately started bunging myself up with painkillers. Fergie read out the team and we had our pre-match discussion, with the boss giving everyone their instructions for the day. The moments leading up to kick-off would be used for motivation only.

With that, it was onto the team bus for the short ride to Hampden. We had a couple of police motorcycle outriders to escort us to the national stadium and the moment they appeared, the nerves started to really get the better of me. Then I was sick on the bus and that just made things worse. Suddenly it wasn't back pain that was causing me to question whether or not I'd be able to play in the match. If I was this nervous a couple of hours before kick-off, would I actually make it to 3pm without having a nervous breakdown?

The lads who seemed to be taking it all in their stride were magnificent though and soon had me laughing away. Some of the other guys simply chose to look out the window - at the M8. Around a mile or so from Hampden the nerves returned. You see all the fans waving flags and either cheering the team bus, or giving you pelters and it starts to dawn on you just how many people have travelled 200 miles to back you. As well as your own hopes and dreams, you also have theirs in your hands. It's quite a responsibility and you want to do it for them as much as for yourself and your family.

It's the biggest day on the Scottish football calendar and when the bus eventually fights its way through the crowds in Mount Florida, you catch your first glimpse of the imposing stadium. When the importance of the occasion really hit home to me was the moment the coach pulled up outside the main entrance to the stadium. There were fans everywhere, police on horseback trying to control the crowds and a mass of supporters cheering and wishing us well. You could almost taste the levels of expectation. It's a massive day out for supporters, but in many ways you can't afford to get caught up in all the drama because you're there to do a professional job.

Then you walk out the tunnel, like hundreds of famous players before you, and the first thing you witness is a sea of colour. There were more than 62,000 people there that day and half were decked out in red and white. Just before lining up to meet cabinet minister Malcolm Rifkind, I looked over to our supporters and banners like

'Fabulous Frankie' were prominent in the crowd. That left a huge lump in my throat. Then it was time for the formalities, the national anthem, the ceremonial meeting of dignitaries, including Mr Rifkind - Hi, I'm Frank - it was pretty surreal and must have been for him too. One minute he would be discussing impending wars and the country's growing economic issues - next he's shaking hands with a bunch of footballers.

And then it's time to do what we were there to do, play the game. As we broke away from the greeting party there was one last opportunity to wave to my family and friends in the main stand. You're on, Frankie. The training top was chucked aside with gusto and the players started hugging one another and dishing out last minute messages of encouragement. The tension was still palpable and that would remain until the first whistle had sounded.

I always enjoy a smirk when I hear people saying that occasions such as a Scottish Cup final should be enjoyed. That's fine, and I agree 100 per cent, but it's not quite as easy as that. And while I can't relax until the referee blows his whistle, the enjoyment factor is still judged on how good a start you make. Lose a goal in the first minute and you're on a downer.

That wasn't a problem for the Dons or yours truly though. With just a couple of minutes on the clock, we were 1-0 to the good. And I was almost quids in.

I'd put £2000 on myself to score the first goal at 7/2, which would have meant a satisfying return of £9000 had I managed to bulge the net first. We were on the attack and John Hewitt was running at the Hearts defence. Both Craig Levein and Sandy Jardine went to close him down. I was in the clear and was screaming for John to square it, but he went for goal on his own and slammed it past Henry Smith for the opener. He'd put us one up and I suppose I couldn't really complain. We were on £7000 a man to win the cup anyway, although there was still plenty of work to do to secure the silverware.

Peter Weir then gathered the ball out wide, sent over a peach of a cross, I dummied it and John lashed it home. Talk about dream starts. Any lingering nerves were well and truly kicked into touch with those goals. Not only that, but it allowed us to grow in confidence and we began to play some nice football. I remember settling down and starting to truly enjoy the occasion for the first time, which, in itself, was so important to me.

Of all the goals I scored in my career, lots of people still mention that dummy to me. I admit it did look really good, although I wouldn't have minded if John had dummied the ball and I'd scored. But it's incredible to think that, 25 years on, I'm remembered for a goal I didn't score.

We went in 2-0 up at the break and it was ours to throw away. After losing the league, Hearts had been unable to pick themselves up in time for the start of the match, so what would their manager be able to do in just ten or 15 minutes? Nothing was the answer, and we scored another to run out comfortable 3-0 winners. Even though I failed to get on the scoresheet, I was delighted we'd won, and that I'd lasted the full 90 minutes. For the last five or ten minutes, my back had started playing up and I was convinced that the gaffer had noticed my lack of mobility. Not much got past him.

In fairness though, he kept me on and I've often wondered if he had an inkling that this just might be my last match. He knew all about the back issues and I wonder if there was a sense of charity in his decision-making. After all, the cup was ours.

But at least he didn't slate the 1986 cup-winning team the way he had chastised an earlier side. After the Dons had hammered Rangers 4-1 in the '82 Scottish Cup final, the gaffer laid into them, saying he'd never seen a team under his charge play so badly. As a team we were spared that ignominy, but on a personal level, my problems were just beginning. Walking up those famous Hampden steps to lift the cup should be the best moment of a player's career - for me, it was anything but.

I held the cup aloft half-heartedly and passed it to the next guy. I shook hands with the dignitaries, got my medal and moved on. There was no great sense of achievement. The others were kissing the cup passionately, hugging it like a long lost brother but I showed no emotion whatsoever. I don't know if there was something lurking at the back of my mind telling me the whole adventure was coming to an end. Or it could've been something else.

In order to get through the day, I'd taken a cocktail of painkillers and the effects were beginning to wear off. I'd never felt so horrible in all my life. We were on our celebratory lap of honour and all I wanted to do was get back to the sanctuary of the dressing room. Once inside, the champagne was flowing and the guys were on a high, singing and dancing around the dressing room with the cup.

Cameras flashed and the joint was jumping.

We left Hampden for a celebratory reception at Loch Lomond with wives, girlfriends and family members. It should've been a night to remember, but at around 8.30pm, I started to feel really awful. It was as though I was on another planet. The pain from my back had returned with a vengeance. The rest of the evening was a blur. I had just become a member of a Scottish Cup winning team and I wasn't enjoying it one bit. It wasn't like me because I could party with the best of them. At least I didn't wake up the following morning with a king-size hangover.

We travelled back up to Aberdeen that night and the following morning we were up bright and breezy for an emotional ride along Union Street on an open top bus. The good people of Aberdeen had turned out in force and the famous old street was a mass of red and white for as far as the eye could see. That afternoon is probably one of the main reasons I hold the city in such high regard. The people are football crazy and back their club to the hilt. Sure, it's easy when you're winning things, but that hasn't always been the case in the Granite City.

Those days were also my most successful in the game. I was scoring goals and managed to win all three domestic competitions. What more could one ask? The Old Firm may have ruled Scottish football for 100 years, but everyone now wanted to beat Aberdeen and the feeling was wonderful.

Afterwards, the players were packed off on a week's holiday to Magaluf and I was certainly ready for a break. I teamed up with Alex McLeish and we sank more than a few drinks, but unfortunately I ended up with the DTs, or the 'horrors', as their quaintly known in these parts. I had far too much to drink and I'm sure this was my body's way of telling me to ease off. I was convinced those little green men were real.

Alex had a good time as well, but he was far more conservative than me and looked after himself. He was always in peak condition and it certainly stood him in good stead throughout his playing career. And he has achieved so much during his time in management as well. To lead your country and your boyhood heroes, Rangers in Alex's case, is every lad's dream. And I firmly believe there's so much more to come from the big man. Couldn't have happened to a nicer guy.

Alex didn't ever really fall foul of Fergie; he was always more of a listener than the type who talked back. Unfortunately, I was the latter. On a number of occasions he urged me not to answer back, and just to let Fergie's words go in one ear and out the other, as I would never win. Unfortunately, that's what I did with his advice. I should've listened.

I still learned a great deal from my time with Fergie. Sometimes you had to bite your tongue, but in saying that, even if you were nice to Fergie he'd still give you the hair dryer treatment.

But the so-called bullying, and I use the term loosely, was good, because he'd make it work to your advantage. He was only ever interested in making me a better player and he definitely succeeded. His goal was to make people the best he could. It's just unfortunate, though, that I didn't really get the opportunity to reap the rewards of his hard work. I would love to have worked with him earlier in my career.

I remember when he took over at Man United and the so-called experts reckoned he would never win anything with a bunch of kids. But that 'bunch of kids', which included David Beckham, Ryan Giggs, Paul Scholes and the Neville brothers, Gary and Phil, eventually brought him many trophies.

What's that old saying about not teaching your granny how to suck eggs?

THE PARTY'S OVER

DESPITE a sensational Scottish Cup final victory, the 1985-86 season had ended on a bit of a downer. Fingers and toes were crossed that a lengthy rest would help prevent further problems with my back. At just 28-years-old, I wasn't quite ready for the knacker's yard.

But the pain had been intense throughout the close season and I knew that a tough battle lay ahead, not just off the park, but on it as well. We'd surrendered our title to Celtic and Fergie was desperate to wrestle it back - at all costs.

Off we headed to Sweden for pre-season and while I wasn't 100 per cent fit, I wanted to take part. We were still a fantastic outfit and the major honours were there for the taking. We had four games lined up in Scandinavia and our first opponents were little-known side Gunnilse IF. We stumbled to a 1-1 draw, but I scored and that helped allay fears of my injury, at least to me. In our second match, against Grohed, just two days later, I got another vital 90 minutes under my belt, although the end result, which wasn't too important, was another 1-1.

The gaffer obviously wanted to utilise the entire squad and I sat out a 3-0 win over Vela before being reinstated for the final match of the tour against the better-known Trolhattan. We brushed them aside by four goals to nil and I was delighted to notch a hat-trick. Injury, what injury?

I'd enjoyed the tour of Sweden, even though we didn't get to see too much of the country. I'm afraid it was all work and no play, which was a pity, because I like nothing better than a bit of 'sight-seeing', especially when Cowboy had been around. We could have been training at Bellahouston Park for all it mattered because it was double sessions. Training in the morning and afternoon and then playing games every other day. It was anything but a jolly. I suppose my priority had been to prove my fitness, so to take part in three games was a positive start.

German giants Stuttgart visited Pittodrie the first Saturday in August and, despite losing 2-0, I enjoyed a decent game. I always enjoyed going up against the best the continent had to offer. Stuttgart were among the big boys in Germany and it was a great test for us.

I wasn't listed for our first Premier League game of the season, a 2-1 loss at Tannadice, but came off the bench against Hibs at home on the Wednesday night, when we chalked up a superb 4-0 win. Was I as happy as my team-mates after that game? Was I heck. It may have been the start of an impressive eight-match unbeaten run for the Dons, but it was also the last time I ever pulled that famous red shirt over my head.

I managed just fifteen minutes against Hibs and I knew there and then that something serious was wrong. That game took place on Wednesday, August 13, but it would be an agonising six months later that the dreaded news would be delivered - that I would never, ever play football again.

Meanwhile, two draws and a defeat at the start of September meant we dropped off the pace at the top of the league. We drew Swiss side, Sion, in the first round of the European Cup Winners' Cup and crashed out 4-2 on aggregate following a humiliating 3-0 loss at their place. It was probably just me and my situation, but I felt that the whole city was on something of a downer.

Late October and early November brought back-to-back Premier League road wins and it looked as though our domestic from was picking up. It proved to be a forlorn hope though.

It's incredible to think that out of all the games played during my time at Aberdeen, I'll always remember a meaningless midweek friendly at Inverness. Don't ask me the score but a massive cloud of gloom descended over the Granite City that night.

And the reason - Fergie handed in his resignation.

The lure of Manchester United had proved too great for the man from Govan and he was on his way south. It was the end of an era at Aberdeen - the most successful in the club's history. Fergie had gone.

While many people at the club struggled to come to terms with his departure, I got on with my own personal fight – to save my career. Six months after my last game for Aberdeen, the rug was finally pulled from under my feet. It was the afternoon of Saturday, February 21, my 29th birthday. We had just brushed aside Falkirk 3-0 at Brockville, and that's when I learned my fate.

As a teenager, I'd endured months of complete darkness and came through the other end. Against all the odds I'd made it as a professional footballer and now, at my absolute peak, I was given the devastating news that I would never kick another ball. I was in pieces.

Back to the match at home to Hibs, my last appearance and when I'd hobbled off, I knew that all wasn't well. But did I ever think it was career ending? Not a chance. I was in pain, lots of it, and realised tough times lay ahead, with a lengthy spell on the sidelines, treatment, surgery perhaps and a period of rehabilitation, but that was all. I would soon be back playing and doing what I did best - knocking in goals for Aberdeen. It was the happiest time of my career and it didn't deserve to be cut short.

I was struggling, but people suffer for their art, it's what they do. I was told there was a small bone floating around in my back (traumatic spondilitis) and that it might have been there since birth. I wasn't too keen on that part of their professional prognosis. I'd always had issues with my back, but nothing that ever restricted me. In one game though, against Raith Rovers in the Scottish Cup, I'd scored a real Roy of the Rovers overhead kick. When I landed I felt slight pain in my back, but didn't ever think anything of it.

Due to the pain and restrictive nature of the injury, I couldn't train every day, and at that level it was something you had to do. It wasn't up for debate. You had to stay on the pace and be as fit, if not fitter, than your opponent. As a striker you have to be lightning quick over ten or 20 yards. The initial burst of speed, that gets you clear of opposing defenders, is a prerequisite. There was no way I could retain that by training just two or three times a week. It would soon go, and I knew it.

To get through the previous season's Scottish Cup final I'd taken powerful painkillers. It's always a gamble, but it worked at the time. But that game was consigned to the record books and the slate had been wiped clean. We were now playing for new honours.

The Hibs game signalled a new regime for me: an endless series of visits to hospitals, surgeons and clinics. Fergie, then his successor, Ian Porterfield, was desperate to get me back playing and, naturally, I was desperate to play again. We were singing from the same hymn sheet.

It was an extremely difficult period. I was still an Aberdeen player and turned up at Pittodrie every day like my team-mates, but while training was a means to an end for them, I was just going through the motions with no game to look forward to at the weekend.

I soon became very close to Tom Scotland, the city of Aberdeen's top surgeon. I made regular pilgrimages to see Tom and he did everything he could to help. I was sent down to Glasgow to see a leading chiropractor. I was a bit sceptical, but willing to try anything. He lifted me up and I soon heard these cracking sounds. I'm convinced that visit did me more harm than good, but what do I know, it was only my body.

Anyway, it soon came down to one particular visit, in the February, and I went along to Aberdeen Hospital for a meeting with a top surgeon. It was there that the final x-rays were taken. As I waited for the results, every possible scenario ran through my head, and each time it ended in a negative conclusion.

Finally, the door opened and in walked the surgeon, with a grave look on his face. He was holding up these huge x-rays and studying them closely. Occasionally, he would look from the x-ray to me, and back again.

Finally, he looked me straight in the eye and said, 'It's not good Frank, I don't think you'll ever play football again'.

I was stunned. Even though this had always been the most likely diagnosis, I couldn't comprehend the enormity of what this guy had just said. It hit me like a bombshell. Surely there was some mistake. I had just turned 29, that day, and was far too young for this to happen. Happy birthday, Frank. Hip-hip hooray.

I thanked him, for what, I don't know, and left the building. I went straight back to Pittodrie and made for the gaffer's office. I couldn't speak to anyone. I didn't even want to tell Ian Porterfield, whom I'd never even played under, but I had no choice. I knocked the door tentatively and walked in.

'It's over', I said.

The gaffer was gutted, he really was. We sat and looked at one another, each unaware of what to say for the best. I knew fine well that my three-year contract was up at the end of the season and I don't mind admitting that I tried to get a new one, but that was a non-starter.

I was so worried about my future. I was in my late 20s and the only thing I'd ever known was at an end. With no trade behind me, how would I survive? What did my future hold? I had a million and one questions, but no one to answer them. I was in a scary place.

I left the stadium feeling incredibly sorry for myself, but returned a couple of days later to clean out my locker. It was then up to the gaffer's office to discuss contractual pay-offs and I was handed £1500 for my troubles. No insurance, no claims, nothing else. It was a bitter pill to swallow.

I said my goodbyes to those I'd come to know as my friends and family. I got on well with everyone at the club and it was awful having to say cheerio. I went down to the dressing room and team-mates that I had grown particularly close to, like Alex McLeish, Peter Weir and Billy Stark, were all in a state of shock. I don't mind admitting there were tears shed, and they weren't all mine.

We had a fantastic group of players at Pittodrie and most of the guys enjoyed socialising with one another. That's what made this situation so difficult to accept. Working day in, day out with all these guys would stop. Just like that. And it wasn't just the players. Our physio Davie Wylie was a great guy and did all he could for me, but to no avail.

That was that. I left the building for the last time and as I walked down Pittodrie Street, the tears started to flow. And it would be quite a while before they stopped. What now?

As the train pulled out of Aberdeen station I was a sorry state. There was £1500 in my pocket and I was carrying a pair of useless football boots - the sum total of two-and-a-half years' hard graft. A career going places had dramatically hit the skids. It was tough leaving my adopted home, but an inbuilt Sat Nav device suggested I should head south to Glasgow and Cadder in particular.

Six months previously I had been on top of the world and banging in goals for fun. Football can give you the most amazing highs, but is also prone to being incredibly cruel just when the world appears to be, quite literally, at your feet. With no plans of any note, I didn't have a clue what was next on the McDougall agenda.

Football had been everything and when given my first break, I had gambled the lot on being a success. And I was, until fate stepped in and put the brakes on my career. And then came the most unexpected of calls.

McDouGOAL

It was a few weeks after I'd settled back in at my gran's house in Tresta Road. She was fussing over me and I was enjoying every minute of it. With the best will in the world though, the call was a couple of years too late. Frank McAvennie was back up in Scotland and playing with Celtic.

'Get yourself over to Celtic Park tomorrow, Billy McNeill wants a look at you', he said, and that was that. How did I feel that night? A mixture of joy and apprehension. The injury hadn't mysteriously disappeared overnight. I'd suck it and see.

The next morning, the training gear was packed neatly into a holdall - not a plastic bag, I wanted to make an impression - and I headed for Parkhead. Celtic were skint at the time and big Billy was no doubt after a bargain. If that was the case, he didn't get it because as you would expect, training was tough. Too tough, in fact. I couldn't handle it and called it a day, but not before I'd given it my best shot.

I was at Celtic for six weeks and no one knew I was there. I would slip in and out of training even though I was desperate for it to work out. It was tough getting so close to winning a deal with your boyhood idols, but I was able to console myself with the fact that I'd played for the best club in Scotland just beforehand.

Once I realised it wasn't going to happen and I told people that I'd been training at Parkhead, a few questioned my decision after I was stretchered off in that cup clash at St Mirren. That was in the past and as I've said previously, I was never one for holding grudges.

At Parkhead, I got talking to Johnny Doyle. He was a real Bhoy at heart and that showed in the way he was treated by the different halves of the Old Firm. Celtic fans loved him and Rangers supporters loathed everything about him. He seemed to revel in it.

During one training session, as we were going through our paces, he asked, 'Why didn't you join us when you had the chance? By all accounts you were a massive Celtic fan and the club wanted you. We couldn't believe it when you chose St Mirren over Celtic. I thought you were off your head'.

I couldn't believe this massive Celtic star had taken such an interest in me. When I explained what had gone on at Clydebank with Jack Steedman, Johnny just shook his head, but I think he viewed me in a different light after that.

Unfortunately, the whole Celtic thing didn't work out. I was philosophical about it and carried on with my life. I wasn't working so I had to sign on the dole. It was a soul-destroying experience. I had never been unemployed in my life and here I was, heading up to the Labour Exchange, in Springburn to collect a weekly giro for £32.

Football had been anything but a hard life, although nowadays you have star players flying off to China or Japan at the drop of a hat to keep their brand name at the top of the pecking order. But they're on thousands of pounds a week - I would've done it for a fraction of that.

What a difference though having to graft on building sites when my career was over. It was £200 for a week's hard labour, but there was no other option. I was so used to having money in my pocket. Believe me, the alternative to work would've been to do myself in, so I took the 'easy' way out.

Working on building sites affected my back just as much as playing football and I had to find an alternative. I gained employment as a part-time barman in the New Mosshouse, known locally as the 'Widows', which was in Possilpark. I'd been a customer at the bar previously, so I knew most of the punters.

During the day, I hung around with my Uncle Robert. He kept greyhounds and raced them at a nearby track, called Ashfield. I enjoyed the greyhounds and soon became involved. I would take the dogs for long walks, getting up at six o'clock in the morning to do so. It was a great way to come to terms with my injury and the end my career. I had lots of time to reflect during these walks and if the dogs didn't know my story beforehand, they certainly did afterwards.

At this point I was having a lot of 'if only' moments. I tried not to let the whole business get me down, but inevitably it does. One moment, football star, next, walking dogs. Actually, it still gets me down to this day, especially during moments of 'quiet reflection'. And you know what? It's as though it all happened yesterday. It's now more than 20 years since I was forced to quit Aberdeen, although it doesn't always feel like that. Time flies.

But while dog-walking may have allowed time for lots of thinking, it wasn't all positives. I was spending more and more time at the track and with that I started gambling. I had always enjoyed a punt, but it soon became a bit more than that.

Frank McGarvey, the former St Mirren and Celtic player, explains in his autobiography how gambling took control of his life. Well, it hadn't yet come to that with me, but I was creeping ever closer to rack and ruin. I worked desperately hard to keep it under control. I didn't have the cash to furnish such an expensive 'hobby' and I had to quit. It was a tough decision to actually carry through, but I managed it and to this day it's something I haven't again taken up.

Robert kept the dogs at kennels behind a pub called the Glen Douglas, which was a mere ten-minute walk from Cadder. Equally, Ashfield was only a 15-minute walk in the opposite direction. Robert's technically my uncle, but I always referred to him as my brother because we grew up in the same house. He was my gran and grandad's son.

Inevitably, I was spending more and more time at Ashfield with the dogs, but I was still surprised when Ashfield Juniors asked me to sign for them. A return to football wasn't something I had ever contemplated. I gave it some serious thought and decided to give it a go and see how the back would bear up.

I suppose I was still a relatively big name in football. It had only been a matter of months since I'd last played for Aberdeen, although going from the highs of the Scottish Cup Final, at Hampden to playing junior football at modest Saracen Park was something of a comedown. But my contract at Aberdeen had been ripped up and I was a free agent.

I played a couple of games for Ashfield, which was literally just over the wall from 'Shire's ground, but the back pain was too much to bear and I was forced to quit – again. Thankfully I didn't ever become a target for the boot boys, but the pain was just too much to bear.

And every time I went in for a challenge, or felt a twinge, the words of my surgeon came back to haunt me. 'If you play on the consequences could be disastrous'. Time to heed that warning, although my brief spell with Ashfield wouldn't be my last.

Eventually, I moved out of my gran's house and into a flat with my younger brother David and his girlfriend, Jane, in Maryhill. David had decided on a change of scenery and headed north from Bury to see if the grass was a nicer shade of green. It wasn't of course, and it was not too long before he decided to go back to England. Only this time he took me with him.

We were sitting having a beer one night when he told me of his plans. Before venturing north, David had worked with Supreme

Windows, and he had already been on the blower to his old boss, Colin Dunne, making arrangements to get his old job back.

It had been around 18 months since I'd left Aberdeen and it was only when he asked if I wanted to go with him I realised there was nothing to keep me in Glasgow, apart from my daughter, Kelly. Naturally I would still keep in touch.

David had taken the liberty of asking Colin about a job for his big brother and he'd agreed. When he told me about it, I accepted. Nothing ventured, and all that. Here I was, a generation later, chasing work south of the border just like dad.

My main problem was a lack of cash. You simply can't make a move of that magnitude without something to fall back on. Sure, I would go and live with my mum, but I was hell bent on paying my way. There was only one thing for it, and that was to sell the trophies and mementoes I'd amassed during my career. I've never been materialistic, but when it came to parting with my football prizes even I was quite sad. Nevertheless, needs must and up for grabs went my Bronze Boot, hat-trick balls, winner's medals, etc.

Of course, there were a few willing buyers, but I ended up punting the lot for just £500. It was tough parting with them, but there was no option. I needed the money just to survive. I know it sounds like a bit of an exaggeration, but it wasn't, I really was down on my luck.

Since then, friends have offered to buy them back on my behalf, but I've refused. I did what I did and I can't afford to look back. It was necessary at the time.

It was 1989 and I stayed with Supreme Windows for around seven or eight years. I'd never worked with UPVC windows before, but learned as I went along and thoroughly enjoyed the experience.

It was a good job. Not quite as fulfilling as banging in hat-tricks against the Old Firm, but fulfilling nevertheless. I ended up quite friendly with Colin, who was a Scottish lad. He also enjoyed a night at the dogs and we got on well.

I was then offered another opportunity to resurrect my football career. At first I wasn't too keen, after my previous experience at Ashfield. This time though, there was a few quid in it. It had been almost two years since I had kicked a ball in earnest and I missed it like crazy, but the words of that surgeon were still ringing in my ears, albeit not as loudly as they once had.

I'd had people at the door trying to sign me virtually from the moment I arrived in Bury, but David pointed me in the right direction. He played for Clitheroe in the North West Counties League and they were a decent outfit. It was probably a similar standard to the top junior level in Scotland.

However, while I knew it wouldn't benefit my health, I also had my crumbling morale to consider. Surely a semi-successful return to the beautiful game would boost it no end. David was a solid player and occupied the right back berth. The club approached me just three weeks after I arrived in Bury, offered £60 a week and I accepted. I decided to play through the pain barrier if that's what it took. I had missed football badly and while I was still gutted at what had gone on at Aberdeen, I was desperate to get back involved again.

I played a full season for Clitheroe and it was a good experience, although my back proved troublesome again and I had to call it a day. There was a real chance of me doing some serious damage had I continued to play, but it was just good to squeeze another season out my aching body and for that I was grateful.

During matches I hardly felt a thing, but the moment the game was over, and I climbed out the shower, the old back stiffened up.

In saying I enjoyed it, I hated playing against teams from Liverpool. The Scousers used to wind me up constantly by grabbing my privates and calling me a Scots git. That really got on my nerves and a few times I was close to giving them it back with interest. I played virtually every week and scored a lot of goals. I remember the first goal I scored and celebrated like I'd just scored the winner in the Scottish Cup final. It felt special, scoring after such a long time out the game.

I was working full-time, but Colin was fantastic and getting time off, especially to travel to away games, was never an issue. Having an understanding boss when you're a part-time player is worth its weight in gold.

I travelled from Bury to Clitheroe every Tuesday and Thursday for training, a round trip of some 50 miles. But after leaving the club I divorced myself from football...until another mate asked if I'd like to play for a Sunday morning pub team.

I had been offered £40 a game, but after just a handful of matches, I suffered a broken leg. This hulking centre-half, who was probably still drunk from the night before, came scything through the back of me and I knew straight away that it wasn't good.

Metaphorically speaking, he had halved me in two. The leg was a mess and there was only one sensible option to take - quit, and this time for good.

In a way, I was hanging on to the fact that I had been a professional footballer, but it wasn't paying the mortgage any more and it was time to hang up the boots.

Knowing, like I did, that I would never again play football was hard to take. Of course, it was the only option I had, but that didn't make it any easier to accept. I had been mucking around in the lower leagues, attempting to hold on to something that had died a painful death. I had to let go.

And once I had accepted my fate, I switched off from the game altogether. I refused to attend matches and made sure the TV stayed off whenever there was football on. It was many, many years before I would ever watch another game.

I enjoyed living in Bury, which has a population of just 60,000. It's a decent place, maybe twice the size of Cadder, but, more importantly, my family was there and that was all that mattered. I had a job and it was good, but the life I was living was far removed from that of a professional footballer. But how many kids actually get to fulfil their dream of playing football for a living. I had lived that dream and, in that respect, I was fortunate.

Just after leaving Clitheroe, I met a lovely girl called Jane while having a drink one night in a pub called The Woolpack, in Bury, which was run by my sister Margaret. It wasn't long before our relationship blossomed and we married in 1992. We set up home in the town and were soon celebrating the birth of my second child. Deanna was born in 1995 and is someone who has made me extremely proud.

Even though things didn't work out with Jane and me and we eventually divorced, we still keep in touch and get on really well. Deanna is a great girl and we see each other often. Jane and I were together for three years and our parting was amicable. As I said before, life's too short...

Not long after the split up, I received a boost when it was announced that Aberdeen were to play Bury in a pre-season friendly at Gigg Lane. The match couldn't come round quickly enough. I was like an excited schoolkid on the day of the game and was delighted to get an invite to the hospitality suite for a couple of drinks prior to kick-off. The room was filled with all the usual ex-players, committee men and wealthy supporters.

I took a walk out to the tunnel and chatted to a few of the Aberdeen squad and backroom guys whom I remembered. I had a brief word with the manager, Alex Miller, and also spoke to an old adversary of mine, Paul Hegarty, who was Miller's assistant.

Without me knowing, a mate of mine had a quiet word with a Bury club official. I was astounded when he approached me and asked if I would make the half time draw, seeing as I was an ex-Dons player. As soon as the players headed in for their half time cuppa I was taken to the side of the park and I don't mind admitting, there were nerves on show. Maybe not as many as the Scottish Cup final, but there were nerves.

There were around two or three thousand Aberdeen fans down for the match and they were making one heck of a din. For a pre-season friendly, the atmosphere was electric. When I walked out onto the park, I don't think too many people noticed. When the mic man announced over the PA system that former Aberdeen player Frank McDougall was making the half-time draw; the away end erupted.

Suddenly, I was transported back in time and it felt as though I'd just scored my fourth goal against Celtic. It was incredibly moving.

After pulling out the winning tickets, I headed over to the terracing where the Dons fans were housed and I was moved to tears. It was such an emotional moment and it was amazing to see all the red scarves and flags. All sorts of memories came flooding back. They chanted my name as if I'd never been away and I signed dozens, no, make that hundreds, of autographs. But I wasn't finished there.

That night I was out on the town with the supporters and we had a ball. The partying went on into the wee small hours and everyone went home happy. It was a feeling of great elation to know that I was still revered in the Granite City. As if I ever doubted it for a minute.

Back-to-back to the nine to five and I had packed in the windows after eight years and moved into gates and railings with Georgian Gates, a company owned by a friend of mine, Gary Howarth. I thought I'd try something different and this fitted the bill perfectly. Again I started learning the game from scratch and was soon made up to gaffer. It was around this time that I met a girl called Jackie, in another Bury pub.

We talked about running our own boozer and in 2000, were handed the keys to our very own bar – The Woolpack. The same place my sister had managed nine or ten years previously for Whitbread. It was sheer coincidence, nothing more. We were desperate to make a real go of the business, although I decided to keep on working, just as an insurance policy. It was tough trying to work around the two but necessary.

We decided to get married, but not until we had the pub up and running and it was once again established in the local community. One of our biggest problems was a lack of parking. The pub was slap bang on a main road, which in itself wasn't a huge problem, but our customers had nowhere to park.

With the biggest majority of the spadework done, we talked about the opening ceremony. Who could we get to open the bar? We wanted a big name and I thought about Fergie. Well, they don't come much bigger than Fergie, certainly not in the Greater Manchester area.

There was one snag though. The night we had set for our grand opening was the night after Manchester United were due to play Real Madrid in a vital Champions League match - in Madrid. I didn't think there was any chance of Fergie being back in time. I decided to ask anyway, not thinking for a moment I could pull it off. I called him at Old Trafford and he said in a flash that he would do it.

'But you're in Madrid the night before', I said.

'You just leave that to me, Frank'.

I was amazed. Not that he was going to try and move heaven and earth to do me a huge favour, because that was the kind of man he was, but that he hadn't called me 'McDougall'.

Seriously though, I asked and he had accepted. I didn't think for a minute he would let me down, but from the moment he agreed, until he arrived at The Woolpack, I was a bundle of nerves. Was it logistically possible for him to get back to Lancashire in time? I would soon find out. It was all over the local papers that Fergie was coming to Bury to open Frank McDougall's pub and the streets were buzzing.

Cue potential problem number two. The last thing I wanted was trouble, as Bury has a massive contingent of Manchester City fans and the rivalry is pretty tasty, to say the least. I had a good contact in the local constabulary and got in touch to explain my concerns. Job done, and on the night, the local cop shop sent sixteen officers and two undercover cops to mingle with punters inside the bar.

As the gala opening edged ever nearer, the sweats got worse. He wouldn't let me down, would he? I had never let Fergie down on the park, although he did catch me having a fly puff on a couple of occasions during training. And then there was the time I got the bus back from training. All these negative little thoughts started creeping into my mind.

But before I knew it, the night was upon me and 6000, that's right, 6000 people lined the streets of Bury to get a glimpse of me, or was it Fergie? There was no sign of him as the clock ticked ever closer to the 6pm opening time. But I knew he wouldn't let me down.

And he didn't, because his car roared into view with a few minutes to spare. He abandoned it directly facing the pub and made his way across to the front door, with a massive grin on his face. I breathed a huge sigh of relief at this wonderful sight and greeted him like a long lost son. Cameras clicked and folk screamed his name and like the star he is, Fergie took it all in his stride.

Then came the opening ceremony. Just before he cut the ribbon, which was red, of course, he said, 'If Frank could pass a pub the way he passed a ball, he'd be worth £50 million'. The crowd lapped it up and so did I. For a split second, I was back in tow with my old boss and it felt wonderful.

Initially I'd had my doubts about asking Fergie to perform the opening ceremony. After all, he was a busy man and it had been quite some time since I'd seen him, but that didn't seem to matter. He was brilliant and I can't thank him enough for that. To rush back from an important Champions League match in Madrid to open a pub for a former player speaks volumes about the man.

Sure, we had our differences at Pittodrie, but when he needed me I stepped up to the plate, and now it was payback time. His son, Jason, accompanied him that night and that also brought back memories. I'd given Jason the boots I'd worn the day I scored four goals against Celtic and he told me he still had them. Listen, they were blue, so what would I want with them?

We went inside The Woolpack after the opening ceremony and Fergie whispered something in his son's ear. Jason nipped outside and was back again in minutes. And with him he had a pile of Manchester United souvenirs for my prize raffle. I was speechless. The pub was packed and even though I knew they had all come to see Fergie, it put The Woolpack on the map and I did okay out of it.

After that there was a real bond between Fergie and me. I appeared on Man Utd TV a few times and we would talk regularly on the phone. He invited me up to the training ground on a number of occasions and again we'd sit and chat about the old days. He came and spoke at a few sportsman's dinners and packed them into The Woolpack. I was always one for trying to attract the biggest names in the business. That's why I'd gone for Fergie in the first place.

After around five months in the pub trade, business started to dip a little and Jackie and I held 'crisis' talks. It was clear that a number of things were the cause of it. Parking was still an issue and there was also a general downturn in the industry. We decided to get out and handed the pub back to the owners, Pubmaster. It had been hard work and, although we hadn't made millions, it was all good experience, which would come in handy a few years later. But it was time to get out because the long hours had left me jaded. I was pretty stressed out.

Jackie and I married in the June of 2000 and our wedding reception was one of the last functions we held at the pub. A few months later though, I just took off for Aberdeen and went on a week-long drinking binge - without the wife. It wasn't the cleverest thing to do, but it was maybe a reaction to the stress I'd suffered trying to make the pub a success.

I hadn't been eating and had lost about three stone in weight. People were constantly telling me that I didn't look good and I suppose it all got to me in the end. I hooked up with a few friends in the Granite City and let my hair down. I knocked it back like there was no tomorrow and, to a certain extent, I had a great time. It was soon time to head back to Bury though and face the music.

Understandably, Jackie was furious, and who could blame her? We worked at it again and things eventually got back to normal. I went back to working with Georgian Gates and not long after, my brother, James, opened up his own gates and railings business and I started working for him.

Through time though, Jackie and I grew apart and decided to go our separate ways. No break up is ever easy and this was certainly no different, but at least it was amicable. I was single again, and it would be a couple of years before I notched up marriage number four.

Despite the back problems, I was still able to play snooker - thank God - and enjoyed my fair share of success south of the border.

I'm quite friendly with three-times world champion John Higgins and was at a club one night with John and the multi-talented 'Rocket' Ronnie O'Sullivan. We played a few frames and despite still knocking in breaks of 60 and 70, I was absolutely nowhere near the standard of these guys.

We had a few drinks during the course of the evening and, as it was a rare night out for the guys, they were letting their hair down. I'd started off at a decent pace, on the drink, and noticed that Ronnie was sinking a few and becoming a bit worse for wear. When opportunity knocks, Frankie Boy is there to take advantage. A few drinks later, I racked up the balls.

'C'mon Ronnie, show me what you're made of.' And of course, Ronnie loves a challenge.

But on this occasion, I was by far the soberer of the two and I whipped his butt on the green baize. How many people, can say that? Not too many I'd imagine.

During the summer of 2006, I was enjoying a few beers with some mates one evening when in walked this girl. As soon as I heard her talking I knew she wasn't local. We got chatting and she asked what I did for a living.

'I'm a painter,' I said, strangely. She looked impressed. 'What do you paint', she asked.

'Houses', I said, laughing.

'Oh, I thought you were an artist'.

She didn't seem too disappointed and we were soon enjoying each other's company, despite the fact she wasn't talking to the next TS Lowry. It transpired that Frank, from Cadder, was soon dating a Brazilian girl by the name of Isabel Baptista and she would soon become the fourth Mrs McDougall. But not before I had sorted out the mandatory problems I seemed to serve up.

She was going through a divorce at the time and I failed to tell her I was still married to Jackie as I hadn't bothered to get a divorce. That caused more than a few problems when it came out because we'd decided to get married and couldn't because I was still hitched.

She wasn't happy at all. That 'wee white lie' definitely put a strain on our relationship. I couldn't believe I'd been so stupid, but thankfully she forgave me. It was a great relief, because I'd grown so close to Isabel and to mess things up due to something so stupid would've been a crying shame.

It wasn't long before Isabel fell pregnant and we were expecting a child. We were over the moon. Tragically, though, she miscarried. A few months later, Isabel was pregnant again, but with a similar outcome. It was a tough time and naturally we were distraught.

We decided she should go home to Brazil for a time and see her family. She was feeling down and it was hoped that a trip home would perk her up. I was soon missing her like mad and scraped the money together to head over to Brasilia for a visit. It was great to be back with Isabel and I was soon at ease in the company of her family.

One day, though, my future brother-in-law, Ricardo, and I headed out on his fishing boat. What could be better than sitting relaxing on a trim little skiff with a bottle of beer and the sunshine? I thought I was Jack the lad and sat there with my top off and a soft hat covering my face.

After around an hour, we stopped at a nearby jetty for a bite to eat and that's when I started to feel strange. I was beetroot red and struggling to eat. I felt awful. Ricardo took me to a nearby hospital and I was admitted straight away. My 'sunburn' turned out to be second degree burns and I was holed up in the local hospital for four days. At one point medics insisted it was 'touch and go', such was the severity of my burns.

I was on a drip and my whole body was shaking. It was an experience I never want to go through again. In fact, if I'm ever in a hot country I make sure I cover up from head to toe. We were engaged while in Brazil and stayed for around four weeks. When we headed back to Bury, I was staying at my mum's place and Isabel was going through her divorce.

We eventually married in our adopted home town and I was soon back working at the gates and railings. My job took me all over England though and it was tough on Isabel, what with the miscarriages still fresh in her mind and me away from home so much. We were renting a generously sized house from a friend of mine, Craig Maxwell, but it was difficult to maintain a decent standard of living with just one wage coming in. We recognised the need to come up with a plan, because living on the edge simply wasn't good for the health.

I put the feelers out and a few folk, including the likes of Alex McLeish, wanted to help. It was nothing more than initial contact, but at least I had made the move.

Isabel then got in touch with a friend of hers and he made a few phone calls. One of our options was to move into the pub trade and we eventually landed the Criterion Bar, in Guild Street, Aberdeen.

It was an extremely popular bar and was situated in the historical harbour part of the city, an area I knew well thanks to some great nights out while a Dons player. And we were informed that the immediate locale was to benefit from massive regeneration, mainly in the form of a multi-million pound shopping complex directly across the road from 'Frank McDougall's Sports Bar.'

When I'd initially heard the bar was in Aberdeen, I got goosebumps. I was delighted because I genuinely do feel comfortable and at home in the city. I love Aberdeen and have lots of friends there, so the move was perfect. Let's be honest, we had to do something and I'd already dabbled in the pub business so it was the most likely way forward, despite Isabel once thinking I was a painter. And while it would be long hours, it was something we would be able to do together.

The pub game is tough and you have to put in the hours, but it's like most things in life, if you work hard enough, you get your rewards. Some nights you can take a decent amount at the bar, but only a small percentage of the takings are actually yours. I'm not complaining though, because it's providing us with a living and I enjoy the banter and the folk you get to meet. I had the pub up for sale at the end of last year, but it's off the market now and it's full steam ahead. I'll probably stick at it until 2013, when the lease expires, and then look for something else. I like a bit of variety.

People often ask if I'd consider getting back into football, in either a coaching or managerial capacity. It's a difficult one because there's so much pressure in the game these days and winning is absolutely everything. Maybe if I'd retired on my terms then the next natural step would've been to coach, but it really was the last thing on my mind when I was forced out the game. A mate of mine, John Brady, called me up when junior side Shotts Bon Accord were looking for a manager, but while it was nice to get the offer, it just wasn't on, due to the pub and the travelling.

And the pressure wouldn't have been too good for the old ticker, especially as I've already suffered a couple of heart attacks. Number one arrived in 2002 when I was busy working at Georgian Gates. I felt slight pains in my chest and tingles in my arm and soon realised that all wasn't well. I went straight to Bury General Hospital and was put on a heart monitor, but was released after a short time. It was a frightening experience nevertheless. The second scare happened around a year later and while it was another small one, it was still a real frightener. It makes you think that you should slow down and make a few adjustments in your life. It's not easy, though.

So the time had come for another cross-border journey and it was with a heavy heart that Isabel and I drove out of Bury en-route to our new life in the north-east of Scotland. Bury was good for me. It was there when I needed it - when there was nothing for me in Scotland.

Of course, I would return, but for now, it was full steam ahead to the Granite City. When I returned to Aberdeen and the Criterion Bar, there was one guy that I was desperate to see again. While at the Dons, Teddy Scott had played a big part in my life and was always there to extinguish the flames of unrest whenever Fergie and I clashed.

Isabel and I decided to pay him a visit in his home town of Ellon. I knew that Teddy lived in Commercial Road, but didn't have a clue where it was or what number he lived at. I eventually found the road and knocked on a random door. 'Do you know where Teddy Scott lives?'

'Aye son, just over there'. I had a hunch that everyone would know Teddy and I was right. I was soon standing at his front door.

His wife answered and immediately asked how I was. I was all the better for standing at Teddy's front door and talking to her, I can tell you.

The legend was soon standing before me and we embraced. It was long and meaningful and followed by a good old chinwag. In all the years I've been around the city of Aberdeen, I've never heard anyone say a bad word about Teddy.

Acquaintances renewed, it was time to get down to business. I was back in Aberdeen and the next chapter in my life was about to begin. It was time to roll the sleeves up and get stuck in. Hard work was something that never frightened me and it would stand me in good stead for my next challenge.

MY FINAL GOAL
(STARRING KING KENNY, ROD & OTHERS)

TO get a decent job these days, you need to have an impressive CV. Somehow though, the Bronze Boot, hat-tricks and winners medals didn't count for much when I was sitting in the Job Centre after leaving the Dons.

My curriculum vitae also included several outings at our national stadium. I played in finals of the Scottish Cup, League Cup, Drybrough Cup and numerous semis.

However, one of the proudest moments of my career arrived in the early days while I was at Clydebank. We were to play Queen's Park in a cup replay, away from home. It was an honour to be involved in the whole Hampden experience, from arriving at the ground in the team bus and walking through the same door as so many famous players had done so before, to settling down in the dressing room and listening to the manager's pre-match talk.

Then it was out onto the famous turf for a warm-up before the actual match itself. It was quite an experience and even though I went on to make numerous appearances at the national stadium, I'll always remember that midweek cup match against Queens.

But as we all know, Hampden had seen better days and by the mid-1990s, plans were at an advanced stage to upgrade, nay, rebuild the place and give Scotland a stadium to be proud of for the new Millennium. Of course, when I left the Dons in 1987, I didn't think I'd ever be in the old place again, unless spectating at a showpiece match, or rocking along to Status Quo.

Unlike Bob Geldof, I don't particularly dislike Mondays, but on one particular occasion, I wasn't exactly having the best start to the week.

It was day one on a new job and the gates I was erecting were posing more than a few problems. Then came the call, straight out of the blue. My old mate Cowboy McCormack was on the blower to inform me that a match was being played on New Year's Day to commemorate the opening of the new Hampden. He invited me to take part in it.

Now that all depended on what he meant by 'taking part'. Was he looking for a flag bearer, or someone to flog pies? At that time I would've been more likely to eat them.

'I want you to play. The least you'll get is a seat on the bench.' He chuckled, before saying, 'You're my star striker. Well, you and Kenny Dalglish.'

King Kenny. What a daft question Cowboy, of course I'll play.

I was playing with Clitheroe at the time in the North-West Counties League, so I was still in relatively good shape. It was something I looked forward to from the moment the call came, to the day and hour I travelled back up the road to Glasgow. I was like an excited nipper playing for the school team for the first time when I caught the train from Manchester to Glasgow. In fact, I was that enthusiastic, I was in the queue for the train half-an-hour or so before the damned thing was due to leave. I even trained prior to the game.

The match, an All Star XI Versus a Queen Park XI, was live on Sky Sports and, probably for the final time, it was an opportunity to play in yet another high profile match.

The train finally chugged into Central Station and I jumped in a taxi to Hampden. The driver was keen to know what was going on in the south side of the city and when I filled him in, he said something about enjoying the 'old crocks' matches. Is that what I was now, an old crock? The conversation gave me food for thought as I climbed the stairs to the impressive new Hampden, before easing my way through the front door. I was soaking up every moment.

The first thing that struck me was the lack of a fanfare, which had heralded my last visit in 1986, as part of the successful Aberdeen side that dismantled a forlorn Hearts XI in front of almost 63,000 people. But I could live with that and was just delighted to have received the invitation from Cowboy in the first place.

I was one of the first to arrive and was shown to an impressive suite to await the arrival of my colleagues-for-a-day. One by one the great and the good of Scottish football made their grand entrance. Tommy Burns, Danny McGrain, Owen Coyle, Billy Stark and Pat Bonner were among them, as was arguably the finest Scottish footballing export, King Kenny. The match organisers had indeed pulled out all the stops, but it was soon obvious that some sort of superstar was taking part.

Suddenly, the door opened and this lengthy entourage filed in, followed by chart-topping singer, Rod Stewart. What a coup. Not far behind Rod came Tony Roper, star of enduring BBC comedy Rab C. Nesbitt. It certainly had all the makings of a fantastic day and, if nothing else, we were assured of some fabulous entertainment. There was no fee for taking part in the match, but I was more than happy to play and even paid my own train fare.

With the kick-off approaching, we made our way down to the fantastic new dressing rooms to prepare for the match. Cowboy handed over the boots he'd picked me up; while they looked a bit on the big side, they'd do. I was hoping they were my passport to the Guinness Book of Records as the scorer of the first ever goal at the new stadium. Standing between history and myself was Mr Dalglish, a few former Queen's Park players and an assortment of others.

My dodgy back wasn't an issue, despite Kenny Dalglish referring to me as 'Frankie Bad Back' during our team talk. He was in great form throughout the pre-match chat, although no doubt the occasion was just a touch more laid back than the three European Cup finals he played in for Liverpool. We were put through our paces before kick-off and I was particularly taken by the footwork of Rod Stewart. He looked more than capable and the stories I'd heard previously about him shunning a pro football career to become a pop star were obviously true.

Kenny and I lined up alongside one another in my dream attacking partnership and the game started at a pretty competitive pace. There were more than 20,000 fans inside Hampden and the all-seated arena was looking better than I'd ever seen it, although some of the old terracing charm had gone.

I've never been the best at passing when I was in front of goal and this game would be no different. Getting that record was in my mind, but I missed three great chances in the first five minutes and I was gutted. Had the opportunity gone? Maybe not. I was clean through on goal and destined to score when, scythe, my legs were taken from me by a no-nonsense Queen's defender. I'd been hauled down just as I was about to pull that lethal right-foot trigger.

I'm convinced I heard the roar of the fans in the traditional Celtic end, despite the stand being empty. Not to worry though, there was still the opportunity to score from 12 yards.

Ten minutes beforehand I wouldn't have got a sniff at taking the spot-kick because the gaffer's instructions before leaving the sanctuary of the dressing room was that if we got a penalty, Rod Stewart was the man. Fair enough, but right at this moment in time, Rod was lying in the treatment room with an ice pack covering a gaping leg wound that would later require 17 stitches. Rod had just met hard-as-nails Queen's Park legend Eddie Hunter.

I finally got to my 41-year-old legs and looked for the ball. I couldn't see it anywhere. Then, I noticed it tucked safely under the arm of Mr Dalglish and was I about to argue with possibly the greatest footballer ever produced by our small nation? No chance, although I swear I saw him flick a wry smile in my direction as he stepped forward to place the ball 12 yards from goal.

Of course, King Kenny stroked the ball home and we were 1-0 up. Sigh. I suppose I should be happy that I had played a part in the first ever goal scored at the new stadium, but the truth is I took no comfort from it at all. But I suppose it's still something to tell the grandkids. That I teamed up with Kenny Dalglish to score the goals that won the match. We eventually won 2-1 and I scored the winner.

If I don't mind saying so myself, it was an excellent goal. I ran all of 80 yards before slotting the ball past the Queens keeper - and collapsing in a heap on the famous Hampden turf. It took a few team-mates to haul me back to my feet just so the game could continue. Had that been a Dons match, I'd have been hooked by Fergie for being in charge of an unfit torso, but he wasn't within 200 miles and I played the entire 90 minutes. God only knows how I got through it. Maybe we'd used all our subs.

I was suddenly thankful for having lasted the course when I saw poor Rod at the end, hobbling around with the weight of the world on his shoulders. It's never easy watching someone receive treatment - especially stitches - in the dressing room after being on the wrong end of a bruising challenge, but it was the funniest thing watching the medics fuss over Rod at half-time.

McDouGOAL

Wee Tony Roper, who is probably best known for playing Jamesie Cotter, in Rab C was watching over Rod as the needle and thread was being weaved through his injured leg. Suddenly, he burst into song and started belting out, 'Wake up Rodney, I think I got something to say to you...' to the tune of one of the crooner's biggest hits. Maybe, he should have sang 'The First Cut is the Deepest, instead!

The pop legend obviously didn't appreciate the comedian's efforts to cheer him up and promptly told him to f*** off. Ironically, it was Tony who had replaced the injured Rod on the park, but he did as he was told and for once he was lost for words. It was a magical moment and I'm sure even Rod had a good laugh about it once the pain had gone.

There were so many good players on display that afternoon and it was good to see the likes of Starky and others. In fact, even Cowboy had a good game and it was something else being in the battle-hardened defender's company, 20 years after we'd first teamed up together. After the match, we were waited on hand and foot by the match sponsors at a fabulous post-match reception.

It was great mixing with the likes of Kenny and Rod and I enjoyed talking to both guys. Then I noticed another idol of mine sitting quietly in the corner chatting to a few admirers. It was the great Jimmy Johnstone, probably the most talented winger ever to jink his way down the flanks of Scottish football. I joined him for a while and was soon listening to a myriad of wonderful stories from a superb career. I could've sat there all night and listened to those tales.

It had been a superb day and I'll forever be indebted to Cowboy for giving me the nod. For just a few hours I was transported back in time to the glory days. It was an honour to play alongside some great players one last time and, so what if Kenny Dalglish got the first ever goal at the revamped national stadium.

I THINK I'M ALONE NOW

YOU can never quite prepare yourself for the type of call I received on the evening of December 23, 2009. It was just after 10pm and my sister Margaret was on the other end of the phone. I couldn't quite take in what she was saying. Apparently, mum had collapsed in her local pub while playing darts and was in a bad way. There had been no warning whatsoever.

She was in a coma and things weren't looking good. Naturally, Margaret was in a state of frenzy and I made arrangements to head south to Bury the following day, Christmas Eve. Mum was a keen darts player and was popular at her local, with many, many friends. She reckoned there was nothing worse than being cooped up in the house, so she liked to get out as often as possible.

The train journey from Aberdeen to Lancashire gave me time to think. My mind jumped back and forward between the period I'd spent in Bury, after I finished playing, and the early years, when I had remained in Glasgow while mum and dad headed south. I thought back 25 years to the moment I received a phone call to say that dad was in hospital and in a bad way. I'd rushed down from Aberdeen, getting there just before he passed away. This seemed awfully like history repeating itself.

It was early evening by the time I reached my destination and I jumped a taxi straight to the hospital. Mum was still in a coma and hadn't regained consciousness since her fall in the pub the night before. It was hard to watch her just lying there and I asked the doctor why she wasn't doing anything to help. How could they just let her lie there like that? She insisted there was nothing they could do.

It was confirmed that she'd suffered a massive brain haemorrhage and in the end, it would prove too much for her to cope with. I sat with mum for almost 24 hours and it was Margaret who eventually suggested I head up to mum's house for a sleep. I was completely done in. Unfortunately, while I was off for a snooze, mum passed away. She died on Christmas Day. As soon as I heard, I went straight back to the hospital and sat with her for a few hours.

I was absolutely distraught. My gran and grandad had been a massive part of my life and brought me up, but when mum died I felt so alone for the first time ever. It was a strange, strange feeling. I spoke to the doctor again and she explained that they had more or less been waiting on all the vital organs closing down. That was so hard to accept. She had been too far gone and her whole life had come down to the family sitting around, waiting for her to slip away. It was a terrible time.

I was so glad I'd seen her though. That meant so much. I reckon it made things easier to accept. When you're heading down on the train it's always at the back of your mind that she may just pass away while you're travelling. Being able to spend time with her made a difference. Chances are mum may not even have known I was by her bedside, but you like to believe that she knew.

I hung around for a while before heading back up the road to Aberdeen. Again, the journey was lengthy. I couldn't wait to get home to Isabel, and she was fantastic. Since mum passed away my brother James has opened a little takeaway food shop called Ma's Kitchen, close to where she lived for 38 years. It's in a tidy wee part of Bury and when James told me I was chuffed. I thought it a really nice touch.

You know, I phoned her at six o'clock in the morning recently. I suddenly thought, 'What the hell am I doing?' I completely forgot. The saving grace for my family is that mum's death was sudden. I don't think she suffered so that's the positive we take from it. I'll miss her, but I have lots of memories to remind me of the good times.

So, what now for Frank McDougall? There is a dream and I may as well share it, because if it comes off, you can say you read it here first. Eventually, Isabel and I are hoping to head back over to Brazil and open a bar in her home city of Brasilia.

And I'd like to - wait for it - run a soccer school. Yes, I know, a Scot teaching the Brazilians how to play football. But why not?

Once upon a time I was nicknamed Zico, so maybe I have what it takes to pass on some of the knowledge I've picked up over the years to a crop of little Brazilian kids who want to play football the Scottish way. And you know what, after the minor heart scares, heading to Brazil might not be a bad idea. After the life I've lived, I reckon a few years in that laid back South American country, with the addition of some decent sun block, may just be the key to longevity.

Naturally there are issues. The first, and most important, centres on my kids. I don't know if I could cope with being on the other side of the world, 7000 miles away. That's a tough one. Lots of soul-searching would have to take place beforehand.

I'm sure it's a case of trial and error. It might be that we head over for an initial period of three months and see how it goes. Who knows, the Brazilians might already know enough about soccer and my services may not be required. I'm currently learning Portuguese because if I do ever go, I'd want to fully embrace their culture.

In saying that, if my dreams of becoming a beach volleyball referee are to be fulfilled, I'd have to move to somewhere like Rio, as Brasilia is totally landlocked. The advantage is that it is a 100 per cent up and coming city. But knowing my luck, Macca would get to officiate at the women's doubles and I'd be left with the men's game.

There are many things in my life that I've achieved that I'm extremely proud of. Football has taken me to places I would never have visited in a million years and has also allowed me to rub shoulders with some of the game's greatest characters.

Whether that has been Abie Monaghan at Glasgow Perthshire, or Sir Alex Ferguson, it's all one and the same because at the end of the day we are all equal and meeting the likes of Abie helped set me on the road to the top. Whether or not I actually reached it is another matter.

Winning the Bronze Boot and claiming a domestic clean sweep of trophies were high points, but scoring four goals for Rangers Athletic in the semi-final of a competition in Edinburgh was equally as important at the time. When all is said and done though, I'm so proud of the fact that I was once the most expensive footballer in the country. When I think back to that period it simply blows my mind.

Frank McDougall, scheme boy, transferred from Clydebank to St Mirren for a whopping £180,000. It's simply mind-boggling. And isn't it ironic that I would enjoy the most successful years of my career when Fergie had paid around half that total to take me to Aberdeen?

It certainly is a funny old game and while I may have been just one tiny cog in the massive football machine, I loved every minute and wouldn't change it for the world. I've had a ball. There are the odd occasions when I realise that had I been born a generation or two later, then my goals could've made me a millionaire. I can't take the blame for that, of course, it's all down to my dad.

So, where do I belong? Wherever life takes me, I suppose. I absolutely adore Glasgow, but at the moment I feel as though I belong to Aberdeen. Doesn't quite fit in with the song though. And then there's Bury, my home for 20 years.

I've had a wonderful career though, and just want to say a big thanks to everyone who played even the smallest part in making it all possible.

You've heard enough from me now, so here's a little word or two from my friends…

BEING FRANK ABOUT FRANK

Sir Alex Ferguson C.B.E.

I WAS well aware of Frank's talents long before I signed him for Aberdeen. Actually, the memory of this takes me back, and still makes me chuckle to this day.

It was around 1977 and I was manager of St Mirren. I'd heard rave reports about this young centre forward who'd been knocking in the goals for Glasgow Perthshire, so I went up to take a look for myself.

Off I went to Possil to take in a Perthshire game and I liked what I saw. This young lad had an eye for goal and technically, he was also very good. 'This one's got a chance', I thought.

By all accounts he was a bit of a scallywag in those days, but he definitely knew where the goal was. You could see it even then and that was all I was interested in. It's a huge step up from the juniors to the Scottish Premier League but some lads just have what it takes.

I arranged for Frank to come along to Love Street for a trial, and he duly turned up on time, which always impresses me. He was around 18 or 19 at the time, came ambling in, along with his brother, and said, 'I'm Frank McDougall and I'm here for a trial'.

I took one look at him and said, 'Okay, but haven't you forgotten something?' He looked confused so I asked him where his boots were. The embarrassed expression said it all. He had forgotten them. It was hardly a great start. Naturally I sent him packing with a flea in his ear and he just turned round and walked away.

I left St Mirren not long afterwards and I believe he had another trial, in which he played a reserve game or two, but I just hope he remembered the proper footwear.

The next time he came onto my radar was in 1984. We'd just lost Mark McGhee to Hamburg for around £300,000 and I knew exactly who I wanted to replace him. Frank had been doing well with St

Mirren and I knew he could do a job for me at Pittodrie. I spoke to my brother, Martin, who was on the coaching staff, at Love Street, and he had nothing but good to say of him.

He was a different type of player to McGhee, who had led the Aberdeen line well, but Frank was a natural born goal scorer, and they are worth their weight in gold. Always have been, and always will be.

I knew I was getting good money for McGhee, but I went in ridiculously low for Frank and initially offered £20,000. Of course, St Mirren chased me, but I eventually got him for £100,000. As far as I was concerned it was a great piece of business.

There was talk of me wanting Frank McAvennie over the Frank I ended up with, but that's nonsense. If the truth be told, I'd probably have taken both, but I got my man. Anyway, McAvennie was beginning to make a bit of a name for himself and I was aware of interest from England, and West Ham in particular, so I knew the fee would be inflated.

St Mirren had a good team at that time, and Frank was playing alongside the likes of McAvennie, Billy Abercromby and Dougie Somner. I'd already taken players such as Peter Weir and Billy Stark north and both had showed up well. I had no hesitation in going back for Frank.

When we're talking natural goal scorers, he was up there with the very best. Possibly the best I've worked with and that's saying something.

In a match between Manchester United and Arsenal last season, Wayne Rooney scored the most amazing goal. He sprinted 20 or 30 yards to get on the end of a pass, controlled it, steadied himself, adjusted his body and scored, all within the space of a few seconds.

There aren't many players capable of scoring such a goal, but Frank is definitely one of them. That was how highly I rated him. He was up there with the very best. Frank was an extremely intelligent footballer. His movement and positional play was very good and, as I've said, he could score goals.

He was also a very good trainer. Let's put it this way, he wouldn't have been allowed to be a 'bad' trainer at Aberdeen; that simply wasn't on. There was no shirking on our training ground, although I've heard the stories.

If I had a criticism, it was that he was vulnerable to some of life's excesses. I'm not going to judge him, but he maybe didn't surround himself with the best of friends. I had to fine him a few times for being out on the town when he shouldn't have been, but he certainly wasn't a difficult player to handle.

Frank may have let himself down when he wasn't with me. I didn't know what he was getting up to so there's always the chance that perhaps his diet wasn't what it could've been. Who knows what might have happened had I been given the opportunity to work with him a lot earlier in his career.

During his first season at Pittodrie, he was outstanding. He scored more than 20 league goals, despite actually missing quite a few games. It was a phenomenal rate, but he absolutely thrived on being surrounded by quality players and, of course, he was one himself.

Should he have been capped by Scotland at that time? Possibly. But there's quite often a number of things that come into the equation when an international cap is on the line. Kenny Dalglish was doing the rounds then and he would've kept most players out the team. A lot of it is down to timing and I'm sure he was in the frame on more than one occasion.

One of Frank's last games for the club was the Scottish Cup final against Hearts in 1986. I didn't realise at the time that he'd been playing with a nasty back injury. It was at the end of the season and it's normal for players to be carrying injuries then. He never complained and, with it being such a huge game, he played on.

It was only after the game that I realised he was struggling quite a bit. We sent him for x-rays soon after and I think he had a cracked vertebrae. He didn't play much, if at all, in his third season with the club and, of course, I left to go to United a few months into the campaign.

At my time of leaving he was attending clinics and hospital and, while it wasn't looking great, he was still battling to save his career. When I heard that it was all over, I was devastated for him. He was at the absolute peak of his career and the next couple of years were shaping up to be his best ever.

It was so tragic that he never got the opportunity to go on and become a great player for Aberdeen, because he was certainly capable and well on his way. What I think was just as tragic though, didn't involve injury, although the disappointment I felt for him on this occasion was unbelievable.

Frank scored four goals against Celtic one afternoon at Pittodrie. It was potentially one of the greatest individual displays I have ever seen on a football field. His goals were simply breathtaking. One with the left foot, another with the right, a volley and a header. The perfect four. Those who were at the game that day witnessed something magical.

However, after the game, we discovered that television technicians had gone on strike and no one had filmed the game. We tried in vain to find out if anyone had recorded it for personal use, but it was all to no avail.

That was a real shame, because there could be no greater legacy than a reminder of the day you scored four incredible goals against one of the top teams in the country. Sadly, Frank doesn't have that to show his grandkids.

Many people have asked if he's the type of player I would've taken to Old Trafford. There is always a place for a prolific goalscorer, but it's difficult to say if such a move would've taken place, although he could certainly have handled playing in England.

We were similar in the way we played the game. Both moved for record Scottish record transfer fees and both goal scorers that liked to let defenders know they'd been in a game.

Frank has always kept in touch, which I've loved, more so when he lived in Lancashire. He would bring some kids to the training ground to watch the players going about their business and we'd always make time for a chat.

He's a very likeable lad and we've always had a great relationship. Of course, I have a soft spot for Frank because he wasn't dealt a particularly great hand, with regards to the injury. That was tough. But he has never complained about his lot and has simply got on with his life. I like that quality in someone.

His association with me may have been short lived, but boy did Frank make an impact at Aberdeen. He deserves a break and I hope he gets one.

All the best, Frank.

Abie Monaghan

GLASGOW Perthshire were an unfashionable club, but we had good players and a good side. There was no money there when Frank joined, so we all knew he was at Keppoch Park for the football.

I'd heard of him beforehand. He had a reputation as a good striker, but I didn't find out just how good until we teamed up on the park. I soon realised he wasn't just 'good', but frighteningly good.

The junior game is a tough grounding and some players simply can't handle it. I was at Maryhill when Tommy Burns, Danny McGrain and Paul Wilson were farmed out by Celtic. They soon realised that life at Lochburn was far removed from their Parkhead 'life'. It was shape up or ship out time. They handled it well and went on to enjoy fantastic careers.

Frank immediately showed one attribute that would stand him in good stead - a temperament second to none. He had all the tricks and that attracted unwanted attention from some tough, uncompromising defenders. But after being dumped on the ground time after time, he would simply pick himself up and get on with it. I don't think I ever saw him react and, as a consequence, he spent far more time on the park than a lot of others.

He was deceptively quick over 20 yards and that was normally enough to get him in front of the defender to nick a goal. He also had the ability to hold off defenders, a la Kenny Dalglish, with that backside of his, which made it doubly hard for defenders to get the ball off him.

Frank was special all right, and I would certainly rate him right up there with the Davie Coopers of the world. Cooper was a phenomenal talent, but so was McDougall. I'm not saying he was almost as good as Cooper – he was as good as him. He was his equal.

It didn't surprise me one bit when he stepped up with both St Mirren and Aberdeen. He was at home in the Premier League. It makes you wonder just how far he could've gone, but for that injury.

Had Alex Ferguson taken him to Man United then the world really would have been his oyster. When someone like Fergie takes you under his wing you must be something special.

I enjoyed playing alongside Frank and he fitted in seamlessly with the rest of the lads. He was a bit younger than the others, but an amazing dry sense of humour made him so popular. He also smiled a lot, which usually led to a smile on the face of the other lads. He could do great things with both feet, but he was also a fantastic team player. I can't remember him ever missing a game or training. He wanted to be there.

As far as I'm concerned, he was always going to make it as a footballer. He had bags of natural talent, that great temperament, a phenomenal eye for goal, and the ability to hold players off, just like Dalglish and Mark McGhee. Frank was as good as these guys.

In fact, James McFadden is probably one of Scotland's most talented players at the moment but, while he's a good player, he's not, in my book, anywhere near as good as Frank.

In terms of his finishing, Frank reminded me of the great Alan Gilzean, who played for both Dundee and Spurs. Gilzean would hang in the air and Frank could do the same. He was brilliant in the air, but was equally at home on the deck - with overhead kicks a speciality.

So many great players have come out of Possil, but Frank has to be the best. 'Shire had a striker by the name of Paddy Turner, who scored for fun, but while he was a phenomenal goal scorer, he didn't have half the tools Frank had.

To think that he came back from being blind as a teenager just makes his story all the more remarkable. I remember he would tell me of how his eyesight was still restricted after his accident.

For someone with such a deficiency, his balance was first class. Apparently there were times when he could only see out of one eye.

I can't imagine a worse fate, so I take my hat off to a unique talent and a seriously good footballer.

Blair Miller

STRIKING up a fruitful partnership with Frank, despite playing together for just one season, was one of the high points in my career. He was an incredible predator.

I'd been at Clydebank the season before he arrived, but had spent most of it in the reserves. Realising we were set for the drop, the gaffer, Bill Munro, gave me the last eight or nine games in preparation for the forthcoming First Division campaign.

Frank duly arrived from Glasgow Perthshire, a ground I knew only too well from my spell in the juniors with Johnstone Burgh. How they could call that football, playing on a black ash surface, I'll never know. I still have the scars to show for it. I'm sure Frank was relishing the opportunity to get back playing on grass again.

We only had pre-season to gel but did it remarkably well. One of my strong points was an ability to win aerial balls, which Frank fed off with relish. He was brilliant with his back to goal and had the physical presence to hold off defenders. Add exquisite close control and a tremendous appetite for the game and you had one hell of a player.

Neither of us were great trainers – goals were our forte.

I like to think I made most of his, but we had tremendous creativity behind us, like Gerry McCabe and Davie Houston, guys capable of threading passes through the eye of a needle.

We were definitely an attacking team, which showed in our goals 'against' record. It was the main catalyst for us missing out on promotion that year.

Frank and I scored almost 60 league and cup goals between us, a phenomenal record in any league. But the First Division was competitive, with teams like Dundee, Kilmarnock and St Johnstone doing the rounds.

Frank and I were in it together and this was never better illustrated than in one particular game. I can't remember the opposition, but I knocked the ball on, he put his head in where it hurts and got between the defender and goalkeeper to head home.

For some reason the defender took him to task for this and had a real go. Within seconds, I had waded in and all hell broke loose. We looked after each other on more than one occasion.

There was a time though when I had good reason to curse Frank, although I don't suppose he knew too much about it.

My dad was good pals with St Mirren chairman Yuill Craig and by the end of the 1978/79 season I was ready to go full-time. Dad promised to have a word with his mate.

I discovered that Saints were keeping tabs on both Frank and I, but was fairly confident that, as I had scored a few more goals, I would get the nod. Either way, I knew it would be a good move for one of us. But with my dad knowing Yuill…

I was married in June of 1979 and the honeymoon was booked for the following fortnight. I had a ball and was excited at the prospect of arriving home to find out that Saints wanted me on a full-time contract.

I had a good job with a bank at the time, and had been there four or five years, but I was desperate for a crack at the big time.

Imagine my horror when I arrived back at Prestwick Airport at 4am, picked up a Daily Record and there, splashed all over the back page, was Frank's cheery face. He had just joined St Mirren for a record Scottish transfer fee and I was left clicking my heels at Kilbowie.

I called my dad and started screaming down the phone at this ungodly hour. He kept telling me to calm down, which is just the worst advice when someone's going off on one. Apparently Jack Steedman thought I was happy working between the bank and Kilbowie.

It was a life-changing moment. Instead of getting to work with one of the most successful managers of all time, Alex Ferguson, I was to remain at the bank and, while I loved my job, it would've been nice to see how far I could've progressed.

I've great memories of Clydebank though, and the season I teamed up with Frank is among the most memorable. We were some double act and got on well off the park as well. He had a great sense of humour and because we were around the same age, we hit it off straight away. If I played even a small part in Frank's development then that makes me happy.

Frank certainly made the most of his opportunities and good luck to him, although having to quit football at 28 must have been so difficult. He still had much to offer. Who knows what he may have gone on to achieve.

What I do know is, although we only played together for one solitary season, what a season it was.

John 'Cowboy' McCormack

I RECKON Frank would've been a Scotland regular if he'd looked after himself off the pitch the way he took care of opposition defences on it. He was an absolute master finisher. Give him the ball at his feet and watch him dazzle you with every trick in the book and a few more to boot.

Ask him to go that extra mile in training though, or stay behind for another session in the gym, and he'd tell you where to go. Frank preferred a few sherbets and a game of snooker. But that's who he is, and that's what we all love about him.

He was the most unpretentious guy in the game. He would get a piece at anyone's door and I love him for it. Frank always has been, and still is, the easiest person to introduce to company. He gets along with everyone and you always get him the one way. Apart from a Tuesday night, that is.

When we were playing together at St Mirren I could never quite work out why he was always at his best in a Tuesday night match. Then it all came out: He went to his granny's straight after training and fuelled up on mince, tatties and doughballs. 'The best in the business', he would say.

We first played together at junior side Duntocher Hibs and then again at Clydebank, before being reacquainted at Love Street. He'll no doubt tell you I've followed him everywhere he goes. I wouldn't dare steal his thunder by telling you the truth.

When Clydebank sold Davie Cooper, they erected the Davie Cooper Floodlights from the proceeds. When they sold Frank to St Mirren, it was the Frank McDougall Stand, but when I left to go to Saints Frank will tell you the Bankies built the John McCormack Toilet. It's an old favourite of his.

But two can play at that game. While at Saints, Doug Somner asked if we wanted to go and see his new house. 'Of course', was our reply. Off we went in the car to East Kilbride and when we arrived, Doug asked what we thought of it. I told him it was a cracker, but Frank just sat there and stared, that famous mystical look etched all over his face.

Finally he said to Doug, 'That's not your house. You're here with us, your wife's at work, and there's smoke coming from the chimney'.

Doug stared at him in disbelief before replying, 'It's a semi-detached ya Muppet.'

Frank is an unconscious comedian. He says something then gives you the 'McDougall Stare'. Somehow he manages to keep a straight face while all around laugh their heads off at his patter.

I signed for St Mirren just in time to look out my passport for the trip to Brazil. We had a great time and stayed in a place just off the Copacabana Beach.

While at St Mirren we would go to the Brabloch Hotel for a pre-match meal at lunchtime on a Saturday. We would always have the same, chicken, which Frank termed 'budgie', due to the lack of meat on it. To make up for this indiscretion he would have a dozen slices of toast.

When it came to football though, Frank was arguably the best finisher I've ever had the good fortune to play with. He was a superb talent and, as I mentioned earlier, had he applied himself more he would have been a Scotland regular.

The truly great players have all the credentials and usually the one ingredient most players are missing is the skill, but Frank had it in abundance. It saddens me though that he didn't scale the dizzy heights others with no greater level of ability have reached. But I wouldn't have changed him for the world.

As an all-round sportsman, he was in a league of his own. As well as being a champion boxer in his youth, he was an absolute whiz with a snooker cue and hit regular breaks of 70 and 75. And when we were in Brazil, he gave more than a few people a lesson on the tennis court, which was perched high up on our hotel roof.

I remember the time we all took part in a charity cricket match. He was hitting everything in sight and scoring runs all over the place. Even the pros couldn't bowl him out. They ended up abandoning the match because it was the only way they could get him out.

So whether it was a tennis, cricket, snooker or football, he was a master of them all. Personally, my football memories of Frank are of this amazing player who scored goals for fun.

But it's not all memories, because we're still in touch with one another and meet up a couple of times a year. He's great company and still the same old Frank – and that's just the way I like it.

Jim Duffy

I WOULD'VE bitten your right arm off to have a player like Frank in any of my teams. Guys like him don't come along too often - the kind you can rely on to come up with the goods when the chips are down.

But not just for his goals. He had a huge personality and an edge to him that I liked. There's no point in filling your team with choirboys. You need players that aren't afraid to put their head in where it hurts. Frank put his head on the line often enough, but got his rewards. He was the Kris Boyd type - a prolific goalscorer of the highest order.

I played against him many times while at Dundee and Morton and he was a real handful as well as extremely deceptive. You'd be nicking balls from him and getting in front to clear the danger then, all of a sudden, he'd find half a yard inside the box and the ball was in the back of the net; just when you thought you were playing him well. You couldn't take your eye off him for a split second.

One game in particular stands out. It was up at Aberdeen and I was handling him pretty well. The game was going our way and he didn't get a sniff. Of course, I was letting him know I was there and on one particular occasion, when I went through the back of him, he was less than complimentary.

I felt it was my job to intimidate him and vice versa. I came off at the end with a few scars to show for the battle. No doubt Frank also had a few, but, more importantly, he wasn't throwing himself all over the place at every opportunity in a bid to get a penalty.

Frank was an honest pro who was good at what he did and that was scoring goals. He was strong and powerful, but that wasn't the only side to his game. He was blessed with a great touch and saw things before others - his football brain worked overtime.

If I had a criticism it would be that he probably didn't work as hard at his game as he could have, and he'd probably agree. But players who can go from being largely ineffective to banging in a winner are worth their weight in gold.

Even though I never played in the same team as Frank, I know for a fact he was a popular guy with team-mates. He has that incredible Glaswegian sense of humour that folk like. Mind you, I could also see him taking stick from his team-mates, but I bet he gave as good as he got.

Along with a couple of others, Frank and I were nominated for the Scottish Player of the Year award one season and, while I just edged it, it wouldn't have been a surprise had the boy from Cadder walked off with the crown.

It was tragic that his career ended prematurely because there was so much more to come. He was just 28 when he got the back injury and the next two or three years would've been his best. I'm sure of that.

Could he have cut it in the English top flight? Absolutely. A good goalscorer can play in any league and if you have the backing of your manager, which he obviously did, and with good players supplying the ammo, then surely more opportunities would have equalled more goals.

Alex Ferguson has shown a love of prolific scorers, although not always those famed for their work ethic. In fact, Frank makes Dimitar Berbatov look like a hyperactive Gabriel Batistuta.

When injury struck, he was just about to start a third term at Pittodrie and had already shown tremendous improvement under Fergie. It's a great pity that we'll never know what he could have achieved.

One thing's for sure though, had he been playing in today's game, he would've scored far more goals than he ever did then.

In Frank's day, he squared up to uncompromising defenders week in week out. Strikers get far more protection nowadays and if a player goes through him he's getting a yellow card. One more and he's off. Frank would've revelled in such freedom.

In that respect he may even have been more suited to today's game than the era he played so successfully in.

One regret might be that he never played for Scotland. He was certainly good enough and showed he could score goals at any level. He might have been a bit too rough and ready for the Scotland set-up at that time, but if that was indeed the case then it was Scotland's loss.

In later years, I would see him up at the greyhound racing at Ashfield and, while he was obviously disappointed at his career being cut short, he never once whinged or moaned about it. He just got on with life and that's one of his enduring qualities.

Billy Abercromby

I KNEW about Frank long before we were team-mates at St Mirren. He was from Cadder and I lived in Ruchhill, which are just a mile or so apart. He had a big reputation as a footballer even then, although our paths hadn't crossed on local pitches as youth players.

When it came to secondary school, I had the option of St Columba or St Augustine's. I chose the former and Frank, the latter, so maybe we were destined to be kept apart until Love Street.

When Jim Clunie signed him for Saints, I had been at the club three or four years and was a first team regular. Frank was a great character and very easy to get on with, so he fitted in effortlessly.

Another thing that endeared him to The Rat Pack, as a few of the more 'outgoing' members of the squad were known, was his incredible vanity. That gave us a right laugh.

Picture the scene. The game's over, Frank is last out the shower and, of course, last at the famous full-length dressing-room mirror. He's standing there, every inch your man about town. Apart from the brown socks, black shoes and tartan Y-fronts.

He was combing his hair like Henry Winkler (The Fonz, from Happy Days) and admiring every inch of himself. He would be there for ages, tending his golden locks with great affection. Despite what Luther may have thought, it wasn't a pretty sight - believe me.

Frank was really down to earth and we became good friends. First time I spoke to him, I thought, 'this guy isn't the full shilling'. Once I got to know him properly though, I realised he definitely wasn't.

As a player, he was nothing less than top drawer. In my 13 years at Love Street he was easily the most clinical striker I played with.

Frank McAvennie was also a great goalscorer, but McDougall had the edge. He was that bit more deadly and had a blinding turn of speed over 20 or 30 yards. He was deceptively quick and both him and Macca would refuse to come off the training ground on a Friday until they'd had their weekly sprints, on which a small wager would inevitably be riding.

Another difference between the two was where they liked the ball played. Macca was happy for you to play the ball into space for him to hunt down, while Frank liked it directly to his feet. He was brilliant with his back to goal.

There was a period when Frank was in and out the team, but this was down to injury and not indifferent form. A fully-fit Luther would almost certainly be an automatic pick. Even on an off day there was every chance he would pop up and knock in a vital goal. He wasn't a bench man - one who would come on and pinch a goal near the end. Frank did his damage from the start.

He was curtailed quite a bit through injuries, none more so than the broken leg he received after a challenge by Danny McGrain.

I wasn't in the least surprised when Frank secured his big move to Aberdeen though.

If anyone could get the best out of him, it was Fergie. For all that Frank was a brilliant guy, he could be quite deep, and a big part of a manager's job is to manage people. Sometimes players need a kick up the backside and, on other occasions, an arm wrapped round them.

Fergie knew how good a goalscorer he was and definitely got the best out him. He had a terrific goals-to-games ratio up at Aberdeen, although that didn't surprise me because he was surrounded by a lot of great players.

I should explain why I've called him 'Luther' a few times. Before a game one day, someone asked Frank who he thought he played like. 'Luther Blizzard...' came the answer. We were all in hysterics. 'What are you all laughing at?' he asked innocently. 'It's Luther BLISSET, ya numpty'. But that was Frank, unconscious comedian to the last.

And do you know what? I reckon he truly believed he was Brazilian legend, Zico. He scored a fantastic goal one day from around 30 yards and I said to him, 'Wow, Frank, that was just like Zico'. It was the worst thing I ever said - he took it to heart.

Tragically, Frank's career was cut short by that awful injury when he was in his late 20s. There was so much more to come. There is one way to illustrate just how sad it was. When I was 28, I was lifting the Scottish Cup at Hampden. Frank's career was over at that age. That's cruel.

It must have been so hard for him to take because football was his life. How do you cope with being told it's all over? That the only thing you've ever been remotely passionate about is at an end. It must have been awful. My heart went out to him, because we were good friends both on and off the park. I really felt for him.

We'd had such a ball at St Mirren and a few of us enjoyed the social side. We'd have a few pints and a game of snooker after training. He was a snooker 'shark' and I don't think I ever came close to beating him.

In fact, he was good at most things. A bit of an all rounder I suppose, just like his body. He was a great character and, sad to say, there aren't too many in the game these days. From the moment he turned up at Love Street, I just knew he would fit in. He did more than just fit in – he was a fantastic player for St Mirren.

Above all that though, he was, and still is, a great friend.

Billy Stark

I JOINED Anniesland Waverley at 13 and went straight into the Under-18s. It was quite a feat for a scrawny winger, but I held my own and stayed till I was 18. Two years before I left, we signed this fair-haired striker, but all I knew of Frank McDougall was that he was from the Possil area of Glasgow, which meant he could probably handle himself.

We played at a good level, had good players and Frank certainly fell into that category. There was far more to him than just popping the ball in the net regularly, although he was as good a finisher as I ever came across.

In Frank's day, most strikers felt that scoring goals was all they had to do; they definitely didn't work as hard as the others. Frank filled that category, but if you got on to him then he would stick the ball in the net and remind you that he had just saved you from a post-match savaging.

He always gave the impression he could handle himself and was streetwise and sharp, but he was also a popular boy in the dressing room. I think the Waverley was good for him. It was such a well-run club and instilled a certain discipline in players, who were expected to wear a shirt and tie to games.

We went our separate ways when we reached 18. I had trials with Rangers and Dumbarton, but was invited to pre-season at Love Street and Fergie signed me on a bus after training. I worked with Fergie for three years before he left for Aberdeen and Jim Clunie took over. Jim signed Frank from Clydebank and we teamed up again. I remembered him from Anniesland, but had also kept tabs on his progress at Kilbowie.

I scored a lot of goals and was probably what you'd term a 'good' finisher – Frank was a 'great' finisher though. That was the difference. I played up front as a boy and I think that's why I scored so many, but Frank was in a different league.

He was also an intelligent player. You wouldn't normally associate intelligence with football players, although you do get some, like Pat Nevin and Brian McClair. You wouldn't instantly put Frank, who was a bit of a Jack-the-Lad, in that category, but there's a football intelligence and Frank had it in abundance.

He knew how to get into scoring positions and bring people into play with his back to goal. His all-round game was superb. He had the lot - a fantastic touch, with an incredible subtlety that few others possessed, he was great in the air, while obviously not the tallest.

Frank was exceptionally good at skipping, which probably accounted for his being fleet of foot, giving him an advantage over many defenders.

But what Frank perhaps lacked in general fitness, he more than made up for with his alertness and ability to read a game. This was never better illustrated than a goal scored by John Hewitt in the Scottish Cup final against Hearts.

Peter Weir got down the wing and crossed low into the box. Frank had run just slightly beyond the front post and realised his chances of scoring were slim. Knowing there was a more than even money chance that Hewitt was running in behind, he stepped over the ball and Hewitt scored.

You have to be totally dialled-in to make a decision like that. How many times do you see a striker try to wrap his foot round the ball and shoot, and it flies hopelessly wide.

There's all that stuff about the 'goalscorer' who sees no one else bar himself and shoots on sight every time. That wasn't Frank. He had a terrific awareness of when to do it by himself, but wasn't one of those blinkered strikers. If someone was in a better position, he played them in.

He thrived on the camaraderie and whole team ethos. Despite his image, and all his dodging and weaving, he desperately wanted to do well for the team. There was a real honesty about him and he didn't want to let his mates down. Players who don't have that are just another player: another goalscorer or defender.

I remember we went on an end-of-season tour of Brazil. St Mirren and Brazil? It just didn't go together.

We met up at Glasgow Airport prior to the flight for a few drinks. Frank joined us. Nothing unusual in that, but as his wife, daughter and mother-in-law had accompanied him to the airport to wave him off, I was a bit surprised he chose to sit with us and not them. It was quite surreal.

There was Frank's family sitting about 50 yards away having a cuppa, while the bold one enjoyed a few beers with the lads.

When the announcement came that our flight was ready for departure, Frank stood up and shouted, 'That's me away' and waved to his family. No kisses or hugs, just a good old-fashioned wave. Brazil was an incredible experience and Frank and some of the guys set up residence in a local hostelry of ill repute called the Sunset Club. In fact, I believe Frank was the host.

I wasn't quite in that crowd, but there were others who feasted on it. I liked a night out but some of the lads took it to the max.

When Frank first joined St Mirren in a record transfer fee the directors were concerned that he stayed above a chip shop, pub and bookies. Let's just say they were on a mission to 'encourage' him to move away from those dreadful temptations.

I'm sure they wanted to protect their investment so they offered some subtle mortgage advice in the hope that he'd dial in and decide to move somewhere a bit quieter. The chairman suggested they might be able to help in terms of getting a mortgage. Frank thanked them and said he'd speak to his wife.

The next day, off he went to the boardroom to give the directors his decision and apparently said to the chairman, 'I had a good talk with Lil last night. We've decided we're happy where we are so we'd rather just have a new three-piece suite if that's okay.' I don't know if Frank ever got his suite, but what he didn't get was what the directors were 'really' offering him.

I wasn't surprised when he followed me to Aberdeen. He'd been doing well at Saints until Alex Miller came in and I don't think they got on.

Fergie didn't just go for the obvious big names though. Frank and I weren't big names, but he always had a game plan and knew exactly who he wanted. Frank was an obvious one. He was brought in to score goals.

Despite losing the likes of Gordon Strachan, Doug Rougvie and Mark McGhee, Fergie knew what was required to land the title and we eventually won it by seven points, setting a new points record in the process. Frank was fantastic that season and hit 22 league goals.

The following term, he scored four against Celtic. It was just such an out-of-this-world performance that made everyone sit up and take notice.

He was inevitably compared to Joe Harper, because, although Eric Black, John Hewitt and Mark McGhee were all excellent players, there hadn't been anyone in the category of wee Joe for a while.

In terms of managing him, Fergie was his rock, and Frank being Frank, he might not have chosen the straight road with a less disciplined manager.

Most players have a bad injury at one time or another, but when it's career-ending it must be 100 times worse. Everyone deals with things differently and I think Frank's way was to spend more time on the snooker table and enjoy a couple of pints along the way.

In terms of footballing ability, he was just reaching his peak at 28. All sorts of scoring records were in his sights - that's for sure.

Frank loved his time at Aberdeen and the punters loved him. It's that supporter thing, where they quite like the guy with a bit of an edge to him. Someone with the ability to go off the rails.

I'm quite a straight, family man and they don't really like that. It's a bit boring.

Who knows if Frank would ever have moved to England? I reckon he would've made the grade down there no problem. If he'd gone to Man Utd, Fergie would've handled him and he would've scored goals. Frank could score goals in any company.

He missed chances like them all, but he had that goal scorer's mentality. His body language was superb and told the world, 'If I miss, I'll be back.' He knew he'd get chances and with his quality, knew he'd score.

Mental toughness was his middle name and he was a confident lad with very few peers.

Gardner Speirs

I WAS coming through the ranks at Love Street when Frank was at St Mirren, but even then he was a huge favourite of mine. He had signed from Clydebank and certainly didn't look out of place in the Premier League.

He had this infectious personality that made him so easy to get on with. I don't think there was a single person at the club who he didn't get along with. At that time most of the players looked forward to training because the banter was so good.

But the most amazing thing about Frank was how good he was. As a striker he was fantastic and had so many different qualities. I suppose you wouldn't say he was the most athletic looking player in the world, but he was so sharp upstairs and so quick over a short distance that he almost invariably had the drop on many great defenders.

He was such a composed finisher with a wonderful touch and linked up well with other players. I can't speak highly enough of him. He was a great lad and an incredible person to be around, and I wasn't one bit surprised when he moved to Aberdeen. They were the top team in the country at the time and had done remarkably well under Alex Ferguson.

It was a big move for Frank and, coming from the West of Scotland, there's always the question mark over fitting in with a team from the north-east, but it would appear that he managed it effortlessly, thanks to his easy-going nature.

And, of course, when you can score a hat-trick against Rangers and four against Celtic it makes it that bit easier to be accepted, whether that's by players or supporters.

I remember watching him against Dundee United, at Tannadice, when he was up against two of the most talented centre backs in the country. Paul Hegarty and Dave Narey were outstanding players, but Frank gave both a torrid time.

And that was the mark of him. He was just so talented, but laid back with it. I've got great memories of Frank as a person, watching him play and playing alongside him.

He was one of those annoying people that could turn their hand to anything. Snooker, rugby, cricket, bowls - you name it, he was good at it.

I understand he also owned a greyhound. My only question though is, 'Who trained it?' Who walked the dog and gave it all its exercise? I reckon it wasn't Frank. I'm sure he had people to do that for him. I'm sure he enjoyed being the dog owner at meetings and such, but as for giving the greyhound its daily exercise and heading out on a six-mile walk, I'm not so sure.

I don't know if it ever won a race, or even finished any, but if that dog was blessed with half the talent of its owner, then I'm sure it would probably have scooped the lot.

It was a dreadful day when Frank had to quit football due to his back injury. I felt for him because he had so much left to offer. Aberdeen were still the dominant force in this country and their supporters would've been looking forward to watching him play for another four or five years. It was a crying shame when he was forced to give it all up.

He was a talented, talented man; a great goal scorer and, more than all that, a funny and genuine guy.

Tony Fitzpatrick

I LEFT St Mirren to sign for Bristol City just as Frank was arriving at the club. That was a pity because I'd earlier taken him to the club for a trial, when he'd left Hearts, but it proved unsuccessful.

Frank wasn't one for resting on his laurels though, and he eventually won his big-money move to Love Street - although Saints could've saved themselves a fortune by taking him on in the first place.

I was Frank's unofficial taxi driver when I returned to St Mirren. I would go up to his granny's in Cadder and pick him up. He was never ready, so I spent quite a lot of time in his granny's house. I would then pick up Frank McAvennie in Summerston and Chic Charnley in Possil before getting Brian Gallagher. What a team they were.

The banter would be flowing all the way to Paisley. They were good days, but the bold McDougall ditched my boring car when Macca bought a cool (well it was then) Ford Capri. Luther would much rather have been seen in Macca's trendy machine than my banger. I missed picking the lads up - like a hole in the head.

That was Frank the man - a top bloke and a great mate - but Frank the player was an entirely different matter altogether. He, perhaps, wasn't the best trainer, but I tell you what, he could play football.

He was a fit guy, mind you; he had to be to play at the top level in Scotland. I'd have to say he is easily one of the best finishers I've ever played with. He was top drawer.

When Alex Ferguson was in the market for a striker at Aberdeen I just knew he was going to target Luther. He was top, top quality and Fergie only ever wanted the best.

Frank had a great touch, exceptional control and could bring people into the game due to his great vision.

That was all well and good, but I'll go back to what I said at the start. Frank was a top bloke and a great mate. In saying that, maybe it's a good thing that I missed out on the trip to Brazil after I heard what that lot got up to.

Ricky McFarlane

I HAD watched Frank a few times while he was with Clydebank and it was obvious he had a real flair for scoring goals. It wasn't long before we had him at Love Street and he was doing the same thing for Saints.

One of Frank's most enduring qualities was his honesty. I'll never forget the look of misery on his face when he came up to me with his week two pay packet in his hands. He said: 'There's a problem with my wages Ricky. I paid this 'Nat Ins thing last week, why do I have to pay it again?'

God love him. There was a great innocence about Frank - a nice kind of naivety. He was a happy big guy and never gave me a minute's problem. He was the butt of many jokes, but was also quick-witted enough to give it back. He was great to have around the dressing room.

At the end of my first season in charge, the club couldn't afford to send us abroad for a break so we headed down to Wembley for the Scotland-England international. We went via Blackpool, which was a big mistake. We stopped at a few bars for some light refreshments. Actually, the beer was flowing.

Frank was sitting next to me and he'd had a few. He said, sincerely, 'Ricky, don't ever depend on me because I'll always let you down.' I couldn't believe what I was hearing. At first I thought he was larking around, but I don't think he was. He was just so honest. Frank was a brilliant footballer, but had he been fitter, he would've been international class for sure.

He was good to work with, took things in and had a great understanding of the game. He was an excellent finisher and no doubt showed that to greater effect at Aberdeen, where he was free to express himself more with people like Jim Leighton, Alex McLeish and Willie Miller behind him.

In saying all that, I cut my nose off to spite my face on many an occasion. In my time as Saints boss, I probably substituted him more than any other. If I thought he'd been on the drink the night before I'd take him off when really I should have left him on. There's this argument with finishers that they're always liable to nip a goal.

Frank was a strongly built boy - physical, but never dirty. At times the press termed him 'controversial', which was up to them, but he was certainly never controversial in the time I knew him.

Give me any player in the country to be one-on-one with a goalkeeper and I'd choose Frank every time. He was in a class of his own in that situation. Cool as a cucumber and deadly to boot.

As for training, Frank did what he had to and that was about it. He wasn't the greatest trainer in the world, but he was still incredibly quick over a certain distance and was remarkably sharp in front of goal.

Probably the only frustration I had with him was getting him up to a good physical standard. Had Frank made it to the senior grade a bit earlier, as a teenager for example, he could have been a far better player. Habits had been established by the time he turned senior.

Scottish players have always enjoyed a drink. It's part of our culture, although it's changing for the better these days. A lot of it is down to lifestyle and how you go about your day-to-day life. A lot of players in the 70s and 80s did what they did, although it never seemed to affect them on the park. They were still fit enough and could run around for 90 minutes.

To be an exceptional trainer, you have to have a very good level of fitness in the first place. If you're not fit enough initially then you'll always lag behind. Frank was normally bringing up the rear.

Frank McAvennie, on the other hand, was a magnificent trainer. The two Franks were big mates, but had different qualities.

Frank had an incredibly big heart and it was shown during St MIrren's trip to Brazil. On a bus journey back from one of our matches, Frank started going round all the lads with a bunnet, asking for a donation for the driver, as a token of our appreciation.

As the driver pulled up outside our hotel, Frank ambled up to him and said. 'Here mate, we had a wee whip round.' No big deal, thought Frank. However, the driver took one look at the contents of the hat, looked up at Frank, back down at the hat and just burst into tears.

Frank had just coerced his team-mates into donating almost two years wages for the driver. He was speechless, and if he voiced his appreciation once, he did it a hundred times. It was an absolutely priceless moment.

Frank may have been a top-quality footballer, of that there is no doubt, but he also had a natural eye for a ball, regardless of shape or size. We once played Paisley side, Ferguslie in a charity cricket match and he hit something like 20 off a few balls.

And on the golf course, he would smack a ball 300 yards straight down the fairway.

When I heard his career had been cut short due to injury I was devastated for him. It would be a tragedy for anyone, but he was in his prime and his goals record was second to none. And remember, he was playing at such a high standard.

Knowing Frank though, I reckon he would have handled it as good as anyone. He had this real bounce-back ability that not a lot of footballers have. He took some pretty tough decisions on the chin throughout his career and dealt with them.

But he still had a great career and will no doubt be remembered for his goals, although there was more to him than just sticking the ball in the net.

He was a fantastic team player and such a popular guy.

You'll have your work cut out trying to track down someone with a negative opinion of Frank. I have nothing but good to say about him.

Craig Paterson

I REMEMBER playing in a Scottish Cup semi-final for Rangers against St Mirren at neutral Celtic Park. We were 1-0 up with around ten minutes to go when I, unfortunately, knocked the ball past our stranded keeper, Peter McCloy, and into my own net. I was sitting in a puddle in the pouring rain feeling incredibly sorry for myself when Frank came over and patted me on the head, saying, 'Well done big man'.

Apart from playing against him on a number of occasions previously, it was my first real face-to-face encounter and he didn't exactly endear himself to me. To be honest, I would tell you my response, but you couldn't print it. When we won the replay though, I was looking for him at the end to shake hands but, if memory serves me right, he was off the park sharpish that night.

I played against Frank a number of times while he was at St Mirren and Aberdeen, and he was one of the best finishers I ever came across. One of these lads that if you gave him half a chance, you knew it would end up in the back of the net.

He was always in and around the box. You didn't have to look too far or chase him out to the wide areas. I'm sure his manager's thinking was, why have him out there? He's not a winger, he's not Jimmy Johnstone; he's the best finisher in the league. So, let's keep him in at the sharp end, a bit like the modern day Kris Boyd.

So he stayed in the middle and any chances that were created, there's a fair chance he'd have them nestling in the back of the net in a split second. He didn't mess around. So he wasn't the most difficult man to find, until you got in the box and then he became a bit elusive. He was difficult to pin down.

In Frank's day, a lot of forwards believed that running more than 15 yards wasn't required. Their mentality was - why should I run from byline to byline, or from one end of the park to the other. I don't have to do that to score goals, so what is the point?

Frank would have to be sharp over ten or 15 yards and that's what his training would be geared towards. Let's face it, when it came to the long slog round the training park, with a couple of heavy medicine balls, forwards were rarely at the front of the queue.

It was all about training to do your specific job back then and Frank knew exactly what he had to do. He had to be sharp in the box and

I'm sure that was all that interested him.

Times may have changed, but I think the forwards of yesteryear would have adapted to the rigours of the modern game. I think you adapt and deal with whatever's put in front of you. And anyway, there's always a place in any era for goalscorers.

You see some players down south with careers spanning maybe seven or eight clubs because there's always somebody crying out for a player who can offer up 15 or 20 goals a season. If you can do that north of the border, then it stands to reason you'll score goals almost anywhere.

The difference with Frank was that he made it look easy.

If he got goal side, you immediately thought, 'goal.' While with other forwards you thought, 'I might just get back here, or he might miss, or it'll come back off the bar', but I think you had the feeling that when Frank had half a chance that was it. There were no second chances.

On a personal level, I just tried to deal with him as best I could. I remember he scored a hat trick against us up at Pittodrie. It's days like that you try to forget when you're career is over, but I'm sure he will remember it forever in all its glory. You know what? I reckon he only had three chances that day. Typical Frank though, they all ended up in the back of the net.

Frank McAvennie

AS Frank and I were being put through our paces on the St Mirren training ground one day, I discovered just how good a 'mate' he could be. I was the new kid on the block and looked to guys like him and Jimmy Bone, the more 'mature' players, to point me in the right direction. And they did just that - well, most of the time.

On one occasion I took a rocket shot to the goolies, which taught me a couple of things. Don't stand in the way while someone's taking their frustration out on the leather and don't trust that pair as far as you can throw them.

I was in agony in the nether regions and the 'concerned' duo was straight over playing the good Samaritan team-mate and coach. 'Here, Macca, spray some of that on and you'll be right as rain'. Well, you listen, don't you?

I can't remember exactly which one of the intrepid pair offered this advice, but naturally I did as I was advised and within seconds the

Ralgex was burning through me like a welder soldering a porthole into the QE2.

Did I give them the satisfaction of seeing my eyes water? No. I turned away. It was agony and I was nearly in tears, but I soldiered on, although seeing them trying to stifle laughter broke my heart. But that's Frank, and we became great mates.

We went to the same school, St Augustine's, in Milton and while I knew of him, due to his reputation as a great footballer, I didn't know him personally. In fact, there's quite an age gap, so much so, in fact, he might even have been the janitor while I was there.

I was a big Celtic fan and when he was leaving Clydebank I was well aware of their interest in him. But they lost out to St Mirren and that was to my advantage. I learned so much from him and 'Papa' Bone.

Frank lived not too far from me so I would pick him up in the morning and he would share his 'wisdom' on the half-hour or so journey to Love Street. That really was an education.

But these were great days. We had a brilliant team spirit, which was only disrupted when Alex Miller took over as manager. Wearing a Rangers top to training didn't exactly endear him to most of the players. I don't think he liked Frank and I because we enjoyed the occasional night on the tiles.

That didn't make us bad professionals because we worked like Trojans on the training ground and did the business on match days. In fact, let me re-word that. I worked like a Trojan on the training ground. Frank was Frank and did his ball work and some light jogging before heading off for a game of snooker.

And listen, it was him that inspired me to become a striker. There I was, working my butt off in midfield - alongside Billy Stark - and scoring quite a few goals, while he would pop up most weeks, net the winner and grab all the headlines, despite doing f*** all else. I wanted a share of the headlines and said as much to Papa Bone.

He gave me my chance up front and not a lot changed. I still worked my arse off and McDougall still got all the plaudits. Seriously though, I reckon Frank is probably the most naturally gifted player I've ever played alongside. He was phenomenal.

I remember Alex Miller and his coach, Erik Sorensen, brought this Dutch guy in to teach us some ball skills. He set up this tricky little course and we watched him ease his way round it, keeping the ball within the cones. But he was making this weird noise as he did so.

We got our chance and Frank was first up. He did it in a canter - making the same noises, which was hilarious - and the Dutch guy stared at him in awe. Frank finished up by flicking the ball up in the air and catching it on the back of his neck. It was unbelievable and this little display proved that the Scots were equally as talented as Johnny Foreigner.

But Miller broke up the 'team' when he sold Frank to Aberdeen, although I was happy that the big man got his move. The gaffer rubbed it in by reminding me 'Just to let you know, I've sold your pal'. Really.

At the same time, I was supposed to go to Celtic, but it never materialised. Alex Miller thought he had broken up the gang, but when Frank left, he brought in Brian Gallagher and Jim Rooney, two guys I knew very well, and suddenly the happy gang had just grown by one.

I eventually left for West Ham, after being recommended to John Lyall by Frank's new employer, Alex Ferguson, so it worked out well for us both. I didn't have to live in McDougall's shadow any more. Whether it was golf, snooker, pool or cricket, Frank was top drawer and his bragging had become intolerable.

But I didn't shake him off for long and we remained just as friendly while we were at different clubs as we did throughout our five years together at St Mirren. I still keep in touch with Frank and 'Cowboy' McCormack and I don't think either friendship will ever die.

Frank taught me a lot about the game and was only too willing to pass on all the tricks of the trade, which isn't a common occurrence these days. I was quite late into the pro game, but Frank was great.

Frank will be the first to admit he didn't work as hard at his game as he maybe should have. You need that little bit extra to make it at international level, although Frank knew exactly where the goal was and that should've counted when it came to caps being dished out.

I played alongside some great strikers, including Tony Cottee, but Frank was up there with them all. These guys will score nine times out of ten, while I would score around seven. I remember him scoring four against Celtic and three against Rangers and being angry with himself because he'd missed another chance in both games.

When I went to West Ham, I couldn't believe the training regime we had at Upton Park. On day one I was waiting for the miles and miles of running to start when I was handed a ball and introduced to the striker's coach.

Of course, we would do a little running later, but for the biggest part of the day we worked with coaches who specialised in our individual field. With that sort of specialised coaching on offer, Frank would've thrived in the English top flight.

He already had all the tricks in his locker but a year or two down south would've made him the complete player. In fact, when he moved to Aberdeen there was an immediate difference in him thanks to his time on the training ground with Fergie.

Frank responded to top class training and it showed in the amount of goals he scored for Aberdeen, which won him the European Bronze Boot. He's a top bloke and a top footballer and I'm proud to call him my mate.

I know him well and have heard all the nicknames, like Gunther, Luther and Zico, but I had my own name for him and it had nothing to do with football. I christened him 'Richard Burton' and not because he was a sharp dresser, but because of the amount of wives he had.

Alex McLeish

THERE'S a myth doing the rounds that I was complicit in getting Frank a move to Pittodrie. Sure, he was a tough opponent and no doubt I voiced this within earshot of Fergie, but to suggest I was behind it is doing a great disservice to Frank. The transfer was down to him - no one else.

He had been banging in the goals for St Mirren and gave us a tough time whenever we met. Although Frank hadn't played under Fergie at Saints, the gaffer knew all about him and had already raided his former club for the likes of Peter Weir and Billy Stark.

At the end of the 1983/84 season, Mark McGhee's move to Hamburg left a gaping hole in the attack. Fergie made his move. In the beginning Mark had taken time to settle and a few of us started thinking, 'this guy's no good', but he turned out to be a shrewd signing. Fergie had a real eye for a striker and produced the magic wand again when he signed McDougall.

Frank was a born finisher and an exceptionally good footballer. He had a terrific understanding of the game and was a great link-up player. There were bags of goals in him and he was as brave as they came. He was what all managers crave. There is no difference between Frank and the very top strikers doing the rounds today.

Fergie had a great recipe for success at Aberdeen: a solid defence and Frank up front to put the ball in the back of the net. Nowadays there are too many strikers who need ten chances to score one or two goals. Frank required just one or two, such were his sharp predatory instincts.

He scored four against Celtic one day and each goal was different. It was an exceptional performance and I've rarely seen anything like it since. I dressed beside him in the changing room and I'll never forget the Monday morning after his one-man demolition of Celtic. We were just about to go out for training when he turned to me with that look of real sincerity and said, 'Alex, from now on don't call me Frank, just call me King.'

Every now and then, it pops into my head and I have a good laugh. Frank is a one-off. He was a great dressing room character and was liked by everyone, without exception. And let's be honest, he did get us a few quid in win bonuses so maybe that was the reason for his popularity.

He had quite a fall-out with Fergie on the training ground one day. I can't remember what it was all about but there was a lot of shouting going on. The gaffer said something to him and Frank answered him back. It went back and forward. There was only ever going to be one winner and it got that bad that Fergie turned to Teddy Scott and said, 'He's suspended till further notice'. Teddy just looked at Frank and motioned him over. He was like a UN peacekeeper and sorted this one out as well.

Frank was a winner and Fergie wasn't daft - he knew he needed Frank's goals and vice versa. A few days later, Fergie got Teddy to tell Frank that he was back in and they had a laugh and a joke about it.

We had a strong dressing room at Pittodrie. There was no room for shrinking violets. I'm certain that was partly responsible for our success, and there was plenty of it. Good footballers, with a strong mentality. You just can't go wrong.

When Frank moved to Aberdeen he also moved into the spotlight. Aberdeen gave him a platform he'd craved and he was just reaching his nadir when injury struck. He was cut down in his prime and but for that back injury, he would've played on well into his 30s.

He could see things instinctively - things that others could see only from the stand. He was very quick in the mind and didn't surrender possession lightly. He reminded me a lot of Tony Cottee, the ex-West Ham and Everton striker, another forward with great awareness, and a guy with plenty of goals in him.

I once told a group of English journalists during a Press conference that the Birmingham dressing room was very similar to the one at Pittodrie during the Fergie era. Fergie maintained that spirit till he left and it was still evident when I left. It's massive.

Rangers and Celtic were stronger and we didn't have the financial muscle to keep up with them, but we knew Fergie was the type of manager who could take us to great things, and with the shrewd signings he made, he did just that.

When he left to take over at Old Trafford, there was chat about who he might take south with him, as managers often do. If Frank hadn't suffered that dreadful injury he could easily have been on his way to Manchester United and I've no doubt he would've scored goals in the Premiership - then or now.

He was quick and, while the whole lifestyle thing is so important these days, he could've adapted. Foreigners come in and can't understand the British passion for a pint. But if Frank were around these days, he would surely have benefited enormously from all the sports science, etc.

There's also the debate about whether or not he should've been capped for his country. Had I been manager of the national team at the time, I wouldn't have hesitated in handing him a Scotland cap. He was one of the very best. I know we were blessed with a lot of quality strikers, such as Kenny Dalglish, Steve Archibald and Andy Gray, but in this era there's no doubt he would be a Scotland regular.

He was a difficult opponent to play against. I was taller than him and you'd think to yourself, 'This is my ball', but he'd nick it away at the last minute. Just when you thought you'd won it.

Frank and I bonded quickly at Aberdeen. We got on really well. My dad, Alex, would come up and watch me play at Aberdeen and it wasn't long before Frank had teamed up with him and they would travel back down to Glasgow on a Saturday night. Invariably they would share a pint and a game of snooker and they became quite close.

Talking about snooker, Frank was an incredible player and would give us all a bit of a pasting on the green baize. He used to challenge Fergie and you can imagine that the gaffer hated losing at anything, but this was one sport that he simply didn't have a hope of winning.

He would be spitting blood as Frank moved round the table, potting balls like Hurricane Higgins and Mr McDougall would make matters ten times worse by offering our beleaguered boss a start.

Frank made an immediate impact with Aberdeen by scoring early. That's always guaranteed to get you into the good books with team-mates and fans alike. We were soon thinking, 'Fergie's picked another cracker'. I'm happy to say that we've always kept in touch and that he's a lifelong pal. Whenever I'm back in Aberdeen, I always make a point of trying to catch up with him.

We first got to know each other some 25 years ago when he signed for Aberdeen. It's a friendship that has lasted since then and it's one that I believe will last for life. He's just too good a guy for that not to be the case.

Frank McDougall - top goalscorer, but more importantly, top bloke.

Eric Black

I PLAYED against Frank a few times when he was at St Mirren and, although we were normally at opposite ends of the park, I was a big admirer. Even then, he was a top class finisher. I wasn't surprised when Alex Ferguson brought him to Aberdeen, not just to replace Mark McGhee, but to add competition for places – and goals. He more or less made a place his own despite the Dons having some great players then.

Frank was a bit older than me, and far more experienced, so I learned a lot from both playing alongside him and watching how he did things on the training ground. He had a great physical presence, but there was much more to him than just barging through defences. He was an intelligent player and showed great variation in his goals. He scored the lot - using both feet, head, tight angles and distance. There wasn't much he couldn't do. Frank also had tremendous composure in front of goal and rarely panicked when one-on-one with a keeper.

From the moment he arrived at Pittodrie, he was welcomed into the fold with open arms: he was incredibly popular. I don't think I ever heard anyone say a bad word against him. One of his best attributes was his infectious sense of humour and the fact he liked to party went down well with most of the lads. He slotted straight in.

I think Frank and I complimented one another on the park. I was only 21 at the time, but we had a great understanding.

At Aberdeen you weren't allowed to shirk your responsibilities in training and Frank was no different. Sure, we preferred to do a lot of our training ground work in and around the goal, but we also had to do the same stuff as the others. We enjoyed our shooting, heading and general ball work though.

I'm sure the hard work paid off because Frank was electric over 20 or 30 yards and that stole him a march on an awful lot of centre backs. He linked the game well, held up play intelligently and brought others into the game. He was a great all-round striker.

He did very well at Aberdeen and who knows what he could've achieved had he not suffered that dreadful injury. Unfortunately, I can sympathise with him 100 per cent, because I went through exactly the same thing, at the same age.

Our dressing room was packed full of top players and strong characters. There's always the chance that a dressing room like that might overwhelm some people, but not Frank. He was one of the lads and soon became a fans' favourite as well. I'm sure they not only enjoyed his goals and skills, but also his non-stop endeavour. He worked tirelessly for the cause.

Fergie's standards were incredibly high and they were never allowed to drop. Again, it takes a certain type of character to be able to withstand that kind of pressure and that's maybe why we were so successful, because we had so many guys that could handle it.

We knew what was required, but we won things every season. It soon became expected of the team and as a player at Aberdeen in those days, you simply had to deliver. Either that or you were out. There was no middle ground. That's where the pressure was and why Fergie filled his dressing room and is still doing so to this day, with big characters.

We worked hard but there was always 'leisure time' and Frank took advantage of that. We had a snooker table at the club and one we used regularly at a bar round the corner from the stadium, which was situated on the beach.

I enjoyed a frame or two and I wasn't bad, but I wasn't in the same league as Mr McDougall. He was an excellent player and took a bit of beating. Let's just say not many of the lads bet against him, such was his amazing consistency on the green baize.

I certainly enjoyed my time at Aberdeen and that was in no small way down to players like Frank, who made sure the team kept on winning. He was a top bloke.

Neale Cooper

FRANK was a cracker. The more I got to know him, the more I liked him. Before he joined Aberdeen, I was well aware of him through his time at St Mirren. Although I was a lot younger, our paths had crossed. But as far as I was concerned he was just another talented player.

I've still got this image of him in my mind. Black and white strip, socks rolled down to his ankles, every inch the lad. He was a fantastic player and caused us more than a few problems. Then he joined us at Pittodrie and I more or less took to him straight away. He liked his game of snooker and a pint and that was right up my street. Suddenly he went from just another opponent to a valued team-mate and good friend.

He was never the greatest trainer, but one of the best finishers I've ever come across. I count myself as extremely fortunate to have played alongside him. Football wise, he was simply an out-and-out goal scorer. Anything in the box and, bang, he'd hit the target. He had a tremendous knack of bagging vital goals and a lot of that was down to his great positional sense and incredible body strength.

He was normally in the right place at the right time, but no one is going to tell me that's always down to good fortune.

Obviously his finest hour came the day he scored four against Celtic. That was quite simply a phenomenal afternoon. But you know what? I always believed Frank was capable of something like that. It didn't surprise me that much. I used to watch him in training and he was an incredible finisher.

He seemed to take great delight in scoring goals and reminded me of Ally McCoist in that respect. The joy when the ball hit the back of the net was etched all over his face. Frank was just that type of boy - a Joe Harper type in many respects. He was just like all the other great goal scorers.

Off the park he was brilliant company as well and we used to indulge in a wee game of snooker, which sort of fitted in with Frank's laddish image. We played one another on more than a few occasions and the only times I ever got near him was when he offered me a start. He was a phenomenal player and I'm convinced that had he not made it as a footballer, a career on the green baize might not have been too unrealistic. He was that good. No, make that brilliant.

I was an Aberdeen boy and Frank was from Glasgow, and brought up a Celtic fan, but we just hit it off. He was a hardy boy, but we became really good friends.

When he was injured it was a massive blow. These things happen in football, but when it happens to someone you're so close it, it takes on an extra significance. It's particularly sad when you think what he still had left to achieve.

You'll never hear me say a bad word about Frank. He is just an all-round good guy and the type of guy you want to go for a pint with. I tell you, he looked after me on more than a few nights out and it's only someone special that does that.

I liked a laugh more than anyone, but I always found an ally in Frank. He was always up for it. He was a very funny person and I still laugh at some of the things he got up to. Maybe I should keep them for another time though.

You'll have gathered by now that I was very, very fond of Frank and still am. I try to get into his pub in Aberdeen to see him and we always end up having a good chuckle about the old days. I wish him all the very best for the future.

Paul Hegarty

KENNY DALGLISH was one of the greatest players of my generation. He had all the ticks, but when he shielded a ball you had little chance of getting it from him.

The first time I played against Frank, he was at St Mirren and I was at Dundee United. He had the most amazing close control and it wasn't long before I was thinking we had another Dalglish on our hands.

But Frank was no one-trick pony. He had that short burst of speed that all good strikers need, he had great awareness and, like all good goalscorers, knew exactly where the target was, even with his back to goal. And he would nick the ball away from you in the air, just when you thought it was yours. He was the complete package. He was definitely blessed with a great footballing brain and was constantly aware of who was around him.

When Fergie snapped him up for Aberdeen it was the start of many personal battles between us. I've heard it said by Frank that I was one of the toughest opponents he ever faced. I take that as a huge compliment, but reckon his memory must be fading because he scored more than his fair share against United when I was around.

I wouldn't say Frank was the quickest player on the deck, but he was certainly lightning fast up top. And, of course, he chipped in with more than his fair share of important goals, which is the mark of a top striker.

Being a striker isn't easy. I know, because that's where I started out, although the least said about that the better. But my short spell up front taught me how difficult the position is so I have great admiration for top-quality strikers.

Frank was great at turning people and bringing others into play. But all he needed was half-a-yard and he was past you - and I'm speaking from personal experience. By that time you'd be hoping his shot was wide of the mark - or stopped by our goalkeeper Hamish McAlpine - although, more often than not, it landed smack between the sticks.

The New Firm, as the media christened Aberdeen and Dundee United, enjoyed a great period of success in that era and we had some great battles with the Dons. Funnily enough, we had a better record at Pittodrie than we did at home against Aberdeen. Alex Ferguson had a great eye for a player and, of course, he still does, and you could see the improvement Frank made under him. He was a good enough player for St Mirren, but he stepped up to the plate with the Dons.

It's fair to say he was a stand-out for both clubs and, but for the injury, his career could've taken yet another move forward.

I would definitely say I enjoyed tussling with Frank. He was a strong lad and capable of mixing it with the best, but he was as honest as the day is long. He wasn't the type to go falling over in the box when you breathed on him.

He never gave you a minute's peace though, buzzing about from kick-off and, on the odd occasion, trying to wind you up. There was never anything nasty though. He would say plenty of things, but it was always tongue-in-cheek. Like a 'nice' wind-up.

It's only when you stop for a moment and look back that you realise just how good the Aberdeen and Dundee United sides of the 1980s actually were. There was quality running throughout both sides. With Frank and the likes of Eric Black alongside him, Dave Narey and I never had a minute to ourselves.

There was one occasion though when I finally thought I'd get some respite. It was the League Cup semi-finals and Hamish had suffered a nasty injury. I took over in goal, which meant someone else had the job of marking Frank. Unfortunately, he popped up in the last minute to score the winner. There was just no getting away from him.

It was incredibly sad when he had to pack it in at 28. At that age you're reaching your peak. You've been through all the hardships of your apprenticeship and all the slogging away trying to make the grade. You're hoping to reap the benefits when you get to your mid-to-late 20s.

Frank had established himself at Aberdeen and deserved so much more from football. He was in the prime of his football career and to be cut down at such an early age must have been so difficult to take. He should still have had so much to look forward to, but sadly it wasn't to be.

I was fortunate to have such a long career, which I appreciated, but a lot of it is down to luck.

The game has changed quite a bit these days, but I reckon Frank would've been a great asset to any team in this day and age. I would liken him to Teddy Sheringham, who used his brain more than his legs when he was getting older. Frank had a similar football brain and was constantly thinking on his feet.

I reckon Frank also had what it takes to play for Scotland. Unfortunately there was an abundance of great strikers around during his era and it didn't happen. He was certainly good enough, that's not in question.

There's no doubt Frank achieved a lot in his career and he has much to look back on and be proud of. At the time, he was playing for one of the top teams in the country and there aren't many players who can say that. He was one of the best in Scotland and I can vouch for that. He was a fantastic striker and really left his mark on the game. I am privileged to have played against him on so many occasions and was touched that he named me as one of his toughest opponents.

He was certainly one of mine.

Dave Bowman

IN THE 1980s, Dundee United-Aberdeen matches were massive, which was in no small way down to the inclusion of players of Frank's calibre. Both sides were challenging at the top of the table and proved they could compete with the Old Firm, even in their own backyard. United and Aberdeen would regularly go down to Glasgow and get positive results.

I played against Frank in the so-called 'New Firm' derbies on a number of occasions and he was a hardy lad. So much so in fact, that I rather doubt he would last that long on the park nowadays. But that's not meant as a slur. He wasn't a dirty player, but you see what players get booked for these days and anyone who saw Frank play will know what I mean.

He was a real handful for our central halves Paul Hegarty and David Narey, and it wouldn't have been the first time they'd come in after playing against him puffing and panting. They certainly didn't relish coming up against Frank.

I've heard it said that one of the toughest defenders Frank played against was 'Heggy' and I'm sure the feeling was mutual. Frank was a Jimmy Bone type of attacker - strong as an ox. He gave defenders a tough time, but his goalscoring record was second to none.

But for someone to score as many goals as he did and not win an international cap was beyond belief. We were crying out for someone to stick the ball in the back of the net and here we had a natural goal scorer desperate to play for his country. It still baffles me as to why he was never given the chance to pull on the dark blue of Scotland. He's definitely a player I would have had in my team in a flash.

Just before Frank was forced to quit, I remember him struggling with a back injury and it seemed to restrict his movement quite a bit. He was trying to play through it, but was eventually forced to throw in the towel when it all became a bit too much.

It's always dreadful when a player has to give up in the prime of his career, but to have to stop at just 28, when it seemed Frank literally had the world at his feet, must have been devastating. Who knows what he would have gone on to achieve? It's one of those football questions that will remain unanswered.

One thing's for sure though. Frank certainly made his mark on the game while he was around and left a fantastic legacy in the shape of a pile of goals. And everyone who was associated with Dundee United at the time will be well aware of the threat he posed to us every time we kicked off. Great player and great goal scorer: that was Frank McDougall.

McDouGOAL

Joe Harper

FRANK and I were both working class lads, out and out goalscorers, similar in height and stature and took no nonsense off supposed 'hard-man' defenders. We never played together - I was way before his time - but I saw him play often enough to know that he was up there with the very best.

Four goals against Celtic, a hat-trick against Rangers, it doesn't really get any better than that. And, although it was an absolute tragedy when his playing career was cut short, he will always be regarded as a legend by Dons fans everywhere. That status is guaranteed.

It was a terrible blow to both Frank and Aberdeen when injury ended his career. He was quite possibly at his peak and had many more good years left in him.

But Frank was more than just a master of the goalscoring art. He held the ball up brilliantly and brought others into the play. And he wasn't easily knocked off the ball either.

He also had a great football brain and I reckon he could've moved back into midfield later in his career if that pre-requisite striker's 'burst of speed' ever deserted him.

He could see things happening before most other players and that gives a forward that important few seconds to nip in ahead of people and do your business.

I'm a great believer in strikers being blessed with a natural talent for scoring goals. I genuinely do believe that. But that quality alone isn't enough to put you on a level playing field with some of the great players.

You must also work hard at your game and I bet if you asked Frank what he was like as a youngster, he'll tell you he spent every waking moment kicking a ball against a wall or playing keepy-uppy.

Practise most things in life relentlessly and you'll eventually become very good at them. And like me he was never afraid to have a pop at goal, or put his head in where it hurts.

He proved that he could score against anyone: from primary school opponents to the best of the Premier League. I'm a great believer that if you're aware of where the goal is then you can score at any level.

Off the park, Frank is a smashing guy. He will talk football till the cows come home. I host a radio show and I've had him on a few times. He's a brilliant guest and the fans love him.

We are both working class guys brought up in the West of Scotland with little airs or graces. All we ever wanted to do was play football and become professional footballers. And at one time we were with arch-rivals Morton and St Mirren.

One thing I'll never be able to understand is just why Frank was never given the opportunity to represent his country. That's a complete mystery, not just to me but also to everyone who was watching their football in the 1980s.

For crying out loud he was top scorer in his country, holder of the European Bronze Boot, and yet he wasn't given a look-in at international level. It's not as if our country was blessed with a clutch of great goalscorers at that time.

If you are scoring 25 goals a season, then you deserve a chance to play for your country. But Scotland bosses tend to pick Rangers or Celtic players ahead of others, even if the guys playing for the so-called 'lesser lights' are banging them in with incredible regularity - and against the big guns.

I was top scorer in Scotland seven out of eight years and only managed four caps, two of which came as a substitute, but I still scored two goals, one in a World Cup qualifier. But Frank should've been in. No doubt about it.

He was still a great player though and had a very good career, despite that awful injury. It would be interesting to see how the remainder of his career would've panned out, although I've no doubt it would've been just as successful as the first part.

He was on a roll at Aberdeen and wasn't just scoring against the smaller teams. The Old Firm, European ties, he loved the big stage and could unlock the best of defences with just a shimmy here or a burst of speed there. Frank could hold his own in any company.

Natural goalscorers are a rare commodity these days and I shudder to think how much Frank would've been worth in today's market.

A WORD FR⚽M THE CO-AUTHOR

IT'S a strange world.

Being asked to help out with Frank's autobiography saw my life rewind 40 years to the age of ten.

I'd moved from Maryhill to Cadder (after being born in Oakbank Hospital - two years after Frank) and the McDougall legend was in its infancy.

He was without question, however, the most talented player in a football-mad scheme. I played against him once. A challenge match - Scotland Boys Club versus Cadder Youth Centre Under-15s, and I was centre-half for the latter. That meant McDougall v. Holmes, just like Brazil v San Marino or David v Goliath; you get my drift?

But there was to be no fairytale ending though and the bold Cado, as he was then known, scored a dozen times. And if he stuck the ball through my legs once, he did it, well, let's not go there.

He was always such an inspirational figure and when he quit Hearts and gave up the game altogether, a scheme was in mourning. Of course, we had shared his pain when the brick came through the window.

But our flag-bearer, with the hopes and dreams of Cadder on his back, had walked away from the type of opportunity we all craved. He soon had the bit between the teeth again and went on to have a fantastic career. He made each and every one of us extremely proud.

It was no surprise to anyone who knew him that he climbed the ladder as rapidly as he did. Glasgow Perthshire, Clydebank, St Mirren, Aberdeen...only the top rung proved elusive and I've absolutely no doubt that was the next step, before that awful injury struck.

Frank has had a tough life. He has worked hard for everything he achieved. He made it happen and I, for one, am proud to have him as a mate. This project took around a year and gave me the opportunity to talk to some fascinating people.

Whenever I approached someone from Frank's footballing past, whether it be Sir Alex Ferguson, Alex McLeish, or Ricky McFarlane, to a man they had nothing but good to say about him.

No one refused to be interviewed for the book and Paul Hegarty was genuinely touched that Frank had named him as his toughest ever opponent, a compliment he returned.

My brother Stephen played alongside Frank at Rangers Athletic. I remember my mum giving them both a lift into the Central Station as they embarked on the first leg of their marathon journey to West Germany. Stephen helped out with many details of Frank's early career.

Frank and I had many sessions (where the strongest liquid that passed our lips was Espresso) and I was able to tell him things about his career.

Staff at Paisley Central Library went above and beyond the call of duty and made sure that volumes of the Paisley Daily Express were available when required. Thanks to David Weir and his fantastic team.

To Gordon Robertson at Clydebank, Davie Preston at Glasgow Perthshire and the staff at Aberdeen Library thank you so much. And to Ross McTavish, many thanks for all your help compiling the book.

At no time was the job anything other than a labour of love. Not once did I huff and puff when getting the laptop out, or while embarking on the 'lengthy' journey north to Dons-land - honest.

My wife Elaine was incredibly patient as I swapped a night at the movies or at a restaurant for a session at the computer.

It's been a pleasure Frank; all the best to you and Isabel for the future, mate.